6gus

French Art of the Eighteenth Century

PAINTINGS

FURNITURE

CERAMICS

GOLD AND SILVERWARE

GILT BRONZE

WOOD PANELING

CARPETS, TAPESTRIES AND TEXTILES

SCULPTURE

INTERIOR DECORATION

COLLECTION CONNAISSANCE DES ARTS

FRENCH ART

of the Eighteenth Century

LONGMANS

LONGMANS, GREEN AND CO LTD
6 & 7 CLIFFORD STREET LONDON W I
THIBAULT HOUSE THIBAULT SQUARE
CAPE TOWN
605-611 LONSDALE STREET MELBOURNE C I

LONGMANS, GREEN AND CO INC
55 FIFTH AVENUE NEW YORK 3

LONGMANS, GREEN AND CO
20 CRANFIELD ROAD TORONTO 16

ORIENT LONGMANS PRIVATE LTD
CALCUTTA BOMBAY MADRAS
DELHI HYDERABAD DACCA

THIS EDITION FIRST PUBLISHED 1957

THIS FIRST VOLUME
IN THE COLLECTION CONNAISSANCE DES ARTS
HAS BEEN ACHIEVED UNDER THE
EDITORIAL SUPERVISION OF

STÉPHANE FANIEL

IN COLLABORATION WITH A DISTINGUISHED PANEL OF EXPERTS:

JEAN CAILLEUX, PAINTINGS
ÉTIENNE LÉVY, FURNITURE
JEAN NICOLIER, CERAMICS
STÉPHANE FANIEL, GOLD AND SILVERWARE
ANDRÉ FILSJEAN, GILT BRONZE
JACQUES LEBRUN, WOOD PANELING
Mlle J. NICLAUSSE, JACQUES THIÉRARD
AND MARCEL THIÉRARD, CARPETS, TAPESTRIES AND TEXTILES
PAUL GOUVERT AND NICOLAS LANDAU, SCULPTURE
ALBERT GILOU, INTERIOR DECORATION

ALBERT GILOU
ART DIRECTOR FOR THE SERIES

FRANCIS SPAR
PRODUCTION SUPERVISOR FOR THE STAFF OF CONNAISSANCE DES ARTS
ASSISTED BY BERNARD GEORGE

The editors of Connaissance des Arts wish to express their thanks for the documents put at their disposal by the directors, archivists and staffs of the following museums : the musées du Louvre, des Arts Décoratifs, Cognacq-Jay, Nissim de Camondo, du Petit-Palais, de la Bibliothèque Nationale; and to express their gratitude to the many collectors, antiquarians, interior decorators, art specialists and amateurs who so freely gave their help and advice. They most particularly wish to acknowledge the help of MM. Bernard Dillée, Cordonnier, Fersen, Grognot and Joinel, Hurtrez, Jansen, Kraemer, Penard y Fernandez, the Baron de Rédé, Mlle Rémy, MM. Rousé-Rivère, Wallraf *(Furniture)*; MM. Lecomte-Ullmann, Le Tallec, Vandermeersch *(Ceramics)*; MM. Baur, Bensimon, Bonnefoy, Christofle, Favre de Thierrens, Puiforcat, La Vieille Russie *(Gold and Silverware)*; MM. Baguès, Diette, Charlot *(Gilt Bronze)*; MM. Grandchamp, Serge Roche (for allowing the use of several pages from his work « Cadres français et étrangers du xve au xviiie siècle » reproduced here on pages 146-7) *(Wood Paneling)*; M. Meunier-Batifaud *(Tapestries)*; Mme Niclausse *(Textiles)*; M. de Nobele *(Bibliography)*.

Photographs are by MM. Bonnefoy, Bulloz, Collas, Dager, Desjardin, Devinoy, Foucault, Franceschi, Giraudon, Kollar, Lévy, Lombard (Lyons), Louis (Nice), Millet, de Miré, Palot, Routhier, Vaulé, Viollet, Vizzavona, from the Archives Photographiques and from the Photothèque.

THE BOOK
AND THE SERIES

This book, devoted to the arts of XVIIIth Century France, is the first in a series intended to comprise a complete pictorial encyclopedia of the plastic arts. The series will record the history of all the various art forms, throughout each period in their development. This will be achieved primarily through pictures—pictures illustrating a very large number of objets d'art, either singly or in relation to contemporary works, in order to clarify their significance, their purpose and their characteristic style.

The growth of styles can best be traced when a prodigal supply of photographic instances accompanies the text. This is the principle which has made the Connaissance des Arts series so successful abroad with the general public. For it allows the pictured examples to speak for themselves, with various objects, periods, and styles defined in succinct captions alone, while each section is prefaced by a short introductory text, broadly setting forth the development of the particular art under discussion.

The volumes in this series will be divided into two separate, although complementary, categories. One will deal with particular periods (such as Romanesque, Gothic, Renaissance, the XVIIth, XVIIIth, XIXth centuries, etc.) the other will deal with the development of a specific art, over the course of several centuries: (including such diversified topics as furniture, ceramics, or goldsmiths' work).

The volumes dealing with individual periods are intended to define the style and essential characteristics of the age they treat. They will illustrate inter-relations between the various arts of a given movement, and will note whatever features the various examples share in common. The books dealing with specific arts will follow their development through the course of several centuries, setting forth the different types of decorative motifs employed, the evolution of forms and their modification under changing social conditions; and the invention and use of new techniques. In this way, the material available in one series will complement the subject matter in the other.

The determining factor in choosing XVIIIth Century French Art as the first volume in the series lay in the enormous wealth of artistic resources displayed in that century.

Precise examples have been used to illustrate in detail the ways in which forms developed during the period. Here the reader has a visual record not only of a succession of changing styles, but also of the thematic unity linking a series of related objects. All the popular decorative motifs used in the various arts are described and their significance to the times explained. Consequently, it is possible to become completely familiar with the characteristic ornaments and decorative motifs of an entire period, while gaining the ability to recognize typical forms, and to place them accurately in their proper era.

Pictures of rare or unusual objects have been avoided; instead, emphasis has been placed on truly representative examples.

For similar reasons, many more objets d'art than paintings are illustrated; since objets d'art, because of the part they played in the daily life of the men and women of the XVIIIth century, are much more apt to embody the fashions and attitudes their owners most appreciated.

Finally, the French XVIIIth century was selected because it was the age when every art attained its highest perfection in France. At that period, the whole world sought inspiration in French works of art, or carefully copied them. When French artisans of the day attempted to imitate works of foreign origin, they usually found that they had, instead, completely assimilated the exotic style and had stamped the resulting "copies" with their own individual characteristics. Imported styles quickly became wholly French styles; imported techniques were soon adapted or improved in France. Chinese and Dresden porcelains, for example, were set in elegant gilt bronze mounts innovated in France. Chinese and Japanese lacquers were used to decorate the finest pieces of French furniture. French influence was so paramount and French technical mastery so complete, that any excess might have been permitted the craftsman of the day. And yet, they were imbued with a classic sense of proportion and good taste that served to keep them well within the proper limits imposed by their media; while imitators of French works seldom showed a comparable degree of self-restraint. When a connoisseur says, "It is not French," he usually means that a specimen is a work of French inspiration, but that it lacks harmony, balance, and restraint.

As the Régence period gradually liberated itself from the somewhat ponderous opulence of the preceding Louis XIV style, it soon managed to attain a perfection and elegance of its own. This style was succeeded by the dramatic exuberance of the Louis XV rococo; but in France the excesses of "rocaille" were never totally unrestrained. With the arrival of the Louis XVI era, a new severity came into fashion, derived from fundamentally architectural and intellectual concepts of style. But despite its origins, Louis XVI décor was never academic or overly conventionalized.

Every facet of French XVIIIth century art is still highly influential today. Innumerable forms came into being then which are now indispensable to the everyday scene, as well as many which will perhaps always continue to be thought classic. The century was remarkable too, for the astonishing degree of perfection achieved in almost every art form—a perfection in conception and execution never surpassed since.

It is hoped that this book will make it possible to clearly distinguish precisely those elements in French XVIIIth century art which are indisputably perfect, and which have become the classics of today.

Portrait of Louis XV. (Right.) Engraving m by Mme de Pompadour, after Guay. This prin now in the Print Room of the Bibliothèque Na nale, where it forms part of a collection of si nine plates which served as the original desi for a series of cameos.

Grandeur et Epaisseur de la Pierre

Louis Quinze

Sardoine Onix de trois couleurs.

PAINTING

Painting in XVIIIth Century France

Painting reached a far more extensive public in France in the XVIIIth century than it had ever enjoyed in earlier periods. The arrival of a distinctly new era of taste, a new way of feeling and perceiving is distinctly apparent both in the new types of subject then chosen by artists, and in the new decorative function that painting was called upon to perform.

After the death of Louis XIV a reaction set in against the austerity that prevailed during the final disastrous years of his reign. This reaction brought about a new freedom of feeling and expression. At the same time, the younger generation of painters revolted against the centralized authoritarian power that Lebrun had exercised as director of the "Académie Royale de Peinture et Sculpture." Artists felt that they should be free to study their own emotions and develop their own technical methods with less constraint; while patrons, too, began to feel a new confidence in their own taste.

A new kind of collector begins to appear

Pictures were no longer commissioned solely for the picture galleries and palaces belonging to royalty, to great statesmen or to the wealthier nobility. A new kind of collector began to appear, who bought pictures purely for his own pleasure— pictures to keep by him as part of his everyday surroundings.

In the "Grand Siècle" it would have been impossible for centers of patronage to exist outside the Court itself; in that century, all artistic patronage necessarily flowed from that one source. But from the very beginning of the Regency of Philippe, Duke of Orléans (1715-1723) the focus of social life began to move away from Court, and to become centered in Parisian society. Commissions no longer came from court circles only, as they had in the XVIIth century. The nobility and the wealthier members of the middle classes began to buy paintings in considerable numbers. These two classes had no great palaces to decorate; their tastes, too, were catholic and created a demand for paintings which would have been wholly unacceptable in the XVIIth century. This new stimulus to contemporary artists gave rise to the new styles of painting which were to become typical of the XVIIIth century.

Occasionally, certain favorite subjects of the previous century, such as history, religion or classical legend, were painted in the Grand Manner; but such treatments were really out of keeping with the temper of the age. A new type of sensibility arose, stimulated by writers like Rousseau, while the "Encyclopédistes" awoke a widespread curiosity—half-scientific and half-exotic— among the general public.

The love of children was an important theme throughout the XVIIIth century. Here this feeling is given perfect expression in the fluid, gay, almost sensual colors used by Fragonard in his portrait of a child. Affection for, and appreciation of youth—emotions that particularly appealed to a century constantly seeking new forms of sensation—are expressed here by a luminous warmth that seems to suffuse the painting ("A Boy as Pierrot"—"L'Enfant blond"). (Color plate at left.)

The triumph of the sketch and the rapidly-executed study

People began to grow interested in the immediate aspect of things. Simplicity of subject matter and spontaneity of treatment were admired far more than were formal compositions. Where the XVIIth century had demanded that art treat the enduring, solid and permanent themes, the XVIIIth century looked to painting for grace and movement. For its classical subjects, the age preferred Venus, with her accompanying cupids, nymphs and nereids, to the fierce, warlike deities of the previous age. Where Louis XIV was painted as a Roman Emperor by Lebrun, the daughters of Louis XV were represented, by Nattier, as Hebe, Flora and Diana.

As the XVIIIth century advanced, rooms tended to become smaller and more richly decorated. Paintings, too, grew smaller and took on a new decorative function, for there was little space to hang them on the richly carved paneling of small interiors. Instead, pictures were chiefly used as over-doors or in the restricted space above wall mirrors.

Easel painting comes into its own

The vogue for small pictures revitalized easel painting, which had played a relatively insignificant role in the previous century. The new limitations in size effected a concentration of interest on subject matter, which had to be pleasing and suitable, so as to harmonize with the décor of small, comfortable private rooms. The chief patrons of artists were financiers, tax-farmers and wealthy businessmen of the new age. Painting had never before played so important a role in everyday life as it did at this period; never had it been so widely admired. Neither had artists ever taken so deep an interest in contemporary life. There was hardly any aspect of the life of the times which was not considered a suitable subject for a painting. And collectors took an unprecedented interest in the personality and style of individual painters.

Painting Genres

Artists executed the principal types of traditional paintings such as portraits, still lifes and landscapes; but also created new genres such as the above-mentioned scenes of everyday life, "fêtes galantes," pastorals ("bergeries"), and exotic subjects.

The portrait painter was increasingly concerned with psychological truth rather than with producing grand official portraits. In Rigaud's work, and in that of many of his contemporaries, the increasing influence of Dutch and Flemish painting is clearly perceptible. Conventional portraits in the Grand Manner gradually gave way to careful portrait studies of the sitter's personality, as revealed in his features. But in portraiture, liberation from the conventions of the past was longer in coming about than it was in any other type of painting. Formal state portraits continued to be painted. All through the century artists were required to make concessions to tradition, particularly in portraying officials and dignitaries of civil and religious life who formed an important part of their clientèle; though even then, artists often showed a new interest in the sitter's personality.

In general, of course, the evolution of the portrait followed the important trends of the period. Spontaneity was preferred to artificiality, both in pose and setting; a painter tried to seize on the characteristic look, expression or attitude that his sitter might naturally assume. Vitality is perhaps the most marked characteristic of portraits from the period. Almost everybody had his portrait painted, from the King down to the simplest middle-class sitter; from Mme. de Pompadour to the ballet dancers at the Opéra.

Nevertheless, even in XVIIIth century society there were always a few portrait painters who continued to be interested in costume and setting rather than in psychology; or in the appearance of the sitter rather than in his feelings. Others were far more analytical in their approach. No psychological subtlety in the make-up of a sitter was inaccessible to Perronneau, Chardin or La Tour. They stripped subjects bare, revealing their pride, their charm, their success, their age; indeed, they reproduced every facet of character. Artists preferred to paint individuals in everyday settings rather than subjects who represented a class or a profession.

The styles of an entire century can be traced in the faces of the sitters of Largillière, Nattier and Mme. Vigée-Lebrun. At first the age is seen to be a trifle pompous, later it is more brilliant and worldly, and at last it becomes serious, sentimental, and reflective.

In still lifes, the subject plays a less and less important role, until, with Desportes, the subject becomes merely the technically perfect representation of a number of wholly unrelated objects. Chardin, the true heir of the great realist movement of the XVIIth century, elevated this omnipresent theme of French painting to the highest realm of art. The common subjects of the still life painter, the "humble objects of everyday life," were given a new and triumphant vitality in his simple but profoundly well-organized groupings, often consisting of nothing but a jug and a glass. Reality is seen in an utterly uncorrupted vision and rendered with complete mastery. His work restates the truth of the well-known saying that there are no privileged spectators, only different ways of looking at things.

Landscape painting, inspired by a newly awakened interest in nature, grew increasingly important as the century advanced. Love of nature appears quite early in the century as the theme in small landscape sketches by Desportes, who was the recognized master of hunting scenes; and it also appears in the work of his successor, Oudry. Hounds—as true-to-life to their originals as any human portrait (indeed, just as their owners wanted them painted)—are depicted in landscape

The figures in this country scene (at right) are very similar to those that appear in **Watteau's** "Fêtes Galantes." Watteau's figures are always the same familiar, sensitive, timorous young lovers, whatever costume he may choose to dress them in. The silhouette of a dress or a hat may provide him with a pretext for an evocative arabesque, but above all, the painter always makes us share the gaiety (whether real or feigned) of his sitters. Their feelings of restrained joy and happiness are one of the permanent aspects of the French character; and they were never given more expressive form than at this particular period. ("Party in the Country.")

Chardin was a master in rendering intimate scenes of everyday family life, like the one reproduced at left. The young governess and her pupil evoke a whole range of feelings far beyond the mere record of a chance pose—feelings which are seized and fixed forever. The simplified color scheme used here is admirably well-suited to the unspectacular kind of scenes which particularly fascinated this artist. Yet Chardin was always able to instill in them a deeply sensitive and personal note of poetry. ("The Young Governess.")

settings which are not artificial studio creations, but scenes which have actually been observed. A love of antiquity and classical architecture, in the manner of Panini, the Italian artist, inspired Hubert Robert; but Robert's ruined Roman temples and arches are bathed in a light found rather in the parks of Saint-Cloud or Versailles than anywhere in Rome.

For the first time, landscape painters are seen to be really in contact with nature itself. The backgrounds of hunting-scenes are real landscapes with real trees and woods. The fountains, wells and springs where elegant couples walk or where washerwomen are busy at their tasks, are all drawn from actual observation and from detailed sketches made "on the spot."

This revolution was nearly over when Hubert Robert, Fragonard and Moreau began to paint. Moreau was especially interested in pure landscape; figures hardly ever appear in his work. He was happiest when painting the countryside of the Ile-de-France, which is the subject of most of his paintings. There is no artificial composition, no conventionalized color-scheme in his work. He never paints Roman ruins, which were merely an echo of the admiration for the antique which played so prominent a part in all the other arts of the period.

In his carefully artificial, deliberately "composed" landscapes, Vernet satisfied the contemporary taste for Italian themes, for the love of nature, and for a nascent romanticism. He combined all the essential elements of the naturalistic landscapes of the period in artificial, "classic" scenes.

Vernet was the popular hero of Diderot's "Salons" (critiques written for the biennial exhibitions of the "Académie," the first art criticism ever to be written for current publication). His work appealed to the newly awakened romantic sensibility and emotionalism of the age, and to the contemporary love of the antique as well. Both themes can often be found at variance with one another in his paintings. When, towards the end of the century, landscape painters altogether abandoned Italianate motifs in their landscapes, in order to express their feeling for nature in its purest form, they achieved a truth to life which seems remarkably modern.

Paintings of scenes from daily life satisfied the almost inexhaustible curiosity about mankind, which was an outstanding characteristic of the age. Daily life is the theme not only of Watteau's "L'Enseigne de Gersaint" and of Drouais' "Portrait of the Meulan Family," but also of Chardin's "Grace before

Meat" and of the "Portrait of Mme. Geoffrin" by Hubert Robert. Family life and middle-class homes were favorite subjects. When artists began painting scenes from the daily life of the poor, they were innovating a subject that was to find widespread acceptance. Under Louis XVI, there was a marked reaction to the elegant, carefree life of society in favor of bourgeois morality; this preference became particularly apparent at Court. In the XVIIth century Le Nain had occasionally painted incidents from everyday life; and Callot had used the theme simply as an excuse for his own lyricism. But the artists of the new age were expected to deal with nothing but true-to-life subjects. Society expected to be shown a truthful, unvarnished image of itself. An ideal reality was no longer the aim; people wanted to savor and enjoy life as it really was. Family life was considered the highest form of worldly existence, and its little rituals were lovingly, and sometimes over-generously consecrated. In Greuze's work, this type of "sensibility," encouraged by philosophical writers like Diderot, sometimes became much too sentimental and emotional. But even in his paintings, as well as in the far more astringent and less emotional subjects of Drouais' portraits, the painter's delight in analyzing the simplest scenes and pastimes of daily life is always apparent.

Exoticism also appealed to a society anxious to increase the dimensions of the actual world of reality; for this was a society for whom the old horizons had vanished just as completely as had the artificial parade and display of the age of Louis XIV. The "Encyclopédistes'" application of the scientific method had pushed back the frontiers of the known world, and men wished to explore it not only physically, but also with their minds and imaginations. The "Compagnie des Indes" (East India Company) had brought back new and exciting themes for artists along with the goods they imported from the Orient; novels too, inspired by Rousseau's theories of the "noble savage," presented the uncivilized world in pleasing colors. Starting from these sources of inspiration, painters began to create imaginary worlds, full of delightful surprises. Everyone loved to be painted with a negro servant at hand; subjects were often shown dressed as a Turk or a Sultana, or perhaps as a peasant or a shepherdess; and paintings with exotic themes were in great vogue. The exotic paintings of Van Loo or Boucher as well as the "singeries" (pictures in which monkeys appear as human beings) of Huet, or the tapestries with "Indian" subjects designed by Desportes, were intended not merely to astonish but to provide an escape from the workaday world.

Fêtes Galantes were the invention of Watteau, whose influence pervades the entire century. His imitators, Lancret, Pater and Mercier, distort and vulgarize the peculiarly fragile sensibility which he distilled in his paintings—the loves, the defeats, the melancholy and the regrets of a society that was becoming continually more refined and free from conventional restraints.

The people in his paintings, though inspired by well-known figures from the Italian Comedy, are quintessentially French. He has breathed into them the life of a world partly of his own creating, but a world that is essentially real. It is an oddly melancholy world of enchanted lovers and their ladies, dressed up for a moment in the costumes of Harlequin or Columbine. But under these disguises, the faces of the painter's companions can be distinguished: Watteau's colleagues, his dealer friends, and, above all, those people of quality who were his principal patrons. After Watteau's death, all poetic qualities disappeared from this type of painting. Succeeding works became merely "escapist" fantasies of elegant, worldly figures posturing in parks, who try but fail to escape their boredom with the grandiloquent poses of the "Grand Siècle."

Legend and mythology no longer spread their decorative emptiness over the vast ceilings and walls of royal palaces, and such themes were no longer required to supply artists with subjects for uninspired academic exercises. Physical conditions were in part responsible for the change, for the small spaces provided by over-doors and mirror panels left little scope for grandiose subjects. When themes from mythology were used by painters, they were interpreted in the dramatic terms of the tragedies of Racine and his imitators; or in the spirit of the comedies of Marivaux.

Towards the end of the century, biblical subjects began to be no more than pretexts for excursions into the picturesque. What interested Boucher and Taunay in the genre was the opportunity it provided for painting a landscape setting, where the play of light and shade meant far more than the sacred or symbolic meaning of the subject itself. Indeed no aspect of history-painting strongly appealed to the artists who made significant contributions to the grace and elegance of XVIIIth century life.

The various types of painting in fashion, and the different kinds of themes appropriate to them, each played their part in creating the special unity of XVIIIth century art. Mythology provided an excuse for amorous or pastoral themes; "fêtes galantes" allowed the pleasures of courtly life to be set against a background of nature, to whose beauties society itself was gradually awakening; history-painting served as a pretext for fanciful "escapist" treatments. Everything that XVIIIth century men and women loved can be found reflected and epitomized in the pictures they chose to have about them on the walls of their rooms.

Even the discovery of Greek and Roman ruins, which affected taste so profoundly from 1750 down to the end of the century, did not alter the essential unity of the period. It led, chiefly, to a new emphasis on proportion, classical restraint and reason, with a consequent subordination of freedom of expression. Roman ruins were highly influential in reshaping the forms of architecture, furniture and objets d'art, but their effect was far less apparent on painting. Their study did produce a certain tendency to compose pictures in a single or very limited number of planes, in the style of bas-reliefs, but it only slightly modified the composition of portraits and genre scenes. In landscape painting, the Italianate, neo-classic style really owes more to Poussin than to Raphael or Giorgone. For when David tried to impose a neo-classicism—derived wholly from antique models—on the age, he failed completely for it had absolutely no correspondence with the feelings or intellectual predisposition of his contemporaries.

The Position of XVIIIth Century Painting Today

There is great interest in XVIIIth century painting in the present day. Collectors now look for paintings which are not merely pleasing, but which are also typical examples of a painter's style and personal manner. At the same time it is important that they harmonize with the decorative setting in the collector's home. The XVIIIth century was perhaps the first historical period to have produced paintings that exactly meet these requirements. Its range is certainly wide enough to satisfy all the varied tastes of modern art-lovers. For the most part, it is attractive and easily understood; and it is entirely successful in interiors which are fashionable today. Its subjects are likely to interest modern art-lovers more than subjects executed in any other period. Technically, its quality is usually fine enough to make it especially appealing today, because of its unusually fluid lines and the use of bright, attractive colors. A hundred years ago it was fashionable to assemble considerable collections of XVIIIth century paintings in appropriate period settings. But today their status, as true masterpieces of art is even more thoroughly appreciated.

JEAN-FRÉDÉRIC SCHALL is numbered, together with Watteau and Prud'hon, among the great XVIIIth century painters of dancers. This picture (from the Nissim de Camondo Museum) was painted circa 1750 and combines the qualities of fine portraiture with a style reminiscent of "fêtes galantes." The most famous ballerinas of the day—Guimard, Saint-Aubin and Taglioni—had Schall paint their portraits. This particular painting, with its careful composition and startling juxtapositions of color, shows the meticulous care Schall employed in an attempt to catch the beauty of a graceful dancer in motion.

THE MOST STRIKING FEATURE of the intimate portrait was the increasing attention paid by artists to the simple poses of daily life. This coincided with the spread of middle-class morality, which was on the increase all through the XVIIIth century despite its outward display of luxury. The effects in portraiture were obtained by the simplest means, as in LÉPICIÉ's portrait of J. Vernet's (his pupil's) son. ("The Little Draughtsman.")

THE GRAND FORMAL PORTRAIT is seen here in its highest development. The expression of the face plays a less important part than pose and setting. The artist, MAURICE QUENTIN DE LA TOUR, has stressed the subject's role in society. Mme. de Pompadour is shown here as a patroness of the arts. Every element in the setting symbolizes this intention, but in contrast with the formal portraits of the previous century, the subject has been shown in a relatively domestic setting. ("Mme. de Pompadour.")

THERE IS A GREAT CONTRAST between this portrait and the one at left. Although the subject is children—throughout the century artists and writers paid great attention to children—it is an official portrait. The setting is given a predominant role in the picture. DROUAIS follows the artificial pastoral style then so fashionable in France. ("Charles of France and Marie-Adélaïde of France.")

IN THIS PORTRAIT of the pious and timid Queen of France, NATTIER has abandoned all the conventional devices which he so often used in his portraits. He is concerned with his subject's mood rather than her position as a queen. Setting and costume are less important than the accurate rendering of the features. ("Portrait of Marie Leczinska.")

THE QUINTESSENCE of the Louis XV portrait is epitomized in this half-length of Beaumarchais by NATTIER. The artist has caught the sitter in a spontaneous though slightly affected pose, which echoes the sinuous lines of the composition. Its lines were meant to blend perfectly with the rococo shapes of the furniture and decoration of the small, fashionable room in which it was doubtless intended to hang. ("Beaumarchais.")

THE LOUIS XVI STYLE is very much in evidence in this portrait, which has been influenced by a reawakened interest in the antique. Simplicity and straight lines are the key-note. The pose is stiff, the composition rectilinear. The predominant feeling is no longer that of wit and elegance, but rather a reserved amiability which is something less than aristocratic. The influence of David's style is clearly seen in this portrait by Mme. LABILLE-GUIARD. ("Robespierre.")

THIS SELF-PORTRAIT of the artist is a triumph of truthful, absolutely objective realism and observation. Neither dress nor setting distracts the spectator's attention from the face, which is treated as if it were an inanimate object in a still-life composition. ("Self-portrait by JEAN-BAPTISTE CHARDIN.")

IMAGINATION plays a major role in this portrait, which is in complete contrast to the one by Chardin. The face is treated as though it were an actor's mask. It is not merely an object, it is a decorative feature. FRAGONARD has arranged the lighting, so as to accentuate the dramatic vitality of the composition. ("An Old Man.")

THE STUDY OF FEMININE PSYCHOLOGY played a great part in the development of the Louis XV style of portraiture. Even though costume becomes very important here, due to the technical skill with which it was rendered, it was not allowed to distract the onlooker's attention from the calm expression on the sitter's face. The mood seems to suggest that she was one of those "cœurs sensibles" whom the Encyclopédistes had made fashionable. Such sitters are often represented either reading or thinking. TOCQUÉ has given his sitter a far-away, dreamy look. ("Mme. de Livry.")

THIS LOUIS XVI PORTRAIT shows how greatly composition was simplified in the latter part of the century. Straight lines again begin to play an important part. Even the fashions in clothes follow the general trend of the evolution of taste, becoming more austere, and less colorful. ("Self-portrait by Mme. VIGÉE-LEBRUN.")

THIS PORTRAIT OF AN ARTIST, by one of his pupils, is typical of the Louis XV style. It is well-balanced, truthful, and excellently posed. It would do credit to the wall of any room. ("Portrait of La Tour" by PERRONNEAU.)

THIS DECORATIVE PORTRAIT is a triumphant example of its type the play of light on the silk of the dress, the pleasant outdoor setting, the pastoral character of the pose, the colors of the flowers, the graciously pretty, though vacant face, are all there solely to give pleasure without evoking the onlooker's response in any other way. ("Portrait of Mme. Bergeret de Grandcour" by F. BOUCHER.) *(Color plate at right.*

SETTING AND COMPOSITION combine into a perfect unity in large formal still lifes like this scene where a hunter has just returned from shooting. The XVIIIth century was passionately devoted to field sport, and numerous official commissions were given for paintings of this type. The influence of Snyders and other Dutch painters can clearly be seen in this elaborate composition by OUDRY. ("Return from the Hunt.")

STILL LIFES sometimes enabled the artist to indulge in the simple pleasure of displaying his technical virtuosity. The gradual refinement of this stylistic exercise seems to correspond with the increasing refinement of the XVIIIth century society. In this famous painting OUDRY has placed a great variety of different whites side by side, ranging from the white porcelain bowl through the white feathers of the duck, the pale color of the wall, the whipped cream, the paper, the candle, and lastly, the silver candle-stick. ("The White Duck.")

OBJECTS OF EVERYDAY USE and the evolution of their shapes can often be better studied in still lifes than anywhere else. Musical instruments play a predominant role in the painting illustrated here, but the other objects add to the effsct of the composition as well, both because of their shapes and textures and because of the skill with which they are rendered. Here DESPORTES has painted a bass-viol resting on an open book, beside a plate of peaches, a porcelain tea service and a silver chocolate pot. ("Still Life with Musical Instruments."

OFTEN STILL LIFES are given a slightly allegoric character both in order to heighten interest and to justify the bringing together of a wide variety of different objects in a single composition. This still life by OUDRY seems to represent "The Five Senses." ("Still Life.")

THIS PICTURE ILLUSTRATES how far the still life had developed since the realistic painters of the XVIIth century began depicting simple assemblages of everyday objects. ROLAND DE LA PORTE has distilled in this painting a deep sense of the intimate life of the entire century. A jug, a glass, a table-napkin, some books, all of whose surfaces are rendered with immense subtlety, stand out against a clear, light-colored background. ("Still Life.")

THE INTERPLAY OF STRAIGHT LINES lends distinction to this still life. There is an absolute, almost abstract, rigor in its composition; the diagonal of the stem of the pipe and the emphatic vertical of the jug are placed so as to divide the composition exactly at the Golden Section. In this painting by JEAN-BAPTISTE CHARDIN, the principal functions of the still life are united: technical virtuosity and the creation of a documentary record. ("The Jug and the Pipe.')

A HINT, a faint suggestion of movement, seems to be implicit in this slightly unsteady composition. It is no longer the mere existence of objects which the artist is evoking. Instead he is creating a scene from which human beings have just departed. It illustrates admirably how every possible facet of still life was exploited during the XVIIIth century, and by none more skilfully than by JEAN-BAPTISTE CHARDIN. ("The White Cloth.")

THIS TYPICAL STILL LIFE, by contrast, differs hardly at all from the flower-pieces of the previous century. It is indeed a type leaving little scope for the unexpected. The taste of the painter, Mme. VALLAYER-COSTER, is manifest in the natural flower arrangement, in her selection of common varieties, and in her subtle coloring. ("Flowers.")

A

B

LOVE OF NATURE (A) was one of the dominant emotions of the XVIIIth century. People dreamed of a life of happiness and virtue, led by peasants in the country. This taste for the pastoral naturally turned artists to the study of agricultural subjects. In this painting OUDRY has enlivened his landscape with a realistic scene of daily life in a farm-house courtyard. ("The Farm.")

THE PICTURESQUE LANDSCAPE (B) also continued to inspire painters. Some sort of figure-subject was usually provided in the foreground as a pretext for the representation of wild, romantic distances, such as appear in the bluish, atmospheric background of this landscape by PILLEMENT. ("Landscape.")

ELABORATELY CONSTRUCTED LANDSCAPE compositions (C and D) in which the charm of nature itself is combined with the more artificial character of French formal gardens were a specialty of certain painters. HUBERT ROBERT was a master of this type which represents one facet of the aesthetic of the period: "art added to nature." Two of his paintings are shown here: (C. "The Fountain" and D. "The Laundresses.")

PASTORAL IDYLLS (E) were often given a dramatic character towards the end of the century. Painters, like the men of letters of the period, were beginning to evidence tendencies that would later flower in the romanticism of the XIXth century. A good example of this is LOUIS WATTEAU DE LILLE's scene of an approaching storm. ("Harvesters Surprised by a Storm.")

C

E

SEASCAPES were a specialty of many landscape painters. Some of them, by giving the setting a theatrical character, anticipated the romantic landscapes of the following century. JOSEPH VERNET, whose landscapes almost invariably contain large areas of sky, was particularly skilled in rendering the play of light and shade. ("Small Italian Landscape.")
(Color plate at left.)

D

LANDSCAPES

A

B

C

DUTCH LANDSCAPE PAINTING influenced French artists (A). FRAGONARD'S study of Dutch paintings directed his attention to their treatment of light and shade; making his work a welcome counterbalance to the academic tendencies of the day. ("The Rustic Bridge.")

SPONTANEITY OF OBSERVATION is combined with precise detail and subtle use of light and shade in the work of the best landscape painters of the second half of the XVIIIth century. This canvas (B) by VERNET is a forerunner of those that Corot was to paint at Mantes one hundred years later. ("The Seine at Nogent.")

VIEW PAINTINGS (C) are not to be confused with landscape proper. Such pictures can only be judged to be documents, unless they are enlivened by close observation of the effects of light, and of clouds in the sky, such as is seen in this painting by LALLEMAND. ("View of Château Montmusard.")

D

THE SCHOOL OF PAINTERS working in the Ile-de-France attached great importance to realism and exact observation. Figures tended to disappear from their compositions. Here nature alone fills the canvas, with its transparent sky, its delicate light, and the subtle shadings of green in the foliage. Such painters as LOUIS MOREAU dispensed with artificial scenes and idealized colorings. ("View of the Countryside near Corbeil.")

THE TASTE FOR FANCIFUL ARCHITECTURAL SUBJECTS in the Italian manner as typified by this painting (E) was a result of the neo-classicism of the times. LACROIX DE MARSEILLE painted this landscape when in Rome. It is composed of a number of real buildings in an imaginary setting. ("Port Scene.")

E

FAMILY SOCIAL LIFE often provided XVIIIth century painters with a suitable theme. A sense of comfort, and a love of intellectual conversation are suggested by this painting by JEAN-FRANÇOIS DE TROY. It seems to evoke some literary salon, like Mme. d'Épinay's or Mme. Geoffrin's, with Fontenelle, Marivaux, or one of the Encyclopédistes reading from his latest work. ("A Reading.")

INTIMATE SCENES of home life are valuable historical documents of the interior decoration of the day; they also gave the painter an excuse to display the charms of a pretty woman. Luxury, which the age had newly acquired, was often evident. In this painting, LANCRET's style is seen to be markedly more sensual than that of his master, Watteau. ("The Dressing Room.")

NO NOBLE FAMILY in the XVIIth century would have allowed itself to be painted at a dressing table. But during the XVIIIth century the taste for refinement and magnificence penetrated every aspect of daily life. Although rooms grew smaller, their appointments became more elegant and more commodious. People of quality began to allow painters to show them surrounded by their luxurious possessions, as in this group by DROUAIS. ("The Comtesse de Meulan in her Dressing Room.")

THE HOME LIFE of middle class families, too, was considered suitable for painting. This was particularly true towards the end of the XVIIIth century, as middle class attitudes grew more widespread. This painting by BOILLY is also an important document on the fashions of 1787. ("The Gohin Family.")

MEN AND WOMEN of the XVIIIth century loved an easy, luxurious life and often combined this taste with a love of nature. All three are found in this painting of a picnic given by a nobleman. The haughtiness and strict etiquette of the age of Louis XIV have disappeared. The love of gaiety and pleasure was the key-note of the times, as well as the subject of many paintings. This picture by VAN LOO was ordered for the private apartments of the Royal Family at Fontainebleau. The ones by LANCRET and DE TROY, reproduced below, were commissioned for the King's dining-room at Versailles. ("The Hunt Breakfast" by Van Loo, opposite; "The Meal of Oysters" by De Troy, below; "Lunch with Ham" by Lancret, at left.)

TOWARD THE END OF THE CENTURY, people began to enjoy looking back nostalgically on the simple pleasures of country living. CHARDIN adds a note of introspection to his scenes of every-day life, whose qualities can be appreciated only gradually, as the viewer learns to absorb their deeper emotional content. ("Grace before Meat.")

MIDDLE-CLASS DINING was considered suitable for paintings, too. These scenes are of interest for their technical skill, and for the portrayal of objects in daily use. The intense calm of the faces is note-worthy. ("The Luncheon" by BOUCHER.)

DUTCH STILL LIFE PAINTERS, like Terborch and Mieris, created a number of paintings intended to be reproduced, later, as engravings. Their French imitators were careful to choose subjects that were in current vogue. In this painting BOILLY has portrayed the rising interest in science and the equal interest in the education of children, which arose from the teachings of Jean-Jacques Rousseau. ("The Optical Glass.") (Color plate opposite.)

A

B

TOWN LIFE (A) is the real subject of WATTEAU's shop-sign, which he painted for the art dealer, Gersaint. In it he has depicted the common everyday activities of a picture-dealer's shop in the XVIIIth century, with XVIIIth century objets d'art. (Detail from "L'Enseigne de Gersaint.")

AN INEXHAUSTIBLE INTEREST in human activities was characteristic of the XVIIIth century. Even scenes of the intimate life of domestic servants were considered suitable subjects for painters. LÉPICIÉ has depicted such a scene (B), giving it a setting which seems to evoke memories of the pictures of threatened virtue, so often painted by Greuze. ("Fanchon Dressing.")

A COMPASSIONATE RECORD of the small details of the life of the poor was often inherent in the work of painters who specialized in rustic scenes (C). Such artists were continuing a tradition founded by Le Nain in the previous century. In this picture, CHARDIN has employed one of the favorite themes in French art—one which was to reappear later in the work of Cézanne and Vuillard. ("The Water Tank.")

THE DOMESTIC LIFE of the wealthy bourgeois accepted into the upper ranks of society was occasionally satirized. In this picture (E), HUBERT ROBERT has, as it were, taken a snapshot of Mme. Geoffrin in her home. She was a well-known blue-stocking, and received the most notable writers and artists of the day in her salon. Here her almost puritanical love of truth and good taste has been slyly set forth in this intimate scene from her private life. ("Mme. Geoffrin Taking Coffee.")

C

STREET SCENES (D) serve as perfect historical documents on the life and customs of the people in the years before the Revolution. This type of painting, which was particularly prevalent in the 1780's, found its inspiration in the work of the lesser Dutch masters of the XVIIth century. PHILIBERT-LOUIS DEBUCOURT is a master of this type of painting, in which common events are transmuted into pictorial art of a high order. ("Celebration in the Paris Markets at the Birth of the Dauphin.")

E

D

IN THE XVIIIth CENTURY artists often gave their pictures a park as a background. The word *"fête galante"* was specially coined to describe the type of painting devised by WATTEAU. It was undoubtedly the most original artistic innovation of the entire century. The word has no exact equivalent in English, but it exactly evokes the figures and atmosphere of Watteau's paintings. ("The Lesson in Love.")

The influence of "Commedia dell'Arte" strongly affected the development of *"fêtes galantes"*. All its theatrical characters—Pierrot, Columbine and Scaramouche—are there. The lovely women never seem wholly absorbed with their suitors, and the men seem hesitant and tongue-tied. They are always placed amidst a setting of leafy trees; and music is never absent. This is the magic domain which Watteau has immortalized on his canvases. ("The Assignation.")

AFTER WATTEAU'S DEATH, the *"fête galante"* gradually became an artificial convention; the dream element completely disappeared. Only the setting remained. Ladies and their lovers assemble in the same leafy groves, but they are mere worldlings now. The genre reached its final phase with S. WATTEAU DE LILLE. ("The Minuet beneath the Oak Trees.")

THERE WERE INNUMERABLE VARIATIONS of the theme of the *"fête galante."* Only the slightest pretext was needed for the composition of groups of amorous couples in outdoor scenes. In this *"fête galante,"* by LANCRET, one is reminded of the groups of peasants skating on the frozen canals of Holland in Van Ostade's paintings. ("Winter" or "The Skaters.")

THE SWING is one of the many devices used in the "fête galante," for it allows both performers and spectators to play a part. It also allows the artist to paint women in graceful poses. Fragonard used such a setting for one of his greatest masterpieces. In this painting (left) PATER has set his version of the theme against a transparent and almost wholly artificial background. ("The Swing.")

EVEN MILITARY LIFE provided a subject for the painters of "fêtes galantes." The terrible last years of the reign of Louis XIV, and the horrors of his campaigns were all forgotten. In this military scene PATER is copying his master Watteau very closely. In spite of its subject, it strikes a note of joy, rather than emphasizing the misery of a campaign against an enemy. ("The Vivandières' Tents in the General's Camp.")

The theatre was the principal influence on the "fête galante" all through the XVIIIth century. The figures grew to resemble actors on a stage, standing before painted scenery. Sometimes the setting was architectural, sometimes leafy. Here the figures' dramatic gestures seem to be repeated by the arabesques of the fountains in these last echoes of the "fête galante" style. (A. "The Fête at St. Cloud" by FRAGONARD; B. "The Dance" by DE LAJOUE.)

A

B

THE OSTENSIBLE THEME of an XVIIIth century painting was often merely an excuse for a display of brilliant invention, combined with the artist's desire to paint seductive bodies and pretty faces. This sketch, one of FRAGONARD'S masterpieces, is one of the finest examples of this kind of painting. (Fragment of sketch for "Rinaldo Delivering Armida.")
(Color plate at right.)

PASTORALS—EXOTIC SUBJECTS

FRANÇOIS BOUCHER was a master of the pastoral comic-opera convention, which the XVIIIth century greatly admired. Lovely girls costumed as shepherdesses or pretty peasants pretend to take part in country occupations, or they engage in tender conversations against hazy blue backgrounds of landscape. ("Cherries.")

PEASANT SCENES are another aspect of the artificial pastoral. They are more true to life, but are still too prettified. The emphasis is on the countryman's leisure rather than on his long hours of work. Country life is usually made to appear pleasantly full of naive virtues, as in this painting by LANCRET, where the peasants have gone harvesting in holiday clothes. (At right, "Summer," or "The Dance.")

A

EIGHTEENTH CENTURY PHILOSOPHERS explored and enlarged the world. Their ideas stimulated the imagination of the ordinary man. There was perhaps more interest in China than in any other remote place and so the taste for "chinoiseries" arose (A). Watteau was one of the first to adopt this fashion, and BOUCHER took the subject up again, both in tapestry designs and in paintings. ("Chinoiserie.")

"TURQUERIES" were another aspect of the wish to flee from everyday life into an ideal dreamland. Here, an XVIIIth century lady has been painted by VAN LOO (B) dressed as a Sultana, attended by her negro servant. ("Sultana Taking Coffee.")

EXOTIC HUNTING SCENES (C) provided opportunities for all sorts of fantasies. An example by VAN LOO is illustrated below. ("Ostrich Hunting.")

THE EXOTIC PASTORAL (D) united both of these types, and suggested the idea of the "noble savage," made popular by Rousseau. This painting by J.-B. LEPRINCE is simply a Boucher pastoral that substitutes Russian peasants for French ones. It was painted in St. Petersburg. ("Musicians in the Fields.")

B

C

D

A

SCENES FROM LEGEND and classical history (A) enjoyed great favor throughout the century. In this picture LEMOYNE adopts the artificial conventions that the imitators of Racine used in constructing their theatrical tragedies. ("The Sacrifice of Iphigenia.")

GRANDIOSE ALLEGORIES went out of fashion as ceiling decorations during the XVIIIth century. Instead, allegorical subjects were treated on smaller canvases (B) like this one by NATOIRE, which were then set into the paneling of the wall. ("Beauty Relighting the Torch of Love.")

BIBLICAL SCENES (C) often served as a pretext for a picturesque subject. Painters were interested in Biblical subjects because they provided opportunities for exotic landscapes, with oriental figures, as in this example by TAUNAY. ("The Preaching of St. John the Baptist.")

MYTHOLOGICAL SUBJECTS in the XVIIth century usually pictured warlike deities of virtuous and imposing appearance. In the XVIIIth century, however, the warriors were dethroned in favor of Venus, Cupid, Bacchus or Aurora, followed by trains of nymphs, fauns, and tritons. The somewhat facile, though brilliant, way in which this type of painting was treated is well illustrated in this painting by LÉPICIÉ (D), though it must be admitted that this genre did not produce the greatest pictures of the period. ("Venus and Adonis.")

B

C

D

FURNITURE

The General Character of XVIIIth Century French Furniture

Furniture styles followed the general trends of the period, and kept changing in the attempt to satisfy an ever-increasing demand for more personal comfort. Furniture became continually more practical and a variety of new types made their appearance. The shapes of traditional pieces evolved gradually and much more furniture was found in XVIIIth century rooms than had been the case in any earlier period.

Monumental forms characteristic of XVIIth century furniture were gradually abandoned—probably the most important development to affect the designing of furniture during the entire century. As the age advanced, a taste for greater comfort arose and the more important role played by women in XVIIIth century society brought with it a demand for smaller pieces that were more imaginative, more elegant and more refined. As furniture became smaller and lighter, right angles and long straight lines gradually disappeared. Rounded forms became increasingly fashionable and the shapes of furniture were more carefully adapted to the needs of everyday existence: the shapes of armchairs, for instance, were more closely adapted to the human body and became well-suited to the wide panniered skirts worn by women of the period.

New types of furniture were evolved to satisfy the requirements of ever more sophisticated and exigent patrons. There was a perpetual spirit of rivalry between architects, sculptors, designers and ornamental engravers, all of whom were continually devising new and original means to attract the patronage of the Court, the nobility and the wealthier members of the middle classes. The basic forms of furniture, like the writing-table, the "bergère" armchair and the sofa, all evolved in a wide variety of different ways. Smaller chairs and tables that could be moved about easily came into existence to allow closer, more intimate social intercourse. The most varied types of furniture were created specially to meet the thousand and one needs of an elegant, sophisticated social life: multiple-purpose tables, tric-trac (game) tables, elaborate toilet-tables, etc.

Great French craftsmen like Cressent, Migeon and Dubois, produced an enormous quantity of furniture of every kind, giving rise to a specifically French style of furnishing that spread throughout Europe. The character of French taste was so strongly marked and so distinctive at this period that foreign cabinetmakers who came to France assimilated it completely and spread it far beyond the frontiers of France.

The new style gave birth to a far greater quantity of furniture than had been made in any earlier age. Pieces of outstanding quality were often commissioned by the King as presents for important courtiers. Furniture was no longer moved from home to home; it remained permanently in the house for which it was made. The richest nobility even possessed different sets of furniture for winter and summer use. People took a close personal interest in their furniture and insisted that it should be of exactly the type and design they required.

The style of this furniture was, of course, the result of the collaboration of a large number of different craftsmen. A carpenter ("menuisier") first made the wooden frame which he assembled from carefully planed and solidly jointed wood. The "ébéniste" (the word derives from "ebony," of which the earliest veneers were made) was a specialist in veneers and marquetry, techniques which had been first introduced into France in the previous century. This marquetry was applied to the plain solid wood frame prepared by the "menuisier." If the piece was not intended for veneering, then a wood-carver would apply the type of decoration in which he specialized, though sometimes the "menuisier" himself would undertake simple carved decoration in relief: stylized floral motifs on a Louis XV chair frame; or an egg and tongue molding or beading on one in the Louis XVI style.

The actual designs for the work executed by the wood-carver were often drawn by a specialist called an ornamental designer, and the plans frequently carried out the principal decorative motifs used in the interior where the furniture was to be housed.

Veneered furniture was given the last finishing touches of elegance by the craftsmen who cast, chased and gilded the mounts ("fondeurs" and "ciseleurs-doreurs"). These mounts, too, were often designed by a specialist in ornamental design. In the case of chairs, sofas, etc., which were never mounted with gilt bronze, the final touches were applied by the painter (or gilder) and the upholsterer.

This collaboration of a variety of highly skilled craftsmen set the seal of artistic success on French works. Soon French fashions spread throughout the length and breadth of Europe, so that everywhere French furniture was sought after and imitated. It is for this reason that it can be maintained, in a certain restricted sense, that there are English, Dutch, German, Italian, Russian and Swedish versions of the Louis XV and Louis XVI styles.

There are several fine pieces of furniture in this drawing room with its carved and waxed oak paneling of the "Régence" period. Against this background the bright colors of the upholstery of the chairs add greatly to the informal character of the room. Two chairs are signed by J. Gourdin and upholstered with detachable cushions of contemporary cut Genoese velvet in dark red. The small Louis XV armchair at the extreme right upholstered with a blue and white damask in a poppy design of traditional character is signed by G. Jacob. The Louis XV "bergère" armchair at the left, upholstered in yellow velvet, is also signed by J. Gourdin. (Color plate at left.)

Forms and Decorations

There is, of course, no style whose evolution exactly corresponds with the dates of the historical or political period from which it takes its name. Just as the "Régence" style really came into existence before the death of Louis XIV, so the true Louis XVI style was born almost in the middle of the reign of Louis XV. In a like manner, something of the monumental character of Boulle furniture persisted for several years after the beginning of the Regency of the Duke of Orléans. Boulle himself lived on until 1732, and his later furniture, while it retained much of its monumental character, already shows signs of becoming a little less rigid in its silhouette. Its mounts become a trifle freer, while their

winged type ("à oreilles"), the "conversational" ("à confidents"), and the intimate ("en tête à tête"). The exact English equivalent to many of these types does not exist. There was a different type of sofa for almost every sort of attitude in which the user might wish to repose. They became smaller, more intimate in character and when they began to take their place in the privacy of women's boudoirs they were given an even wider variety of feminine names, the "turquoise," the "paphos," the "duchesse," the "veilleuse," etc.

"Today," wrote Voltaire, "social behavior is easier than in the past. Ladies can be seen reclining on sofas or day-beds without causing embarrassment to their friends and acquaintances." The type of day-bed known as a "duchesse" was easily movable because it separated into two parts: a "bergère" armchair with an unusually long seat and a little chair

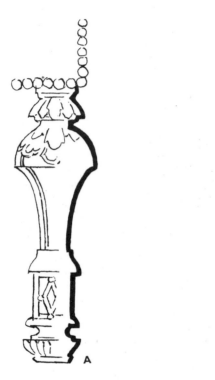

The evolution of styles of furniture in the XVIIIth century can be followed clearly in the changes in shape of the legs of chairs, tables, etc., as well as in their decoration. At the beginning of the century, chair-legs still in the Louis XIV style (A) are straight; similarly at the end of the century under Louis XVI, legs became straight once again (H). Between these two extremes the lines of the leg grow progressively more "cabriole". Under the "Régence" period (B) the curve only departs a little from the straight line, but under the Louis XV period it gradually took on the shape of an elongated "S" (C, D, E). Throughout the period when these changes are taking place, carved decoration

covers almost the entire surface of the leg. At first this decoration is geometrical, then under Louis XV sinuous floral elements begin to appear (B, C). At the same time ornament tended to play a more prominent part at the top of the leg to give emphasis to the curve of the knee. During the transitional period between the Louis XV and Louis XVI styles the leg preserved its curving shape longer than any other part of the furniture. Even while it remained curved, however, neo-classical motifs began to appear in the decoration. At the end of the century, legs returned again to the rectilinear shape found in antique art (G, H), just as the decoration became purely classical.

forms even occasionally make use of the volutes, shells, plant-forms and rock work ("rocaille") of the succeeding period.

The Louis XV style developed at an historical moment when the general organization of social life was growing somewhat freer. "The Louis XV style," Michelet wrote, "marks a return to a feeling of joy in living itself, and to a warmer regard for human values."

*The shapes of furniture
were dictated by the search for comfort*

The age demanded more practical, more comfortable furniture and furniture better adapted to its every need. The skill and imagination of contemporary craftsmen brought into being more and more pieces of furniture devised for specialized purposes. The traditional type of sofa developed into a variety of different species, the gondola shape, the basket shape, the

with a low back which could be set at the foot of the larger part so as to convert it into a sofa. The "duchesse brisée" included a third section, a sort of stool or pouf which occupied the central section and extended the length of the seat of the "bergère" section.

The curves and counter-curves of the Louis XV style grew ever more sinuous; they were particularly well adapted to this type of furniture. Starting as simple arc-forms the characteristic curves of the period approximated more and more closely to a pronounced C-curve and eventually developed a counter-curve of S-shape.

Chairs were made to invite the sitter to sink into them. The "bergère" type of armchair, which came into existence in the "Régence" period, was adapted to those cosy corners of the room which the comfort-loving were less and less willing to quit. Mme. Victoire, Louis XV's daughter, is said to have claimed that her "bergère" armchair, of which (like the other comforts of living) she was excessively fond, was the one thing which had saved her from having to enter a convent.

On the smaller types of chair the arms were set well back behind the front edge of the seat so as to accommodate the wide, panniered skirts which had come into fashion circa 1715, though the change did not actually affect furniture until about ten years later.

The chest of drawers was no longer merely a coffer set on feet and intended to hold every sort of possession. It was given an elegance of outline and, in its interior fittings, a really functional beauty which enabled it to hold its own in spite of changes of fashion and taste. The centers of the front and sides gradually became bowed and "bombé" in shape. Its feet grew increasingly curved and more slender; their extremities were fitted with little "shoes" of gilt bronze. Chests of drawers were sometimes veneered with patterns of

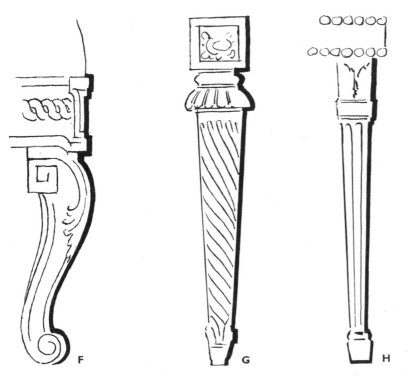

F G H

flowers which seemed to be scattered over the entire surface in an arbitrary and almost natural fashion.

The writing table, an invention of the previous century, changes rather less than most types of furniture. The corner-mounts in the form of acanthus leaves and female "espagno-lette" heads are now of more subtle form. Smaller and more elaborately decorated writing tables, specially designed for women's use, begin to appear.

The qualities of balance and solidity in furniture begin to be less obvious. Pieces are supported on small graceful elongated legs with hoofed feet which appear incapable of supporting any weight, yet add greatly to the elegant, refined appearance of furniture and do, in fact, continue to perform their function with complete success.

The so-called "rocaille" phase of the rococo movement is the one important contribution made by foreign ornamental designers to the evolution of taste. It was the creation of men like the Italian Meissonier, from Turin, and of Oppenord, from Holland.

"Rocaille" plays a predominant role in interior decoration

There was a tendency for foreign ornamental designers to create ever freer and more fluid forms, allowing unbridled

rein to their imagination. They paid less and less attention to formal restraints and restrictions. But even when their designs abandoned all traditional character or when the use of asymmetrical motifs produced totally unbalanced forms—as happened in the later development of the rococo in certain other countries—the innate classicism and natural good taste of the native craftsmen called on to execute them, restored an essential element of balance and harmony.

Unknown decorators carried the love of refinement and elegance, a taste for exquisite detail and the desire to please, to their utmost limits. Furniture was produced in the most varied color schemes. The ebony marquetry, which had originally given its name to the "ébénistes" responsible for veneering, was displaced by more colorful woods—tulip-wood, king-wood, purple-wood and a wide variety of other exotic types—and contributed greatly to the colorful effect of contemporary furniture. The favorite marquetry for furniture was of geometrical or floral design, but the use of lacquer was also almost equally fashionable and introduced another range of even brighter color into schemes of decoration. Painting, too, achieved a new importance in furnishing. Chair frames in particular were painted with delicate colors which harmonized with the upholstery.

Bérain, at the end of the XVIIth century, had accustomed people to the use of fantastic elements in decoration. The marble tops of Toro's side-tables often rest on fantastic monsters such as appear among the cupids and birds which decorated the cornices of contemporary rooms. Cressent's chests of drawers grew ever more "bombé" in shape, their sides and ends seem almost to billow outwards. They are richly mounted with gilt bronze which adapted its forms from the decorative motifs of the wall paneling. Sometimes chests were veneered with lacquer in the Chinese style. The brothers Martin succeeded in imitating in a lacquer of their own invention, the bright colors and ornamental forms which were so much applauded when they were first imported from the Far East on lacquer boxes and screens. This was known as "Vernis Martin." Chair frames, too, gradually adopted the sinuous lines of the paneling of the walls.

The rococo style used a new range of more sharply acute angles; more abrupt turns; pierced and denticulated forms; and misshapen cartouches. Pineau, Oppenord, Slodtz, and Meissonier all poured out a vast number of "picturesque" designs intended for use by cabinetmakers. The word "picturesque" began to be used by contemporaries to describe certain furniture designs dating from just before the middle of the century.

The Louis XV style obtained its rich effects by the use of gilt, elaborate carving, and sumptuous gilt bronze mounts. The Louis XVI style was to obtain an entirely different kind of effect, depending primarily on harmony of proportions.

Circa 1750 a reaction set in against the excesses of the rococo. This reaction led to a new stylistic synthesis. After a transitional period during which craftsmen were hesitant about abandoning the old style in favor of an entirely new one, an almost complete break was made at last. When Mme. Du Barry gave a reception for the opening of her new Château de Louveciennes in 1770, it was apparent that the Louis XV style, the most completely French of all styles, had given way to the Louis XVI style, whose predominant characteristic was the use of forms and decorative motifs borrowed from architecture and antique classical art.

Architectural forms come into fashion once again

In 1754 Cochin wrote his "Humble Supplication to Goldsmiths, Bronze-Chasers and Wood-Carvers." This contains the following passage: "At least let us hope that when things are intended to be square, they will not be twisted and distorted; ... we beg them (the wood-carvers) to realize that when we supply them with good straight pieces of wood it is ruinously expensive to have them cut into elaborately sinuous shapes..."

Curves began to be abandoned in favor of straight lines. At the same time rather fewer types of furniture were made, but at any rate the tendency to multiply new forms indefinitely was checked. Antiquity, with its rectilinear shapes and its right-angles, now set the style for furniture. The shapes, the silhouettes and the moldings of furniture all became simpler. Craftsmen like Georges Jacob knew how to make use of square shapes, straight lines and nicely calculated proportions in order to produce calm symmetrical effects.

Little by little, peg-top feet, fluted legs, etc., replaced the supple and sinuous forms of the slender legs with hoofed feet of the previous period. Stiff, upright caryatids at the corners took the place of gilt bronze mounts in the form of women. On chairs, the arm supports returned to their natural place above the front legs again. Towards the end of the Transitional period they were generally of baluster shape and usually decorated with narrow flutes. This remained the predominant type down to the end of the Louis XVI period.

Decorative elements taken from antiquity are sometimes found in use even before the new forms themselves begin to come into existence. Transitional period taste and fashion began quickly to turn towards ornaments in what was then called the "Greek style": ovoli, beading and acanthus-leaf motifs took the place of scrolls and rococo shapes. At the beginning, that was felt by many to be a sufficient concession to "the antique," and such decorative motifs were used on the curving shapes characteristic of the Louis XV style—especially on the typical cabriole legs of the period — for some time before true Louis XVI shapes came into existence.

Decoration becomes more restrained and more linear

In general it may be said that the forms of gilt bronze mounts grew more attenuated. Drawers and the dropfronts of secrétaires were merely framed with thin gilt-bronze moldings and furniture mounts generally became more severe and thinner; their ornaments were usually borrowed from the Doric or the Corinthian styles.

Small rosettes began to be used at the corners of secrétaires or at the ends of moldings which sometimes took the form of swags of drapery, instead of following classical models. Delicate garlands appeared in the centers of doors or on the capitals of columns. Emblematic trophies symbolizing music, gardening or some other favorite activity of the period also were used.

In marquetry, floral motifs were replaced by motifs of a geometrical character such as lozenge-shapes, circles or rectangles. Nevertheless, the total effect of the Louis XVI style is pleasing and the frequent use of ribbons and medallions, for instance, as a decorative adjunct to trophies of a pastoral character, has a charming and delicate effect.

Copies

At Paris a prosperous and well organized industry distributed an enormous number of copies of French XVIIIth century furniture throughout the world and thus greatly increased its fame.

In addition, rustic cupboards and chests of drawers of a Louis XV character were made in country districts long after Louis XVI, Directoire, Empire and Restoration styles had passed out of fashion in Paris. This was due to the long period required for a new style to penetrate from Paris to the provinces.

About a hundred years ago when taste began to turn back to the XVIIIth century, the fabrication of pieces in the various styles of the period became a commercial enterprise. Some thirty years ago there was a large store in Paris dealing in

both genuine antiques and modern copies. Two Louis XV cupboards could be seen standing side by side there, one a genuine period piece, the other an exact reproduction produced in the workshops attached to the store. Their prices varied, the one costing about four times the price of the other. The more costly piece was the reproduction.

There was a market for both types of furniture. Around 1900 the same situation existed with regard to veneered furniture. Wealthy middle-class clients were prepared to pay far more for copies produced in the Faubourg Saint-Antoine workshops than for original pieces in the hands of antique dealers. Fashion, the fact that the ordinary man-in-the-street knew little about values, and the advantage of being able to order a complete suite of furniture, all contributed to the existence of an enormous industry devoted solely to the reproduction of XVIIIth century furniture. In furniture as in fashion, the predominance of French taste was world-wide and French craftsmen in making these reproductions at least showed that they had lost none of their traditional skill.

This was manifest in the finest creations of the makers of these modern reproductions. They were masterpieces of their kind and the craftsman's signature on such a piece of furniture (for they frequently and proudly signed their pieces) adds considerably to their value even today. These faithfully well-made copies, reproduced in considerable numbers, played their part too in familiarizing a large public with the character and the forms of XVIIIth century furniture. The Wallace Collection in London, for instance, possesses an extraordinarily fine reproduction of the famous cylinder-topped desk (now in the Louvre) which was made for Louis XV. The reproduction has played an important part in making the English appreciate this masterpiece.

All the modern reproductions, whether they be interpretations or faithful copies of their originals, are still greatly sought after in Europe, in the Orient and in South America. They are still the object of a very active business which is handled by specialists dealing only in this kind of furniture.

XVIIIth Century Furniture Today

It is still occasionally possible to find not only important châteaux but even modest private houses in the provinces, still possessing all their original XVIIIth century furnishings. It is a privilege to see these for they convey something that no museum can offer. They distil the charm and the vitality of objects seen in their natural setting.

The principal reason why XVIIIth century furniture continues to remain in fashion has no connection with its speculative value or its value as an investment. It is rather that it is particularly well adapted to take its place in the simple, somewhat bare interiors of modern dwellings.

Nothing "tells" better against bare light-colored walls than a display cabinet, a bookcase, a writing table or a pair of wall-lights. The bare character of modern settings emphasizes the subtlety of the shapes of the objects themselves, shows them off and brings out their essential character.

Apart from their usefulness—and XVIIIth century furniture of all sorts is extremely well adapted for everyday use—such pieces bring a harmony and a sense of quality into modern interiors that nothing produced in our day can quite equal. For they exemplify the perfect combination of the artist's imagination with the craftsman's technical skill—where both are developed to the highest level of achievement.

This Louis XV cupboard *is outstandingly elegant, owing to brilliant scarlet panels of Chinese lacquer, with which the doors are decorated. The main body of the piece is veneered with tulip wood, and the panels of lacquer are enclosed in rococo frames of gilt bronze which, like the rest of the mounts of the piece, are of the finest quality. The piece is stamped by B. V. R. B. The slightly curving sides of the piece are veneered with floral designs in various woods, a style frequently adopted by this craftsman. Its size is: height: 5' 6"; breadth: 4' 7"; depth: 1' 3-3/4". (Color plate at right.)*

CHESTS OF DRAWERS (COMMODES)

A

A. THE LUXURY of the age of Louis XIV is still evident in this chest of drawers attributed to Cressent. In spite of the richness of its decoration, its shape is more functional than Boulle commodes of the previous century, which were architectural monuments of vast size and little convenience.

B. THE PATTERN of the veneers, usually of kingwood, plays an increasingly important part in the decoration of chests of drawers during the *Régence* period. The one illustrated here contains two tiers of drawers; its sinuous outlines are emphasized by a delicate beading of gilt bronze.

C. THIS CHEST OF DRAWERS is richly ornamented with gilt bronze and contains three tiers of drawers without any divisions between. The gilt bronze mounts are particularly rich and spread over the entire surface of the piece. The drawer handles are hardly visible for they form part of this gilt bronze decoration. This type of chest of drawers with short legs, and a lower edge coming almost down to the ground, is typical of the period and was reproduced by almost all the craftsmen of the time with varying degrees of richness in the decoration.

THE EARLIEST CHESTS OF DRAWERS date from the end of the reign of Louis XIV. They derived from decorative but impractical types of furniture: coffers and lidded chests. The idea of incorporating several drawers in these coffers gave rise to the utilitarian chest of drawers.

D. THE TOP DRAWER of this early Louis XV chest of drawers is unusual, for it is fitted as a writing desk. The design of the marquetry is rare, including *singeries* (scenes in which monkeys are shown in the attitudes of human beings). The piece is typical of the work of the great cabinetmaker Dubois.

B

C

D

A

C

THE SILHOUETTE OF THE LOUIS XV CHEST OF DRAWERS gradually became more sinuous, and increasingly rococo.

A. THE RED LACQUER PANELS are the most striking features of this chest of drawers. Its somewhat sober shape is offset by the gilt bronze mounts. Its small size suggests it was intended for the small, elegant rooms then coming into fashion.

D

B

B. THE ROCOCO MOUNTS of this piece of furniture show that it dates from the middle of the Louis XV period. They divide the front of the piece, which is veneered with black and gold Chinese lacquer, into three compartments. The central one is shaped like a shield from which raised scrolls emerge to form the handles of the drawers.

C. THE TRANSITIONAL CHEST OF DRAWERS between the Louis XV and Louis XVI types retains its cabriole legs as can be seen in the examples illustrated under C, D, and E here. At the same time, the rectilinear and classical forms of the Louis XVI period are foreshadowed in the designs of the body. Still lifes of domestic utensils and various other utilitarian objects, represented in marquetry, are characteristic of the work of the cabinetmaker Topino. This commode in the Transitional style has a body which is in the purest Louis XVI style, containing an upper drawer fitted with writing materials.

D. THE CABINETMAKER RIESENER made this Transitional chest of drawers. The interruption of the faces of the drawers by a marquetry panel, as well as the unusual character of the legs, are highly original features.

E. GEOMETRICAL MARQUETRY consisting of circles enclosing rosettes was often employed on this type of furniture right down to the end of the XVIIIth century. This chest of drawers, stamped by Dautriche, contains three tiers of drawers. The upper tier is mounted along the front and side with an elegant gilt bronze frieze.

E

A

THE LOUIS XVI CHEST OF DRAWERS was the most practical piece of furniture devised by the eighteenth century. The chest of drawers usually contained three tiers of drawers, sometimes with, and sometimes without, a division between them.

B

A. THE SHORT FEET and squat shape of this chest of drawers are extremely rare. It seems to be a sort of revival, on a reduced scale, of the "Commodes-tombeaux" (tomb-shaped chests of drawers) of the Louis XIV period.

B and C. ROUNDED CORNERS and tapering, fluted feet are the characteristics of these two Louis XVI chests of drawers. They differ chiefly in the richness of the gilt bronze mounts, although both have a bronze molding outlining the drawers.

D. LOUIS XVI CRAFTSMEN were able to work in the most varied materials: lacquer, shell, bronze, ebony, mahogany. Elaborate combinations of rich materials are characteristic of the style and are well illustrated by this piece of furniture intended to stand between two windows. It is not a chest of drawers though it derives from that piece of furniture. This example with its rich decoration (panels of black and gold lacquer framed with red shell) is signed by Weisweiler.

C

D

AN EXTRAORDINARY TECHNICAL SKILL and an outstanding decorative sense are the most striking features of this drop-front secrétaire made by Martin Carlin. It is ornamented with the gilt bronze festoons which are characteristic of Carlin's style, and the drop-front is inlaid with panels of marble mosaic.
(Color plate opposite.)

A

B

DROP-FRONT SECRÉTAIRES came into general use soon after the end of the *Régence* period and enjoyed an almost uninterrupted vogue. The drop-front operates on exactly the same principle as our modern desks. Generally, this type of furniture was intended to be used by women. This accounts for the extraordinary refinement of finish and luxurious character of their decoration.

A. IN THE EARLY LOUIS XV PERIOD this type of furniture was usually veneered with a simple tulip-wood marquetry. In the small secrétaire illustrated the sides curve inwards, and the front is of a delicate bow shape. A search for appealing forms was characteristic both of the period and of the work of the cabinetmaker Migeon, by whom the piece is signed. It measures only 43-1/4 " high.

B. THE MOST SOUGHT-AFTER SECRÉTAIRES of the Louis XV period nowadays are those veneered with lacquer panels, framed in elegant moldings of gilt bronze. The one illustrated was made by the cabinet maker Cuvelier.

C. THE UPPER PART OF THIS SECRÉTAIRE is shaped somewhat like the roof of a Chinese pagoda. This is characteristic of the taste for exoticism which was typical of one phase of the Louis XV style. The entire outline of the piece is sinuous. The drop-front and the door below are both veneered with panels of red and gold lacquer. The piece is signed by the well-known cabinetmaker Leleu.

C

D. SMALL, ELEGANT AND EXPENSIVELY DESIGNED pieces of the Louis XV period sometimes have the drop-front and the doors below of tambour design, that is to say formed by narrow slats of wood which slide sideways into grooves within the interior of the piece. These slats are treated just as if they were the ordinary wooden surface of a secrétaire. They are sometimes veneered with simple geometrical marquetry, sometimes with designs of flowers, etc., as is the case in the drop-front secrétaire illustrated opposite, which is stamped by Nicolas Petit.

D

A

B

B. THE MARQUETRY known as "*à la reine*" (in the queen's style) is often found on pieces which date from towards the end of the century. It frequently appears on pieces specially executed for Queen Marie-Antoinette. Her favorite floral motifs are enclosed in the trellis pattern of the marquetry, and the garlands of gilt bronze and medallions with an allegorical subject are types of decoration she particularly favored.

A. THE ARCHITECTURAL CHARACTER of the piece is emphasized when the marquetry is divided into separate panels. On the late Louis XV drop-front secrétaire illustrated above the marquetry is divided into four panels, each veneered with a similar floral bouquet.

C. THE DROP-FRONT SECRÉTAIRE illustrated at left has only a single door below the drop-front, whereas there are usually two. In this instance it is veneered with a simple geometric marquetry. A set of drawers is usually built into the interior of the cupboard behind the door. This drop-front secrétaire bears the stamp R. V. L. C.

D. THIS DROP-FRONT SECRÉTAIRE is the work of the cabinetmaker Jean-Henri Riesener and illustrates the balance and sense of proportion which is characteristic of Louis XVI furniture. Each panel is framed by a gilt bronze molding in low relief. The key-hole escutcheons on the doors, the circular handles of the drawers, the lambrequin in the centre of the base in front and the two rosettes with which the feet are mounted, are all of chased, gilt bronze. This piece, with its cut corners, is typical of the simple forms which the greatest craftsmen of the period were prepared to use when they were not working for royalty.

C

D

A

A. THE FIRST STAGE in the evolution of the Louis XV bookcase was taken when grilled doors replaced the solid doors used on bookcases of the previous century. This bookcase is veneered with tulip-wood and richly mounted in chased, gilt bronze in the form of masks and foliated scrolls of a type characteristic of the *Régence* period.

D. THIS BOOKCASE, veneered with mahogany, combines the forms of two different types of furniture: the drop-front secrétaire, and the chest of drawers. It dates from the end of the XVIIIth century and its style already foreshadows a type of furniture which was to appear in the early years of the XIXth century.

D

B

BOOKCASES, like so much furniture we use to-day, first came into being at the end of the XVIIth century. Louis XIV bookcases in the Boulle style show how quickly the form was perfected, and thenceforward the only variations are those due to changes in the trend of decoration.

B. THIS MAGNIFICENT LOUIS XV BOOKCASE is veneered with an attractive marquetry of rare design in sycamore and kingwood. The sinuous outline of the door-panel is emphasized by a delicate molding of gilt bronze. The piece is the work of the cabinetmaker J.-C. Saunier.

C. ELEGANCE AND REFINEMENT are the outstanding characteristics of all furniture intended for use in the small harmonious boudoirs of this period. They are to be seen in the fashionable proportions of this small bookcase with its marble top.

C

A

B

CORNER CUPBOARDS

A. THE ORIENTAL CHARACTER of the gilt bronze mounts of this piece, as well as the black and gold lacquer with which it is veneered, illustrate the taste for the exotic which prevailed during the middle years of Louis XV's reign. The lower edge of this corner cupboard, with its sinuous form, is given an unusual degree of prominence.

B. THE FRONT OF THIS CORNER CUPBOARD is of an elaborately curved and bowed form. It is veneered with sprays of flowers enclosed in a rich framework of gilt bronze typical of the early Louis XV style. On this corner cupboard by Dubois a third foot is set in the center of the front.

C. THE NEO-CLASSIC GILT BRONZE MOUNTS of this Louis XVI corner cupboard take the form of a wave motif in the frieze, classical medallions on the corners, together with flutes, swags and flaming urns.

D. THE SOBER LINES of this corner cupboard give it perfect architectural balance. It is the work of the cabinetmaker J.-L. Cosson.

CORNER CUPBOARDS were of a strictly utilitarian character before becoming purely decorative pieces of furniture. They formed part of the wall paneling and generally contained shelves, very often fitted with water tanks, basins, bowls, etc., intended for the service of the table or for toilet use. When eventually they were introduced into drawing rooms they took on all the elegant shapes and decorative forms of the setting in which they were destined to be used.

C

D

A

B

A. THE TRUE WRITING TABLE begins to appear during the *Régence* period. It is the successor of the typical Boulle writing table, and its ancestry goes back to the Louis XIII writing tables surmounted by a nest of drawers. It usually contained three drawers, like the one illustrated here. The top is covered with leather which took the place of a coarse cotton material called "bu-reau" with which such pieces were originally covered, and from which the French word for desk, "bureau" has been derived.

C. THE FASHION FOR WRITING TABLES reached its height during the Louis XV period. This type of furniture, originally devised to be used by men, began to be made for women also, during the middle of the century. It then became a boudoir writing desk and was invariably small. The restricted size and rich decoration of the example illustrated are typical of a mid-Louis XV writing desk.

C

B. A CARTONNIER is a set of shelves and drawers intended to hold papers, writing materials, etc. It is exceedingly rare to find one forming an integral part of the writing table like the example illustrated here. This one is quite unusually small (4' 3" × 2' 3-1/2") and dates from the Louis XV period.

D. THE CYLINDER-TOP DESK was devised to allow papers to be rapidly put out of sight. The one illustrated here was made by Riesener for the French Crown; it is in the early Louis XVI style though it dates from somewhat later. The legs are slightly curved, reminiscent of the Louis XV style, while the body and especially the gilt bronze mounts, are in the fully developed Louis XVI style.

D

WRITING TABLES

B. THIS SMALL, ELEGANT, AND REFINED CYLINDER-TOPPED DESK, made by Riesener for Marie-Antoinette for the Tuileries Palace, is an illustration of how well formal types of furniture could be adapted for feminine use.

A. THE FRONT OF THIS LOUIS XVI WRITING TABLE can be pulled out to increase the writing surface. This arrangement is very unusual in the case of a large writing table like the one illustrated. It is, however, not uncommonly met with in small writing tables, where the top can quite frequently be extended, and supported on an extra pair of legs.

B

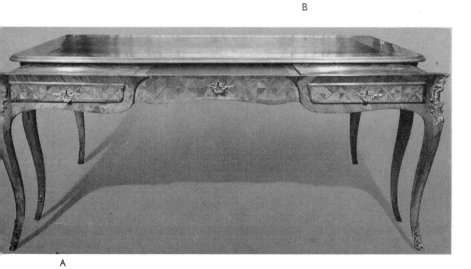

A

C

C. THIS IMPRESSIVE WRITING TABLE is notable for its exceptionally refined gilt bronze decoration: the frieze is in an interlacing design, while the keyhole is flanked by large sprays of oak leaves.

D. THIS TYPICAL LOUIS XVI WRITING TABLE contains three drawers and is supported on four tapering, fluted legs. The gilt bronze mounts are of the simplest character; the drawers lightly emphasized by a delicate molding. The legs are shod with gilt bronze feet of classical design.

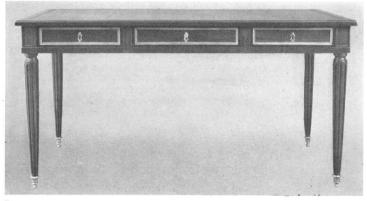

D

A

B

C

SMALL TABLES constitute the aristocracy of XVIIIth century furniture, demonstrating the fertility of contemporary cabinetmakers' ideas better than other pieces. They were born of the need for small portable tables which could be utilized for a wide variety of purposes. Ultimately various specialized types were devised for use as gaming tables, bedside tables, what-nots, etc.

F. THIS SMALL LOUIS XV TABLE exemplifies all the characteristic elements of the style of its period.

F

D

A, B and C. THESE ARE GAME TABLES, or tric-trac tables as they are sometimes called. They have three features: the top can be reversed; it is covered with leather on one side and material on the other, for writing or playing cards. The interior contains the pieces required for the game. The two forms, square and rectangular, in which the gaming table is found from the *Régence* period right down to the end of the XVIIIth century, are both illustrated here.

D. THIS WRITING TABLE dates from the *Régence* period. It is of carved wood, and was usually covered either with a tablecloth, or with an elegant piece of needlework.

E

E. THIS TABLE, BY TOPINO, has marquetry around the frieze imitating the forms of gilt bronze, so that mounts have been dispensed with. The top is veneered with a marquetry panel of high quality representing a still life containing a vase, a book, a pen, and an envelope.

G. HEXAGONAL LEGS with a shelf fitted between them are the outstanding features of this beautiful writing table by Carlin. The gilt bronze mounts, in the purest Louis XVI style, stand out beautifully against the black ebony veneer.

H. THE GILT BRONZE mounts of this writing table have been treated with the greatest subtlety and freedom by its maker, Riesener. It is a masterpiece which shows the extraordinary degree of accomplishment of which the great cabinetmakers of the latter part of the century were capable.

G

H

IS SMALL TABLE BY R. V. L. C. combines the elegance of the Louis XV e and the refinement of the Louis XVI. It is of painted wood, mounted h gilt bronze, and a plaque of Sèvres porcelain forms the top. *(Color plate opposite.)*

A'

A

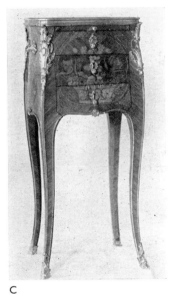

B

B. THE SMALL SIZE and almost square shape of this table (it is only 14″ wide) made it well adapted to the small rooms in fashion during the Louis XV period.

C. THIS WORK TABLE contains three drawers just as did the contemporary chest of drawers. It is in the Louis XV style and bears the stamp of Delorme. The upper drawer opens at the side.

A. THIS SMALL LOUIS XV TABLE by Boudin has perhaps more appearance of strength than elegance of proportions, but its top is a masterpiece of multicolored marquetry. It is inlaid in the center with a landscape in the style of C.-J. Vernet.

D. THE GREAT CABINETMAKERS of the period exercised all their ingenuity in devising small writing tables intended to be used by women. The top of this one is inlaid with floral marquetry of flowing design and sinuous outline. Its cabriole legs are mounted on feet of gilt bronze scrolls.

C

D

E. THIS TABLE by Nicolas Petit with its sober lines and simple, plain veneer is a typical example of the small tables of the Louis XV period.

E

B. THIS "DRUM-SHAPED" TABLE is by Boudin. This kind of table usually had only a single compartment in the interior, but it is sometimes fitted with three drawers.

B

C. OVAL TABLES were particularly fashionable in the Louis XVI period. The top, the drawer, and the shelf between the legs of this table are all of quite admirable proportions.

C

A. AN ORIGINAL FEATURE of this writing table in the Transitional manner is the fact that drawers at each side spring open when a small button is pressed. It is stamped by Topino. The shelf between the legs is kidney-shaped to allow room for the sitter's legs.

D. THIS LITTLE TABLE by Weisweiler illustrates the characteristically pure lines and refined shapes of Louis XVI furniture. The top and shelf are marble, framed in a molding of gilt bronze.

F. SMALL TABLES of this unusual design, which resemble gueridon tables with two tops, came into use towards the end of the Louis XVI period. The circular top is of Chinese black and gold lacquer. The lower shelf, veneered with a scrolled marquetry, can be opened in two semi-circular flaps. This piece is by Gaspar Schneider, who became a master-craftsman in 1786.

D

E. THE NEO-CLASSIC CHA-RACTER of this Louis XVI table is emphasized by the presence of a classical ewer, set on the crossing of the stretchers.

E

F

53

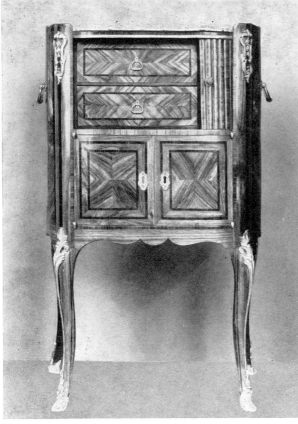

A

B

BEDSIDE TABLES were intended, as their name implies, for use in the bedroom. Certain types known as "en-cas" (for emergency use) were intended to be laid with a light supper which could be eaten during the night. They were frequently provided with handles at each end so that they could be easily moved.

C. PIERCED CORNER MOUNTS simulated in marquetry are a remarkable feature of this Louis XV bedside table of an elegant and original shape. The lower part is open.

A and B. TABLES OF THE "EN-CAS" type were often fitted with a slatted shutter which could be slid aside to reveal a set of drawers. The top was often of marble so that breakfast or supper could be served upon it. The lower part, closed either with one or two doors, was known as the "necessary" cupboard. These tables both date from the first half of the XVIIIth century.

D. THIS BEDSIDE TABLE in the Transitional style veneered with marquetry incorporating Chinese figures was designed by Topino.

D

E. THIS KIDNEY-SHAPED BEDSIDE table is in the Transitional style and bears the stamp of the cabinetmaker Carlin.

E

F. THE RECTANGULAR SHAPE of this small table with its veneer of trellis design, enclosing quatrefoils in marquetry of various colored woods, is typical of the Louis XVI style. It is signed by G. Kemp.

F

A'

B

C

D

THE BONHEUR-DU-JOUR first appeared in the middle of the XVIIIth century. It is a piece of furniture intended for women, and combines a writing desk and a toilet-table. It takes its name from the speed with which it achieved success with the public.

A. THE ORIGINAL FEATURE of this *bonheur-du-jour* is its oval shape. The marquetry can easily be recognized as the work of Topino. The gilt bronze mounts and cabriole legs show that it dates from the Transitional period.

B. A NEST OF DRAWERS is often to be found resting on the upper part of a *bonheur-du-jour*. The one illustrated here, in the late Louis XV style, has two drawers in the body of the piece.

C. THIS COMBINED DESK AND *bonheur-du-jour* of light colored satinwood is inlaid with two oval plaques of Sèvres porcelain. It bears the stamp of Saunier.

D. THE LOWER STAGE of this *bonheur-du-jour* is in the form of a lean-to desk. The design of the marquetry is of the type sometime known as "*à la reine*" (see above p. 45) and the gilt bronze ornaments are of that neo-classic form in full favor towards the end of the XVIIIth century.

A

B

C

B. THIS LOUIS XV INVALID TABLE contains no mechanism at all. The upper part with its four short legs can be lifted off and placed on the bed. It was the work of the cabinetmaker Criaerd.

C. THE SMALL SIZE of the top of this heart-shaped toilet table can be increased by an ingenious device. Drawers in the shape of butterfly wings spring out at each side when a button is pressed. Pieces of this type were very fashionable during the Transitional period. The one shown has the stamp of the cabinetmaker Cordié.

D

MECHANICAL DEVICES were sometimes used in the construction of a piece of furniture so that it could be adapted to a variety of purposes. This was a specialty of numerous German cabinetmakers such as Weisweiler, Rœntgen, Canabas and Œben, who worked in Paris.

A. THIS LOUIS XVI WRITING TABLE by Weisweiler is veneered with amboyna wood inlaid with ebony. Satinwood is used for the lining of the drawers. A system of rods and ratchets concealed in the legs enables the top to be raised so as to provide space on the second table top beneath.

E. MECHANICAL FEATURES and multiple functions were better adapted to the Louis XVI style than to any other. In this combined writing table and toilet table a mechanical device releases a mirror, a reading desk, a large drawer and two smaller ones fitted with small bottles for perfumes or toilet unguents. It was designed by David Rœntgen.

D. THIS MECHANICAL MUSIC-STAND or reading-desk in the Louis XVI style is the work of the accomplished master cabinetmaker Canabas. When folded it has the appearance of a small table resting on a single central leg with three feet.

E

E′

A

TOILET-TABLES first appeared during the Louis XV period. They were not intended for women only. Models exist which were particularly designed for masculine use.

A. THE TYPICAL LOUIS XV TOILET-TABLE is in the form of a table with a drawer in the center of the front and a top which opens as three separate panels. The one illustrated here, by Peridiez, is veneered with various wood and inlaid with a floral marquetry.

B. THE TOILET COMPARTMENTS separated by a space for the knees are the notable feature of this Louis XV toilet-table by Migeon. The one at the left usually contained toilet utensils as well as perfume bottles and cream jars.

B

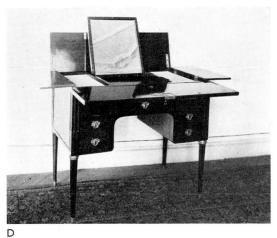

D

E. THIS SMALL TALLBOY (or chiffonier) dates from the early Louis XV period, and contains eight drawers. It is the work of the cabinetmaker Dubois.

D. THE RECTILINEAR LINES of the Louis XVI toilet-table give it an austere character which foreshadows the Empire style. The principles of its construction are the same as those of the Louis XV period.

C. THE CHIFFONIER (tallboy), sometimes known as a "semainier" (i.e. it contained a drawer for each day of the week), is a piece comprising numerous drawers one above the other. This practical piece of furniture appeared towards the middle of the XVIIIth century. The Louis XVI example illustrated is veneered with black and gold lacquer in the Chinese manner, and signed G.-A. Bruns.

E

C

A.

A. THE VIGOR OF THE CARVING of the frame of this Louis XV *bergère* armchair emphasizes the majestic elegance of its shape. The front legs are carved with an open flower enclosed in a heart-shaped cartouche.

B.

F.

B. THIS LOUIS XV WINGED BERGÈRE ARMCHAIR was made by the chairmaker Tilliard. The upholstery insures comfort and the wings give protection from the draught.

F. SQUARE SHAPES and straight legs are characteristic of late XVIIIth century chairs. Larger *bergère* armchairs, are known as "*marquises.*"

D. THE VOLUMINOUS ROBES which were in fashion during the Louis XV period frequently made it necessary for the arm rests of small *bergère* armchairs to be set well back behind the front edge of the seat.

C.

C. AN UPHOLSTERED LEDGE along the top rail of the back of this chair known as a "*bergère ponteuse*" (gaming chair) is its outstanding feature, designed so that onlookers could supervise a friend's card game.

E.

E. THE SCROLLED SHAPE OF THE BACK of this armchair is very rare. It dates from the Transitional period between the Louis XV and Louis XVI styles, although the straight legs with their twisted flutes are already in the full Louis XVI style.

DURING THE RÉGENCE PERIOD chairs began to be designed for greater comfort. The backs were inclined slightly and the legs made rather shorter. In the so-called "*bergère*" (the word occurs occasionally in XVIIIth century English inventories as "Berger") padded cushioning was first used. The sides of the chair are upholstered, and the arms distinctly more curved.

D.

A

B

C

A. ARMCHAIRS of unstained carved wood from the early XVIIIth century are often upholstered with tapestry enclosing a single floral medallion.

B. THE FLAT-BACKED RÉGENCE ARMCHAIR illustrated here is characterized by the refinement of the carving, the sinuous frame, the cabriole legs.

C. CANING CAME INTO FASHION for armchairs about the beginning of the XVIIIth century. This light upholstery was employed during the Louis XV period by many of the greatest chairmakers but gradually passed out of use as the Louis XVI period advanced.

D. THIS ARMCHAIR with flat upright back upholstered with detachable cushions dates from the Louis XV period, and is signed by Tilliard.

D

E

E. THE TYPICAL LOUIS XV armchair, perhaps the most perfectly designed French chair, no longer shows Italian influences as did the Louis XIV armchair, and does not imitate classical models. This armchair, made by Blanchard, this a perfect example of the type.

F. THE CARVING of the arm supports, the legs, and of the frame around the seat of this Transitional armchair is already inspired by neo-classic motifs characteristic of the Louis XVI period, although it still preserves the general form of the Louis XV chair.

G. THE CHAIR WITH A MEDALLION BACK is one of the commonest types of Louis XVI armchair. It exists in several forms: oval, lightly curving to fit the sitter's back, or it may have a flat, nearly round back. This latter shape was particularly favored for large chairs. The one illustrated is by J.-B. Meunier.

F

G

A

B

C

A. THE CHARACTERISTIC FEATURES of this *Régence* chair are its flat back, its cane upholstery, the cross stretcher joining the legs, and the flowing sculpture carved in low relief.

B. THE ELEGANCE of the Louis XV chair is epitomized in the simple carved moldings and the double curves of the frame of this chair, which is the work of Sulpice Brizard.

C. THE RICHLY PATTERNED UPHOLSTERY of this chair by Nogaret of Lyons makes it suitable for a drawing room.

D. THIS CHAIR called a *cabriolet* dates from the last years of the Louis XV style. It has a violin-shaped back, slightly curved to fit the sitter's back.

F. A LYRE, CARVED AND ENCLOSED within the frame of a rectangular or round-topped chair back is one of the most remarkable motifs devised by Louis XVI chairmakers. This one is signed by Dupin. Its frame is of gilt wood, upholstered in plain silk velvet piped around its edges. This model was repeated under the Directoire and the Empire.

E. THE "ANSE DE PANIER" (basket-handled) back of this chair was one in the large repertory of forms available during the Louis XVI period. The one illustrated here is the work of Dupin.

G. THE SQUARE - BACKED CHAIR, its frame simply molded, is perhaps the most sought after Louis XVI chair today. It was originally devised by the celebrated chairmaker Georges Jacob, and repeated both by him and his imitators.

D

E

F

G

THE FRAME OF THIS RÉGENCE SOFA is elegantly carved with pomegranates, shells and rococo forms. It is richly upholstered with tapestry woven with poppies and birds.

THIS LOUIS XV BASKET-SHAPED SOFA is one of the most sought-after types today. The back is of sinuous outline and is prolonged into armrests which envelope the sitter. It bears the stamp of Henri Amand.

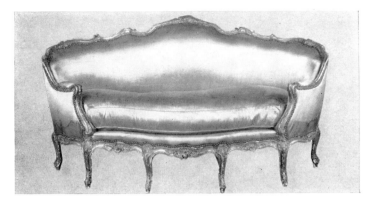

A SOFA invariably formed a part of a complete set of XVIIIth century furniture. Such a suite would usually include one or two sofas, a pair of *marquises*, four *bergère* armchairs, twelve armchairs (fauteuils), twelve chairs, some stools and one or two screens. The sofa was the most important, and numerous types exist such as the square sofa with open arms, the basket-shaped sofa and the winged sofa. These are perhaps most sought-after today.

THE LOUIS XV SOFA illustrated here is of a particularly rich design. Its most outstanding feature is the bold shape of the back, and the open upholstered arms. Beneath the seat the frame is carved with floral motifs, cartouches, and sprays. It bears the stamp of the chairmaker Tilliard.

THIS CORNER SOFA is a very rare specimen. The frame is carved with plain molding which emphasizes its shape. In this it resembles a large number of chairs of the late Louis XVI period. The finest designs for these were created by the great chairmakers Georges Jacob and Séné.

THIS TYPE OF SOFA with its scroll-shaped ends is typical of the Louis XVI style. It hardly differs from daybeds of the period.

CERAMICS

Porcelain and Faience in the XVIIIth Century

Porcelain and faience enjoyed an immense vogue during the whole of the XVIIIth century. They were extensively employed in fields where their use had hitherto been the exception. In addition they served a far wider public than they had in the past. A new creative impulse seemed to inspire the ceramicists of the XVIIIth century and their products were greatly influenced by other arts.

From the very beginning of the century a completely new field opened to the ceramic arts. A variety of factors contributed to this development. Louis XIV's many wars had ruined the French treasury and caused the King to compel his subjects to send their gold and silver plate to the mint to be melted down; he also issued edicts limiting the uses to which precious metals might be put. Saint-Simon tells us that the King set an example by sending his magnificent silver to the melting pot and then deciding to replace these masterpieces with faience. His example was followed everywhere; the fashion for faience gained in popularity and henceforward new and unexpected opportunities opened before the owners of faience factories at Rouen and elsewhere.

Another fashion arose: the vogue for small objects of a purely decorative character. More and more small, precious "objets d'art" were made of china. Many of them were given an even more luxurious character by being mounted, either in silver, as in the case of boxes and other small objects (p. 80, C, 82, B, and 83, E), or in gilt bronze, as in the case of vases and statuettes (p. 65). The vogue for these tiny works of art was immense and a factory like Mennecy devoted itself almost entirely to their manufacture.

This fashion for small objects, like the fashion for increasingly smaller rooms, spread to foreign factories. There, china objects began to be made on a smaller scale than ever before. The large dishes, wall-fountains, and basins of the Louis XIV and even of the "Régence" period gave way progressively to smaller objects better suited for daily use (footnote 1).

A wider public began to interest itself in china and to have an influence on its decoration. In imitation of the King, the nobility began to have their table services made of faience, especially in the second half of the century, when the demand for table services and other utilitarian objects became widespread. For a vast public, objects in porcelain, which had formerly been unknown except in the upper ranks of society, began to become almost essential luxuries. The "Compagnie des Indes" (East India Company) imported incredible quantities of porcelain and created an immense public for it. French porcelain manufacturers also sought to profit from this ever-increasing market (footnote 2). To meet the varied needs of this new public, a large number of factories came into existence: Strasbourg, Niderviller, Lille, Sinceny, Sceaux, Chantilly, Mennecy, Vincennes, Sèvres, etc. The factories which had already been established in the XVIIth century enjoyed a new prosperity: Rouen, Moustiers, Marseilles, St. Cloud (footnote 3). Some of the greatest persons in the kingdom (footnote 4) took factories under their protection, with far-reaching effects on the high reputation of French china.

Numerous technical innovations were introduced: to the traditional type of faience decorated in "high temperature" colors were successively added "soft paste" porcelain, faiences decorated in "low temperature" colors, then "hard paste" porcelains, whose basic constituent was kaolin clay, and lastly the "pipe clays." At first these materials were used in rare and costly objects which were purchased by the richest classes alone, but gradually the expensive new methods and new styles passed out of fashion. When they did so, their makers turned to a new market: to the less demanding middle classes.

This development occurred in almost all the great factories. After a brilliant period when working for wealthy patrons, they sought wider outlets for their products, often to the detriment of their artistic excellence. This did not occur simultaneously everywhere; circumstances differed from factory to factory.

When, for instance, the Vincennes factory was at the height of its success in 1750, Rouen was already on the way to producing simpler wares. Under Louis XV, money was lavished on the porcelain factories with a prodigal hand; the directors of the factories responded by devising new and more astonishing types of designs, as well as inventing increasingly important manufacturing techniques. Under Louis XVI, however, the changing trends of taste brought a new balance and harmony to ceramic design. Factories also became more interested in supplying a less specialized and a less sophisticated public.

Other arts exercised considerable influence during the XVIIIth century in extending the high reputation of faience and porcelain and in enriching its designs.

Although famous painters occasionally provided designs for porcelain and faience, in general the forms of ceramic decoration were distinctive and original (footnote 5). When themes were borrowed from paintings they were usually interpreted fairly freely, as were the seascapes of Vernet, which were copied at Marseilles (p. 67). More often they were reduced in scale so as to play merely a small part in the decoration: such as the cupids after Boucher (p. 85, A), "fête galante" scenes after Watteau, etc. At the beginning of the century large central reserves had sometimes been painted with scenes like the "hunts" of Tempesta (p. 68, D). But these reserves grew less and less important under Louis XV (p. 70, E) and eventually became simple medallions during

---

Faiences decorated in "high temperature" colors are vividly ornamental. On this Sinceny porcelain tray there are two coats of arms in the decorative scheme which is of the traditional Rouen—or rather "Sino-Rouen"—type. The influence of Chinese patterns, which were imitated at Rouen for many years, can still be seen in the style in which the flowers and birds are painted. But in this example there is also an element of the rococo; for the composition has much greater complexity than its Chinese prototype.

1. "I must confess that the Dresden porcelain cost me rather a lot, but then I bought eight complete table-services, besides what I spent on framing my mirrors in Dresden porcelain, as well as in buying chandeliers, clocks and a toilet service for my dressing-room. Indeed my passion for Dresden stops just this side of idolatry. I am really Dresden porcelain from head to foot." Letter from a lady of the court of Louis XV, cited by Émile Bourgeois. ("Le Biscuit de Sèvres au XVIIIe siècle," Paris, 1909.)

the Louis XVI period (p. 77, E). Sculptors, in particular, exercised a direct influence on ceramics, since they were often called upon to create and even to execute groups of figures on a small scale, as well as statuettes. Cyfflé, who was both a sculptor and a ceramic worker, carried out his own models in "terre de Lorraine" at Lunéville. Niderviller had an important workshop of sculptors, but at the Vincennes-Sèvres factory, in particular, there was an exceptionally large number of famous sculptors amongst the modelers employed: Falconet, Defernex, Bouchardon, Lemoyne, Clodion, Pajou, etc. In these various factories, innumerable groups of lovers, peasants, etc., were produced (p. 75, E, and 85, D), as well as statuettes of children (p. 75, F, and 85, B) or mythological subjects (p. 79, E). Other factories specialised in figures representing the "Streetcries of Paris" (p. 75, D, and 79, A), and towards the end of the century allegoric subjects, often of a very cold academic character, began to appear. The Royal factory at Sèvres employed its sculptors in designing shapes of vases as well as the more important pieces for table services. This explains the extraordinary effectiveness of their forms, as can be seen in the chamber candlesticks (p. 87, D), the soup-tureens (p. 87, A), or the vases (p. 86) illustrated. This last object was probably commissioned as a Royal gift.

Silver exercised rather less influence on the forms of porcelain and faience. It was only at the factory known as "du Pont-aux-Choux" at Paris that the forms of silver and metal work were exactly copied. This factory employed goldsmiths to design its models (p. 79, C and D). All these varied contributions, either due to indirect influences or to direct borrowings, gave an added vitality to the ceramic arts in France.

Shapes

Each center of production, and sometimes each individual workshop, had its own exclusive shapes. They were inspired by prevailing Parisian fashions, and were very rarely copied from pieces produced at rival establishments. In the earlier part of the century certain foreign influences persisted: a slight Italian influence at Moustiers, for instance, and a pronounced German influence at Strasbourg.

The shapes of Louis XIV faiences were simple: round, oval, or rectilinear in the case of dishes, flower pots and bowls (p. 68, A, B, D). Larger and more imposing pieces, like wall-fountains and large decorative ewers, remained massive and somewhat architectural in character, but their lines were always balanced and harmonious (p. 68, E). At St. Cloud these forms were enriched with gadrooning only.

Shapes derived from the Far East were imitated at St. Cloud, Chantilly, and Mennecy in their so-called "Korean" designs. They were simple, clear and precise (p. 82, D and H). Their influence persisted even when the direct copying of Oriental models gave way to French styles.

Louis XV shapes were adopted everywhere, but not always with equal success. For many years the most popular styles included: plates and dishes with lobed or shaped borders; soup-tureens with sinuous outlines, supported on small scrolled legs, with lids surmounted with a knob in the form of flowers, fruit or animals; and decorations of rococo forms, scrolls and volutes. The shapes adopted at the Vincennes-Sèvres factory were particularly satisfactory, for this factory had never been influenced by Chinese porcelains (p. 84, A, and 86). At Niderviller and Lunéville shapes were restrained and elegant (p. 75, B, and 78, A), and of a most vivaciously baroque character at Strasbourg (p. 74, D). At Marseilles, free and imaginative shapes were used right down to the end of the century (p. 77, A and F) and throughout the period Rouen continued to use somewhat heavy shapes (p. 70, C).

The severe shapes peculiar to the Louis XVI style with its pilasters, flutings, straight lines, etc., were seldom adopted for faience, because faience paste was much more suitable for fluently composed and subtle forms. Marseilles (p. 67) or Sceaux (p. 76, E), were never successful in this severe Louis XVI style, and the St. Clément factory (p. 78, B and E) was hardly more successful. On the other hand, the porcelain factories at Niderviller (p. 89, A) and especially those at Sèvres (p. 88, A) and Paris (p. 89, D), adapted them with far greater success.

Decoration

At the beginning of the century, the most outstanding decorative motif was the "lambrequin," first created at the Rouen factory, where it was used with excellent effect from the end of the XVIIth century onwards. It is essentially a symmetrical design arranged to converge towards a central point, generally decorated with a coat of arms or a small scene of figures or a landscape (p. 68, A and B). When, after melting down his silver, the King extended his patronage to the faience factories lambrequin designs came into widespread use. The motif allows for much variation and adaptation. Originally, and indeed almost always, it was executed in blue and white, though eventually a touch of red was sometimes added (footnote 6).

Such decorative motifs as "hunting scenes," after Tempesta, continued to be used for some years at Moustiers. They were generally painted blue and white. This type, too, was an inheritance from the XVIIth century; doubtless the last vestige of an Italian influence which was at one time of great importance at this factory (p. 68, D). Soon it was replaced by a new type of decoration inspired by Bérain. The compositions in this style were symmetrical, just as were the "lambrequin" designs, but they were symmetrical in relation to a vertical axis rather than to a central point. Arabesques, pilasters and garlands framed the cartouches; and the reserves were painted with fantastic animals seated on brackets, etc. The entire design was drawn with extreme precision in blue on a white ground (p. 68, C). There was more elegance than strength in the "Bérain" style of the "Régence" period, and the shapes on which it was used already showed a tendancy to become lighter and more elegant.

Far Eastern art influenced French ceramics greatly during the XVIIIth century, but this influence varied from factory to

---

2. *Every factory produced table services. Faience factories like Rouen (with its famous "cornucopia" decoration, p. 70, C), Strasbourg (flowers, p. 74, C and E), Marseilles (flowers, landscapes, p. 77, A and D), Moustiers (grotesques, p. 71, B; the "potato flower," p. 71, E) and the porcelain factories of Sèvres (from the "Royal" services, p. 87, A and exceptional pieces like the "Buffon table service," p. 87, B, down to those with simple floral decoration with or without "cabbage leaf" motifs, p. 87, C) or Chantilly (carnation, floral sprays, p. 82, E and F). The Parisian factories devoted themselves to this type of production, using fairly simple schemes of decoration (flowers in various colors, p. 89, D) and sprays of flowers scattered all over the surface (p. 89, E).*

3. *The sole exception to this was the Nevers factory, whose former excellent output was no longer maintained during the XVIIIth century.*

4. *The Prince de Condé with his famous collection of "kakiemon" (Korean) porcelain was the founder of the Chantilly factory. Every year at Versailles, the King, as proprietor of the Sèvres factory, organized a sale of the best pieces produced there. Courtiers were eager to make numerous purchases even though prices were high, in order to please their sovereign.*

5. *Pictures were hardly ever copied directly on porcelain or faience, as had been the case in the XVIth century at Lyons, or as is sometimes done today. The type of decoration invented by the Bérain family was indeed closely copied at Moustiers, just as Tempesta's hunting scenes were, but such rare examples are exceptional and date only from the beginning of the century.*

6. *Its success was so great that it was copied everywhere both in France and abroad. The Lille factory made especially skilful use of the "lambrequin"*

factory, and it is important to distinguish the different results.

Extreme instances occur where an attempt has been made to copy or exactly imitate Oriental porcelains. At the soft-paste porcelain factories, especially at Chantilly during its earliest period, the workers attempted to duplicate a type of porcelain which was already greatly admired. This was the "Korean" porcelain which was reproduced with remarkable fidelity at Chantilly (p. 81, 82, A, D, H), and imitated with a warmer range of color, a greater freedom of design and a rather more vigorous composition, at St. Cloud (p. 80, E and D). In the early years of the Mennecy factory, too, the same types were imitated (p. 83, A).

"Blancs de Chine" (white glazed porcelain) were imitated with even greater success. The creamy appearance of the French soft-paste porcelain very closely approximated the special paste used for the "Chinese" white porcelain, especially at St. Cloud (p. 80, C). At Mennecy and Chantilly (footnote 7) also, Oriental figures, and objects decorated with flowers in

"The Spring" is a very exceptional piece of porcelain from two points of view. First on account of its size (length 17" without the bronze mounts), for soft paste porcelain is much more suitable for pieces of smaller size; it is of an exceedingly fragile nature and warps or collapses very easily while being heated. Secondly it is exceptional on account of the charming color scheme. Almost all the groups produced at the Vincennes-Sèvres factory were white, either being merely glazed or more frequently left in the biscuit state. This piece, which bears the date-letter for 1756, is enriched with magnificent gilt-bronze mounts which, in addition to providing the base, appear around the figure itself in the form of a lizard, sprays of foliage and a palm tree.

relief were produced with modeling in clean-cut lines.

Chinese styles heavily influenced the Rouen faience-makers. Ming blue and white porcelain was already being copied at this factory when the century began (footnote 8). The paste used for these copies remained exactly the same as that used for pieces decorated in the "lambrequin" style. This last type of decoration was later enlivened with a few touches of red, added to the initial blue and white pattern. Eventually polychrome decoration prevailed over the earlier and simpler styles (p. 69, A and F). Circa 1725, these colors were especially

pattern (p. 68, A); Strasbourg in its earlier years adopted it also (p. 68, F); Leroi, at Marseilles, used it for a much longer period, introducing variations and adapting it to shapes of a Louis XV character (p. 69, G). It was even used on St. Cloud porcelains with an extraordinarily elegant effect (p. 80, B).

7. Eventually "whites" were produced in a less imitative style and in French shapes. These were frequently decorated with gadrooning (p. 80, A) and in relief with plants of a less exotic character than those used on Oriental models, as well as with large flowers in the "French" style. Statuettes of European figures and other objects (especially candy boxes) were also produced in this beautiful material, without any decoration whatever.

8. The same was true at Nevers, where models in the "Chinese" style in blue and white, which had continued in use since about 1650, were still being made well on into the early years of the XVIIIth century.

9. This theme was adopted by other faience factories, notably Lunéville, where it was used successfully in large, vigorous and decorative scenes (p. 78, D), and rather less successfully at the Les Islettes factory. It was also used in very gay colors by Férat at Moustiers as well (p. 71, F). A type of "chinoiserie" in the style of Pillement, rapidly and gaily drawn, was sometimes used at Moustiers as well as at Marseilles (p. 71, H). Porcelain was comparatively seldom decorated with Chinese figures though occasionally they are used on a small scale on the hard paste porcelains of Sèvres, Strasbourg and Paris.

10. The shapes of certain pieces produced at Sèvres, Niderviller (p. 75, B), at Lunéville (p. 78, A), are very gaily emphasized or outlined with scrolls in relief, decorated either with gilding, with bright red, or with several bright colors.

11. Nevertheless certain instances must be mentioned, notably the Royal busts (as well as those of Bonaparte) produced in biscuit porcelain at Sèvres,

used to produce quite accurate copies of the so-called "famille verte" Chinese K'ang-H'si porcelain.

But soon the attempt to imitate Oriental models exactly (p. 69, E) gave way to a new development: the so-called Sino-Rouen style (p. 70, C) which continued in use to the end of the century and was imitated by numerous faience factories, such as Lille (p. 69, B) and especially Sinceny (p. 62). This style was distinguished by highly original Chinese scenes.

At most factories, Chinese pieces were no longer used as exact models; but many exotic, amusing and fantastic subjects continued to be rendered in the "Chinese" style, with little relationship either to Oriental art or to reality. Ceramic decorators like the numerous painters and interior decorators of the period, used "chinoiseries" with complete freedom and imagination. The most remarkable examples of this class are the decorations of Strasbourg faiences which were carefully drawn and painted in bright, gay "low temperature" colors (p. 72 and 74, G). (footnote 9)

Decoration in the naturalistic style included the use of flowers, birds, and landscapes as well as "trompe-l'œil."

Occasionally naturalistic decoration shows signs of the influence of Dresden porcelain, but in fact it really derives from a long-established French taste and was widely used. Flowers, in particular, became a favorite form of decoration. Those used on Strasbourg faiences were perhaps the most beautiful of all, owing to their perfection of design, the precision with which they were drawn, the seriousness with which the originals were studied, and because of the astonishing range of colors used at the factory (p. 72, 74, C and D). Strasbourg flowers inspired those used at the Niderviller factory (p. 75, B) where they were painted in a softer and more harmonious range of color. They also inspired those used at Sceaux (p. 76, A) and, in a lesser degree, those used by the Marseilles factory (p. 77, A and F). At Marseilles they were treated with a fanciful charm, being small, light, painted in bright colors and arranged in bunches or garlands.

The curious "trompe-l'œil" designs were related to this "naturalistic" style. Sometimes they took the form of simulated fruit set out on a plate, or sometimes imitated an engraving laid on a simulated background of wood with a pronounced grain (p. 75, A): especially successful examples of these "trompe-l'œil" were the large dishes in animal or vegetable form: ducks, hens, cabbages, or bunches of asparagus (p. 74, A and B; 76, C and D). These original table decorations were a particular specialty of the Strasbourg and Sceaux factories.

The rococo style was more influential on the shapes than on the decoration of china. This is well illustrated by the products of the Marseilles factory. Nevertheless, rococo motifs were very widely used. At Rouen, for instance, they were sometimes combined with the "Sino-Norman" style and occasionally some rococo motif would almost cover an entire piece (p. 70, A). At Strasbourg the bravura of the rococo style was used with even greater effectiveness (p. 74, E and F). In general, however, rococo decoration was subordinated—often being used for details, such as the frames surrounding landscapes painted by Fauchier at Marseilles (p. 70, D). On soft-paste porcelain, the rococo style appeared in the borders enclosing the colored grounds (p. 86), in the shapes of the reserves, and in their gilded framework (p. 87, A). (footnote 10.)

Certain exclusive themes and styles of decoration were used in many areas. Fish and shell decorations, for instance, are typical of Marseilles (p. 73 and 77, C). Faience with a yellow ground was a specialty of the southern French factories (Marseilles, p. 77, F, Montpellier). Faiences decorated with a background resembling grained wood, or with landscapes painted in pink and white, were almost always the work of the Niderviller factory (p. 75, A and C). Grotesque figures were a specialty of Moustiers (p. 71, B, and 73), and decorations in the Chinese style in "low temperature" colors were particularly used in factories situated in the eastern part of France. Porcelain with a colored glaze appeared circa 1740, and is generally confined to pieces made at the Vincennes-Sèvres factory. Its special privileges as a Royal factory made it easier to develop and patent new technical methods, and the factory carefully protected its discoveries (p. 86 and 87, A).

Historical themes, or subjects from family or everyday life were very widely used. By this means ceramic art was brought into close relation to public events and particular individuals. Nevertheless the great events of history left hardly any mark on porcelain and faience design (footnote 11). The pieces inspired by family themes, and others in the popular style of peasant art, were produced at numerous minor factories whose products cannot be considered works of art. Nevertheless such trends sometimes influenced the great factories.

At Marseilles, Leroi inscribed plates with verses from popular songs, as exemplified by the popular type known as "à la Camargo" (p. 71, C). Plates were occasionally decorated with playing cards (p. 69, D), and numerous examples bear the name of the owner and a date; the latter were often wedding or birthday presents. They were a specialty of the Nevers factory (p. 71, D). Jugs, sometimes in the form of figures, bearing the name of the person who had ordered them together with a date, were made at Rouen and Sinceny (p. 70, B). Occasionally a piece is found with a satiric or comic inscription, for instance, a plate dedicated to a certain "Francis Gaillard, who does not intend to give it up" (footnote 12).

XVIIIth Century Porcelain and Faience Today

Formerly, avid collectors could amass hundreds of pieces of valuable ceramics, without really knowing their value, or the way they should be displayed. This is not the case today. Nor, on the other hand, can china be collected nowadays for everyday use, because the breakage risks entailed are obvious. Nevertheless, traditional services like the so-called "cabbage leaf" design used at Sèvres, the "floral pattern" used at Chantilly, and the "bouquet" or "barbeaux" design of the Paris factories are still reasonably commonplace. They sometimes still serve their original purpose as household china. Vases, too, are often found in use and many have been very successfully made into lamps.

Nowadays the problem of collecting ceramics falls midway between the regrettable method of assembling a vast unwieldy collection, and the worse one of putting valuable pieces into daily use. Usually a limited number of pieces are selected for the decoration of a room. Vases, plant pots, etc., take their natural place on furniture; soup-tureens and large decorative dishes are set on side-tables, and small objects like boxes and saucers can be set out on tables about the room. This produces a splendid decorative effect. The more rare and fragile types can be displayed in well-lit cabinets built into the wall. The personal taste of the collector can find limitless opportunities of expression in the choice itself, and in the display of the various pieces.

---

and groups of historical figures (Henri IV and Sully) made in "terre de Lorraine." There were certain pieces whose handles were given the form of a dolphin in celebration of the birth of the eldest son ("dauphin") of Louis XVI, but most notable of all were certain pieces produced during the Revolutionary period (p. 88, C). By far the most important are the series of plates decorated with revolutionary devices.

12. Sometimes these inscriptions were not without wit, as for instance this short poem which was probably taken from a popular song: "My husband has gone away—To travel in Austria.—He has forbidden me to make love.—But I cannot do without it—I cheat, I cheat, I cheat." ("Mon mari s'en est allé — Voyager en Autriche. — Il m'a défendu d'aimer — Mais, ne pouvant m'en passer, — Je triche, je triche, je triche.")

PERFUME BURNER, in the form of a vase, made of Marseilles faïence at the Veuve Perrin factory. The shape is very unusual. The landscape painting with its scene of the port, the sailboat, the rocky foreground and the hazy vista, is a typical example of the Marseilles style. Landscapes painted at the Veuve Perrin factory usually pictured incidents from daily living. Scenes of fishermen hauling in their nets, such as this one, were often used.

A

B

C

E

D

F

ALMOST ALL LOUIS XIV FAIENCE was decorated in blue and white. Shapes were very simple: circular, oval, and sometimes, in the case of serving dishes, with cut corners. There are three chief types of decoration. The principal one is the "lambrequin," a pattern reminiscent of lace or wrought iron converging symettrically towards a central coat-of-arms, as on the Lille plate (A) or towards a small central scroll subject, as on the two-handled Rouen tray (B) which is decorated in red and blue. This pattern is easily adapted to pieces of widely differing shapes such as the helmet-shaped Rouen jug (E) which represents a form frequently adopted. Although the lambrequin pattern was invented at Rouen, it was widely imitated elsewhere. On the Strasbourg soup-tureen dating from about 1735 (F) it is combined with an unusual

feature in which a piece of fruit forms the lid handle. German influence (Strasbourg was very near the border) is responsible for the somewhat heavy shape, and for the curious feet in the form of crayfish. A detail of Rouen lambrequin faience is illustrated in color (p. 72, A), as well as a variant of the type made at Marseilles (p. 69, G); an instance of its use on Saint-Cloud soft-paste porcelain is also illustrated (p. 80, B). Examples made at the Moustiers factory appear here: lamberquins appear in a lacy border at the edge of the plate (D) the center of which is decorated with a hunting scene after Tempesta, set in a wide margin. A lambrequin border also appears on the slightly later *Régence* dish (C). Here the center of the plate is decorated with the imaginative and graceful pattern invented by Bérain.

SCENES WITH FIGURES painted in blue and white began to be employed at Rouen at the beginning of the XVIIIth century, where decoration copied from Chinese originals had already been used for a considerable period, on shapes identical to those pieces decorated in the lambrequin style. Later pieces with oriental patterns were decorated in blue and red, and subsequently in a wide variety of colors. At first they were quite dark but they grew successively lighter and more transparent. Sometimes the copies closely resembled the originals, as in this plate with "Chinamen in black costume" (A). The addition of black greatly enriched the range of color at Rouen. It is found on the plate decorated in the so-called "cock" style which is an exact imitation of porcelain plates of the K'ien-Lung period (E). On the large tray (F), the Chinese style is used with greater freedom, and the small figure made at Lille (B) departs still further from its Chinese prototype. The plate (C), made by Leroi at Marseilles, is an almost completely imaginary creation. On the Sinceny plate (D) a familiar motif of playing cards is combined with flowers and birds in the Sino-Rouen style. The Rouen type of lambrequin was adapted by Leroi at Marseilles with an interesting modification. In this dish with its lobed edge (G), he has transferred the lambrequin decoration from the border to the center, enlarging the individual elements greatly and arranging them to spread symmetrically outwards towards a relatively sparsely decorated border.

B

C

D

E

F

G

A

THE VERY LARGE ROCOCO MOTIF which covers a large part of the body of this Rouen jug (A) is exceptional in the prominent role it plays. It is in strong contrast to the traditional form of the jug itself.

B

TRUE ROCOCO seldom constitutes more than a detail of faience decoration. It provides the polychrome frame of the landscape painted in yellow on a dish made at Marseilles (D) by Fauchier. A rococo cartouche, too, appears on the Lille plate (p. 72, B) and encloses an inscribed ribbon. Louis XV forms, on the other hand, were quickly adopted for the shapes of vases and soup-tureens and for the sinuous designs of handles and borders of plates. The one illustrated, made by Fauchier in Marseilles (E), is typical. Its polychrome decoration consists of a landscape in "natural" colors, surrounded by large flowers in the same style. Numbers of pieces of faience were made with inscriptions bearing the owners' names. An example is the Sinceny jug in the form of a figure seated on a barrel (B), inscribed with the owner's name and the date 1771. Such pieces were usually presented on the occasion of a birth or a marriage.

ROUEN FAIENCE tended to be somewhat heavy in shape, and the traditional "cornucopia" decoration in the Sino-Rouen style was over-worked during the XVIIIth century and became somewhat commonplace (C). (See p. 72.)

C

D

E

A

B

C

D

E

A. THREE TYPES OF DECORATION enjoyed great success at Moustiers. The richest, the "medallion" type (A), consisted of small polychrome scenes, usually from mythology, enclosed in circular or oval borders. The decoration is completed with floral garlands. The soft colors seem to melt into the beautiful creamy glaze and make the products of this factory particularly attractive. Grotesque figures in the style of Callot (B) are painted in green, yellow or violet in the so-called "cameo" style: occasionally two or even more colors were used (p. 73). The appeal of these Callot figures, or of the fantastic animals scattered over the surface without any apparent pattern, lies in the spirited way in which they are painted. The floral decoration known as "potato flowers" (E), on the other hand, is of an almost peasant-like simplicity and charm. The Nevers plate (D) with its religious subject, is also inscribed with the owner's name. A more sophisticated type is the plate by Leroi made at Marseilles and painted with a portrait of the well-known dancer, Camargo (C), shown flanked by musicians and accompanied by couplets from a song. The painting is in a soft blue, melting slightly into the glaze.

B. "LOW TEMPERATURE" DECORATIONS were used at Moustiers in the Férat workshop: flowers, landscapes and chinoiseries accompanied sometimes by an unusual but typical decoration on the edge of the plate, (F). Another type of decoration by Férat of small, gay Chinamen in a fantastic setting in the style of Pillement, was imitated at Marseilles by the Veuve Perrin (H). Only one other workshop, Le Vavasseur (G), adopted the "low temperature" colors. The works produced there were strong and decorative but somewhat coarse.

G

F

H

IN THESE TWO EXAMPLES OF ROUEN FAIENCE, both in " high temperature " colors, there is a striking contrast. The first, known as the " lambrequin " or " radiating " style is noble and well-balanced : it is executed with two colors only: blue and red. This exemplifies the aristocratic style of the early years of the century. The " cornucopia " style (below) was produced during the Louis XV period and exemplifies the rise of middle-class taste. The composition, although not without vigor, depends heavily on a wide range of colors for its appeal. The "Sino Rouen " style in which the flowers are painted is copied from Chinese porcelain.

LILLE FAIENCE, always imitated that of Rouen and consistently employed " high temperature " colors. The workmen had just sufficient talent to copy the " lambrequin " type of decoration. The decoration of Lille faience lacked vitality and strength, as can be seen in the rococo form illustrated below. This rare piece of faience is inscribed with the owner's family name ; on the reverse is a polychrome shield with the inscription: Lille 1767.

STRASBOURG had the honor of inventing " low temperature " faience colors, where the method was put to brilliant use for many years, especially for floral designs painted in natural colors, and carefully drawn with great attention to detail. The factory developed a wide range of strong but subtle colors, featuring the famous "Cassius purple." In floral patterns, the largest bouquet of flowers was usually placed to one side of the plate and balanced by two smaller bouquets placed near the opposite border. The Chinese scenes, on the other hand, were usually painted in the center of the plate, surrounded by a bit of landscape.

AT SCEAUX, " LOW TEMPERATURE " COLORS were used from the first, where the making of ceramics was profoundly influenced by the nearby factory at Strasbourg. The Strasbourg style of painting in " natural " colors was adopted as well. In the series of designs known as " birds and cut fruit " (illustrated above) the drawing is precise, almost crisp, and the colors are so strong they nearly clash with one another. More yielding lines and softer colors are found in another similar series of designs, also used at Mennecy (see page 83 F).

APREY was one of the minor factories which occasionally created pieces more or less successfully decorated in "low temperature" colors. But they were generally copied from the work of other factories. The bird designs, a Sceaux copy, were carefully executed but were lacking in the precise line, the sense of design and the color of their originals. Occasionally the flower painting in the so-called "fat" manner displayed a certain sense of style, but this occurred rarely.

MARSEILLES FAIENCE usually pictured sea subjects and fishermen, painted in "low temperature" colors. The decoration used at this factory was notable for its remarkably imaginative treatment and its gaiety. Animated seashore scenes were clearly inspired by the locality, as were the unique decorations in which fish appear. Shells, seaweed, fish nets and tackle, as well as an occasional ear of wheat (seen below) were often incorporated in these designs. These Marseilles fish (which are usually placed towards the edge of the plate) form an amusing and or iginal type of "trompe l'œil" decoration.

THE EVOLUTION OF MOUSTIERS DECORATION is as easily divided into two distinct types as is that of Rouen. The two examples shown here, painted in "high temperature" colors, are full of contrast. The first is a hunting scene after Tempesta, in blue and white, executed in a broad, decorative style. Below, the painter has given an attractive, satirical character to the cleverly drawn figures of his grotesques. The creamy glaze and harmonious colors show how highly technical skill had been developed at Moustiers. But in spite of their pleasing decorative qualities, Moustiers faïences lacked vigor.

NEVERS FAIENCE had become quite decadent by the beginning of the XVIIIth century. A few hackneyed designs copied from those of the preceding century were executed in "high temperature" colors. Occasionally, too, Chinese figures in blue and white were used, but this fashion did not last long. Neither did the occasional use of polychrome scenes from the novel "Astrée". Both were completely devoid of the vigorous treatment that had formerly brought so much fame to the Nevers-Italian style. Thus design, composition and color were dull.

A

E

B

C

THE STRASBOURG FACTORY flourished under three successive generations of skilled directors. The first was Charles-François Hannong, who founded the factory in 1721, and specialized in pieces decorated in the Rouen style (see p. 68, F). His son, Paul Hannong, succeeded him in 1732 and caused a total revolution not only in the style of faience produced at Strasbourg, but throughout the whole of Europe, when, about 1748, he invented the "low temperature" type of decoration. This procedure, which was henceforward adopted exclusively at his factory, provided a rich palette of strong colors which the workers employed at Strasbourg used with extraordinary skill. Paul Hannong was an indefatigable inventor creating new shapes and new styles of decoration. The great flower patterns painted in "natural" colors were drawn with remarkable attention to detail and unrivalled spontaneity (C). They were imitated everywhere with varying degrees of success. From about 1750 onwards he also employed rococo forms in an extremely bold manner, producing elaborate pieces decorated with birds' heads, shells, huge scrolls, and flowers in relief, all executed with great vigor (E). He also created numerous "trompe-l'œil" types of faience, lidded dishes of animal (B), or vegetable (A) form, and his cruets and sauce-boats in the form of ships (F) are imbued with the same original spirit. The output of the factory under the direction of his son, Joseph Hannong, between 1762 and 1782 was much less wide-ranging. During this period the factory specialized in decoration with flowers. The arrangement of the floral bouquets became looser and more elegant, but perhaps a trifle more commonplace and lacking in spontaneity. Even so they were always painted with an astonishing mastery of technique (D). The only interesting innovation during this period was the decoration known as "the Chinese style". This was of a markedly imaginative character, painted in gay, strong colors, and brilliantly executed by the skilled craftsmen of the factory (G). These "Chinese" types of decoration were very widely imitated, especially in the eastern part of France, but with varying degrees of skill which seldom equaled the perfection of their originals.

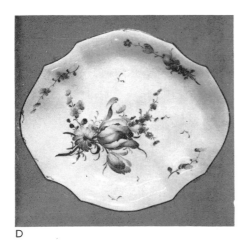

D

F

G

B

AT NIDERVILLER, the Strasbourg style was given an original character: the soft transparent colors produce delicately harmonious effects, the decoration is elegant and the shapes are refined (B). This factory specialized in carefully drawn, loosely composed landscapes painted with great atmosphere in pink (sometimes slightly violet) on a white ground (C). Such landscapes also appear in the same pink or sometimes painted in grisaille, as simulated engravings, usually bearing a date and an artist's name. The one illustrated (A) is inscribed "A. Niderviller" and is signed "Deutsch;" it dates from about 1772. The engraving is painted in *trompe-l'œil* to give the appearance of a print pinned on a piece of wood, the grain of which is skilfully imitated.

C

THE NIDERVILLER FACTORY was chiefly famed, however, for its attractive and delicately formed figures. The Niderviller modelers were particularly skilful in rendering the charm of children (F. "The Bowl of Soup") or the fresh naïvety of a peasant girl's face (D. "The Artichoke Seller"), or the lively exchanges of a flirting couple (E). Their success is largely due to the perfection of their fresh and harmonious colors.

D   E   F

A

B

C

THE SCEAUX FACTORY was founded in 1748, and quickly turned for inspiration to Strasbourg, then at the height of its success. Sceaux flowers are skilfully rendered in a wide range of colors, but lack the freshness of their Strasbourg originals. The bold frieze of leaves on the borders of some Sceaux pieces (A) is one of the most original and successful of this factory's inventions.

MANY PLATES are of a shape peculiar to this factory: the edge is notched and decorated with a comb-like motif painted in blue (B). Such plates are often decorated with bordered landscapes, framed with flowers and fruits. Fruit motifs, particularly, were often found at Sceaux, either in the form of whole or cut fruits, and very often combined with other types of decoration.

"TROMPE-L'ŒIL"PIECES (C and D) were generally made at Sceaux in the style of those produced by the Hannong family at Strasbourg. They are, however, somewhat lacking in the vitality, the brilliant modeling and the bright coloring of the Strasbourg examples.

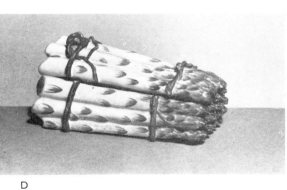

D

E

F

THE SCEAUX FACTORY made great use of birds in its decorations, throughout its existence (E). With the coming of the Louis XVI style, shapes began to change a little; the handles of this vase, for instance (E), show the influence of the new manner. At the same time the range of colors begins to be modified to correspond more closely with the softer colors used on the soft-paste porcelain of the period (F).

A

B

C

IMAGINATION, GAIETY AND AN EXTRAORDINARY FREE-DOM in the composition of the decoration are the special characteristics of the Marseilles factories. Louis XV shapes were quickly adopted there and only abandoned with reluctance long after the Louis XV period was over. The Marseilles type of floral decoration aims at attractiveness rather than verisimilitude. It was much admired and extremely successful (A). Other typical Marseilles decorations are of the type known as "The Menagerie" (B) and "Fish and Fishing Tackle" (C). The use of a yellow ground was a specialty of the southern French factories, and was much used at Marseilles by Fauchier in his "high temperature" pieces, and by the Veuve Perrin for "low temperature" decoration. In pieces produced at the latter factory, charming floral bouquets stand out in bright red against the beautiful yellow ground (F).

D

VEUVE PERRIN was in charge of one of the most important and famous of the faience factories of Marseilles. Her productions were often painted with landscapes and scenes of the daily life of Provence. The lids of such pieces were often surmounted by flowers in relief, by a group of fishes, or, as here, by a dog (D).

THE FAIENCE-MAKER ROBERT did not decorate his pieces with peasant scenes. Instead he preferred to use people of quality, shown either dancing or walking. His flowers, like those decorating the spaces around the central landscape, gradually changed their character and become smaller and more elegant (E). Bonnefoi, another faience-maker, turned still further away from the homely vitality of the scenes adopted by the Veuve Perrin. Under his influence Marseilles faience became more sophisticated, more elegant, and more restrained in its type of decoration (G) during the Louis XVI period.

F

G

LUNÉVILLE was the residence of Stanislas Leczinski, King of Poland and Duke of Lorraine, and Louis XV's father-in-law. He was the protector of the faience factory which, from that fact alone, gained a certain fame. The Lunéville factory was deeply influenced by nearby Strasbourg. Nevertheless its productions have a character of their own. Lunéville flowers are small, with long curving leaves emerging distinctly on alternate sides of the stalk; they are intermediate between the minutely finished flowers characteristic of the Alsacian factories like Strasbourg and the rustic type of flowers of the second-class factories. Colorings are fresh and clear, although the elements show little gradation in their shading.

A

B

C

THE ST. CLÉMENT FACTORY was situated in small village about nine miles from Lunéville the history of the two factories as well as t pieces they produced have sometimes be confused with one another. The princip characteristic of St. Clément faience was t use of very carefully drawn birds, painted bright colors in imitation of Sceaux. Above this factory specialized in works in the sever Louis XVI style—a noteworthy exception faience manufacture. The very fine, clo grained paste adapted itself readily to t rather severe forms of classical capitals, mo ings, fluting, and the straight lines of t new style (B). In addition these rectiline forms were well adapted to take the sort carefully drawn, precise decoration whi was characteristic of St. Clément (

D

A CHARACTERISTIC IDIOSYNCRACY at Lunéville was the frequent use of gently scrolled foliations, touched with red, green and yellow (A) on the borders. A certain number of "high temperature" pieces continued to be made, but for the most part they were confined to large garden figures in the form of seated lions, sometimes with polychrome decoration and sometimes merely glazed a uniform blue of a slightly violet tone (C). Decoration in the "Chinese style" is much more abundant at Lunéville than at Strasbourg. If the extreme elegance and delicacy of the Strasbourg originals is lacking, they are painted with the same rich range of colors, and are vastly superior to pieces produced in small factories like the one at Les Islettes with which Lunéville is often confused. Figure subjects are usually on a fairly large scale; they are pleasingly posed, sometimes in scenes of a rather elaborate character set in landscape treated in a somewhat more detailed manner, and occasionally fantastic animals are also used as a decorative motif (D).

E

A

B

IN 1743, "LE PONT-AUX-CHOUX," a Parisian factory, began to produce cream wares in imitation of those made in England. The "pipe clay" faience, as it is called, which was produced there was of a very high quality. It could be easily shaped into rather complex imitations of metalwork designs, and was often decorated with original motifs, such as masks, flowers and birds (D). The decoration consists of applied motifs in relief: flowers on a ribbed background (C) or on a granulated one. Scenes with figures are rarer (B).

THE SAME WHITE CLAY, left in the "biscuit" state, was used with great spirit by the sculptor Cyfflé, who produced his celebrated "Terres de Lorraine" at Lunéville, usually mythological groups (E. "Venus and Adonis"), children's games, or "Cries of Paris" (A. "The Tinker").

C

D

E

A

SAINT-CLOUD was, without doubt, the most aristocratic of French porcelains. The factory, founded at the end of the XVIIth century, continued until 1766, when it closed without ever having fallen into decadence. The paste is beautiful, soft, very creamy and transparent.

B

C

THE TYPES OF DECORATION used are few; the lambrequin type (see p. 68) in blue, sometimes of a very deep color, is the most frequently used (B). The "whites" (glazed but unpainted pieces) were one of the most admired products of the factory, for the character of the paste lent itself admirably to this type. At first, the factory copied Chinese originals exactly (C); later they were modified by the adoption of French decorative details: gadrooning in the Louis XIV style (A), and "natural" flowers in relief.

AT SAINT-CLOUD, polychrome decoration is always of the "Korean" type. Far Eastern models are imitated less exactly than at Chantilly. The designs are more original and always in perfect taste (E); sometimes individual elements of the "Korean" style are used on an enlarged scale (D); the colors are much warmer than those used at Chantilly, especially the rather strong blues and yellows.

D

E

AT FIRST IT SEEMS STRANGE that such unusual and slavishly copied pieces of porcelain in the so-called "Korean" style should ever have become fashionable in France. But this sort of oriental china was very highly prized in the earlier part of the century. Pieces such as this were not, of course, actually made in Korea. The name was first applied to them during the XIXth century. They were really of Japanese origin, and the style is said to have been created by a potter namel Kakiyemon. At Chantilly, the style was imitated with complete success, as this illustration shows. Not only were the techniques of production, the pastes, the designs and the colors of the glaze copied with remarkable fidelity, but even the very spirit and feeling of the "Korean" pieces were caught by craftsmen in the Chantilly factory.

CHANTILLY SOFT-PASTE PORCELAIN

AT CHANTILLY two different types of porcelain of a very different character were produced. In the early period, which began in 1725 and lasted for about 20 years, the "Korean" style was the only one used. The paste was whiter than at Saint-Cloud, and much closer to the oriental type which it copied. The forms, too, are very exactly imitated as is the decoration, which is precise, somewhat severe, and executed in light, transparent colors applied evenly and outlined with a narrow black line. The statuettes produced always represented oriental figures (A). The decorative motifs varied very little. They were either flowers (H), legendary monsters, or figures, usually small and few in number (D).

A

IN THE SECOND PERIOD floral decoration became more French in character (C) as did the shapes, though for a considerable time they continued to retain something of the character of the oriental types which originally inspired the factory. Some of the bird decorations used retain a certain telltale severity in the execution (G), in spite of the generally French character of the design. Numerous small boxes both in the "Korean" and the French manner were made at Chantilly in the form of animals (B) or figures, mounted with silver. Eventually table services in a soft blue and white porcelain became an important part of the factory's output. A large number of plates and small pieces decorated in the so-called "spray" (E) or "carnation" (F) styles have come down to us, though soup-tureens are hardly ever found. In spite of the simplicity of the decoration, these pieces are very pleasant to look at because of the fine quality of the paste.

C

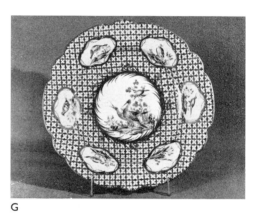

B

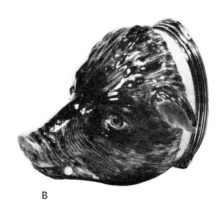

E

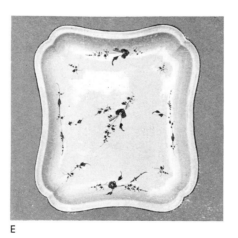

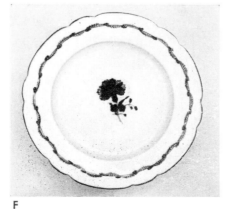

F

G

H

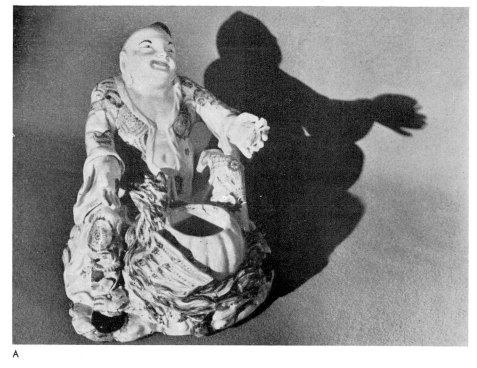

THE "KOREAN" STYLE was used at Mennecy for a much shorter time than at Chantilly, and hardly ever used for knife-handles, boxes or figures (A), which were often unusually small. The paste is more creamy than Chantilly and the colors stronger; the decorative motifs, too, are smaller and more tightly drawn.

FOR THE MOST PART THE PRODUCTS of this factory were decorated in the "natural" style. Flowers, especially, were used on innumerable pieces. Occasionally these were large and important (C), but generally they were of small size: cups, sugar basins, cream jugs and innumerable powder-jars. Plates, except for a small group decorated with landscapes in a central medallion, are almost unknown.

A

MENNECY PORCELAIN FIGURES were generally inspired by Dresden, such as certain birds (B), and groups either left in the unpainted white glazed state, or painted in a variety of colors. Children playing, or pastorals (D), were the favorite subjects. These objects were always of extremely small size; they were decorative and imaginative toys rather than pieces intended to play an important part in the decoration of a room.

B

C

NUMEROUS SMALL BOXES, either for sweets or snuff, were produced at Mennecy, sometimes being left white, and sometimes painted. They were given the most variegated forms: small coffers, baskets, chests of drawers (on which small floral bouquets were painted on a ribbed ground or on a basket-work background in low relief), shoes, fruit, animals, and very often figures (E).

MENNECY AND SCEAUX were under a common management for a time, and so types of decoration common to both factories are known: decorations with fruits and especially with birds (F) made at Mennecy have a remarkable similarity in design and color to those produced at Sceaux.

D

E

F

1. ALTOGETHER NEW SHAPES were created as can be seen by this soup-tureen presented by Louis XVI in 1777 to his brother-in-law, the Emperor of Austria. The piece is executed in hard-paste porcelain, decorated in a style very similar to that used for soft-paste varieties. Neither the rich floral pattern nor the lavish use of gold makes up for the austerity of the porcelain itself and the contrast between it and the delicate soft-paste piece, illustrated below and also manufactured in Sèvres, is very striking.

2. THE GREAT SOUP-TUREENS which formed part of the large dinner services "en pâte tendre," usually ordered as presents for foreign royalty or princely families, were really intended for display rather than for use. The decoration illustrated here is particularly rich. The gold decorated background and the scenes of birds perched on the branches of trees are classic features. The tureen is painted in the strong, clear colors which earned the factory a well-deserved reputation, even in its early days.

A

B

C

FIGURES AND GROUPS painted in a variety of colors both in Vincennes and Sèvres porcelain are rare. They are almost always left either in the white "biscuit" state or merely glazed white. Biscuit porcelain (with a matt surface to which no glaze was applied) was an innovation of Vincennes which enjoyed a very considerable success, due to the fine grain and creamy color of the paste, as well as to the skill of the well-known artists employed by the factory especially to model these pieces. (D. "Jealousy" by Van der Vorst, after Boucher; B. Sèvres, "The Schoolmistress" by Falconet.)

IN 1738 SOME WORKMEN who had fled from Chantilly founded a factory in the old Chateau at Vincennes. In 1756 it was moved to Sèvres after having been raised to the rank of a Royal factory some little time earlier. The patent was for porcelain in the "Dresden style" which clearly indicates that, at the time of foundation, there was no intention to imitate oriental porcelain. In fact, the first pieces produced imitated Dresden (E), but the quality of the paste and the colors which blended so attractively into the glaze gave it a "velvety" effect unrivalled by any other factory. The good taste of the directors and their inventive powers, as well as the fact that numerous skilled artists and chemists were employed, soon earned for "French porcelain" such a high reputation that the initial attempt at imitation was quickly abandoned. In a few years all the various types of decoration eventually to establish the supremacy of Sèvres porcelain were already in use: amongst the most important were the floral decorations used on table services as well as on the individual and imaginative creations of the factory's modelers (C); the cameo-style painting in blue and white or pink and white; the painted figures; and the cupids, after Boucher (A). Other specialties of the factory were the "flying birds" and the high quality of the gilding which was elaborately chased and used either as a part of the decoration or as a frame around it. In addition a range of rich colors was invented: Sèvres blue, turquoise blue, apple green, pale yellow and the aristocratic "rose pompadour."

E

D

THIS VASE OF SOFT-PASTE PORCELAIN would have been attributed to Vincennes if it were not for the fact that, combined with the mark of the Royal factory (two interlaced L's, the King's initials), it bears the date-letter G corresponding to the year 1759, which makes it certain that it must have been made at Sèvres itself. On this piece the famous "ROSE POMPADOUR" ground is combined with a green which adds greatly to its beauty. Its shape is superbly conceived, the curves of the decoration both divide the areas of color from one another and unify the composition as a whole. The elegant piercing shows great understanding of the subtleties of the Louis XV style.

The pieces made at Sèvres were remarkably varied and abundant. It is by far the most important French porcelain factory. Innumerable table services were made there. Some, like this one given by Louis XV to the King of Denmark, are very celebrated. The decoration consists of floral bouquets, painted in variegated colors in reserves on a lapis-blue ground enriched with a pebbled-gilt decoration. This service included eight soup-tureens and deep dishes (A). It has remained in the hands of the ruling family of Denmark ever since it was made.

A

B

THE TABLE SERVICE known as the "Buffon" service, copied, with scrupulous exactitude, engravings of birds in Buffon's famous "Natural History". On the back of each plate is an inscription giving the name of the particular bird painted on the front (B). The border is decorated with an elegant "partridge-eye" pattern in a soft green which, in certain examples, is ornamented with three small medallions, each painted with a bird.

THE MODELERS at the Vincennes-Sèvres factory had an extraordinarily sure taste. This chamber candlestick—dating from 1752—is notable for its subtle rococo form (D, Vincennes) and is a masterpiece of unstudied elegance.

THE SIMPLEST TABLE SERVICES were usually decorated with flowers painted in natural colors: small sprays disposed over the surface were combined with simple blue filets, or with scrolled and interlacing shapes along the borders. Sometimes large decorations of the "comb" type in deep blue, known as the "cabbage-leaf" pattern, give remarkable strength to a traditional design (C).

C

D

A

B

THE LOUIS XVI STYLE was handled particularly successfully at Sèvres. Classical forms, although severe, were generally softened by some detail, such as the subtly modeled handles, which prevented the piece from having too chilling an effect (A). The decoration was often on a lapis-blue ground, always very popular at the factory, and usually accompanied the traditional pastoral scenes. In the Louis XVI period they were enclosed in a border of semi-classical type.

DURING THE DIRECTOIRE PERIOD there was a change in the forms of pieces which were modeled in the antique style, and a new range of colors was introduced with unusual tones and daring color contrasts. Thus the mauve ground of the jug (B) serves as a background for decorative motifs in green and gold. At other times a bright orange-yellow contrasts with lavender-blue ribbons painted with dark red patterns. The success of these audacious—though carefully calculated—effects is undeniable. They foreshadow the flowering of new stylistic formulæ which, in the early XIXth century, were to supplant the traditional motifs in use for so long. During the Revolutionary period the factory was only occasionally in operation, and the productions of this period are, for the first time, sometimes of mediocre quality. Nevertheless certain Revolutionary pieces are interesting not only for their quality but also for the contemporary themes used in their decoration (C): trophies including Phrygian bonnets, fasces, masonic triangles, and an open book with the title "French Constitution." Around the rim, a tricolor ribbon is twisted around a torus molding of leaves.

C

HARD-PASTE PORCELAIN, which began to be made about 1770, unlike the other technical innovations of the period, did not call forth work of the highest quality. The rich did not pour out large sums of money to acquire pieces of this type. On the contrary, it was the commercial opportunity of producing hard-paste porcelain at low prices which really brought it into common use. This explains why hard-paste porcelain is generally pleasant, but facile and commonplace. Only at Sèvres was it really decorated in an attractive manner.

A

C

PORCELAIN made of kaolin clay came into use only in the Empire period. During the Directoire period the rich "Egyptian" style of decoration foreshadowed the porcelain that the Paris factories were soon to produce in considerable quantities (C). During the XVIIIth century Parisian factories concentrated on making table services. A floral decoration was usually adopted: bunches of flowers in natural colors (A and D) or the "spray" design (E).

D

E

AT MARSEILLES, ROBERT had already begun to produce porcelain with elegant decoration as early as 1760. He particularly favored landscapes. From 1765 onwards Niderviller began to abandon the production of faience in favour of porcelain, and sometimes produced interesting pieces in which the Louis XVI style was very skilfully used (B).

B

GOLD AND SILVERWARE

Goldsmiths' Work in the XVIIIth Century

The art of the goldsmith was intimately linked with the triumphs and troubles of the century. It symbolized the luxury of the age, and reflected its changing fortunes, just as its forms reflected the everyday life of the century.

Insofar as it reflects the grandeur and display of the age it perpetuates the influence of Louis XIV. The monumental objects of silver produced for the King in the previous century were intended to bear witness to his splendor and royal might. Louis XIV commissioned huge drinking vessels, "torchères," even carriages made of solid silver, as well as monumental pieces intended only for display, to add to the magnificence of his surroundings. In addition he enriched the Church treasuries with much goldsmiths' work. Luxurious commissions of this sort continued to be given to French craftsmen in the XVIIIth century; they spread the fame of French goldsmiths' work throughout Europe. Foreign courts ordered large quantities of French silver; the commissions given by the Kings of Portugal, for instance, are justly famed. Silver also reflects the political vicissitudes of the day, just as the social changes of the period can be seen in its changing shapes. From the earliest times, goldsmiths' work had provided a reserve of bullion, which it was customary to melt down in time of war, or as the circumstances of the times demanded. Like other kings, Louis XIV kept his reserve of specie for just this purpose. During his reign, no less than forty ordinances and sumptuary edicts concerning the melting down of silver and gold were issued. There was a wide variety of reasons for these edicts, but the final result was an almost total destruction of the finest silver of the period. Only the memory of this wonderful display of silver is preserved today in documents, inventories, tapestries and engravings.

The melting down of so much gold and silver quite obviously had unfortunate æsthetic consequences, but it is perhaps less self evident that the various sumptuary edicts had an important influence on the evolution of goldsmiths' work. Certain laws, for instance, limited the weight of pieces, or forbade overly elaborate or over-charged decoration. As a result the rich, solemn and highly decorated display pieces, which had been in vogue in the previous period, tended to disappear at the end of the reign of "le Roi Soleil." But this had a favorable effect, for it encouraged restraint, good taste and simplicity in the making of gold and silver objects.

At a period when society was undergoing profound changes, the fortunes of this art closely followed the vicissitudes of daily life. From the beginning of the Regency of the Duke of Orléans, social change was rapid. New classes came into existence. The professional men and businessmen drawn from the middle classes wished to become the owners of gold and silver plate, as well as all the other appurtenances of wealth, which, in the previous century, could have belonged only to persons of the highest rank. Silver, by its nature, is particularly well suited to objects intended for constant use—for pieces which are almost utensils. At the beginning of the century the character of the luxury arts began to change. Goldsmiths ceased to produce objects intended for display alone; they turned their talents towards the production of more ordinary, more functional pieces.

It was only in the XVIIIth century that gold and silver objects for purely secular use began to play an important part in daily life. Society became less mobile; families moved less and less frequently from house to house and with the coming of a taste for entertaining in one's own home, a new art came into existence—the art of dining. Numerous documents survive which list the appropriate numbers of plates, dishes, etc., required for the entertainment of a particular number of guests. Every noble family of importance possessed its own "establishment" ("Maison") of silver based on the size of the King's "establishment." There was a special "establishment" of cutlery for the use of the servants, for the kitchen staff, for the bakery staff and the butler. There were game-dishes and pieces intended for table decoration only; almost every type of cutlery that we know today was devised at this period. These included such rare pieces as oyster-forks, ice-spoons, traveling services or hunting services, and folding knives and forks which could be kept in richly decorated cases. Some of the specialized pieces invented in the XVIIIth century have now gone entirely out of use; today, examples of a salt-fork or a combined knife and fork for oysters can only be found in the hands of collectors. At this time it became more general to serve sweetmeats at the table, and special equipment was devised for this purpose. Silver-gilt, regarded as almost an essential where table-silver was concerned, was used to create richer effects on pieces of all kinds. Both the silversmiths and the craftsmen who made knife-handles lavished all their skill and artistry on their particular specialty so that table services of the period are quite as elegant as any other XVIIIth century objets d'art.

The art (or the craft) of the goldsmith has hardly changed at all in the course of history. Even today goldsmiths still do their work by hand. The XVIIIth century craftsmen had such outstanding skill in manipulating metal that their work has never been equaled since.

The basic characteristic to which French XVIIIth century goldsmiths' work owes its high reputation, is the fact that it evolved a type of piece which was practical and, at the same time, elegant. The permanent factors underlying all metal-work were perfectly understood and developed to their highest point; the manners and needs of the age were studied with extraordinary care. As a consequence, the craftsmen of the period became the greatest in the world.

ome fine pieces of French silver. At the top: a pair of three-branch andelabra of silver, cast and chased by the royal goldsmith F.-T. Germain 757). At the top in the center: soup-tureen or dish for game pie made for e French Court in 1756 by the master-goldsmith Balzac; the silver plates f lobed-oval shape at each side of the soup-tureen date from the XVIIIth century, s do the small Chinese porcelain jugs with silver mounts. The two large shes (9-1/2" in diameter, one of silvered metal, the other of silver) date from e late XVIIth century. In the center: a silver entrée dish, its borders chased ith filets, ribbons and foliage and with handles at each end, made by Thomas ermain. The vegetable dish filled with fruit in the foreground was made 1757 by the master-goldsmith E.-P. Balzac. It is engraved with the arms f the Duc d'Orléans. At each side of it are silver wine coolers made in aris by E.-P. Balzac in 1759. The silver goblet with applied decoration, the extreme left, dates from the XVIIIth century. At the extreme right a silver sugar sifter made by Nicolas Besnier (1732). (Color plate at left.)

Shapes and Decorations

Eighteenth century goldsmiths' work cannot be entirely separated from that performed toward the end of the XVIIth century. It is not merely that the two periods are closely linked owing to the fact that the reign of Louis XIV extended well on into the XVIIIth century, but also because all the fundamental circumstances pertinent to XVIIIth century goldsmiths' work were already operative in the latter part of the XVIIth century.

The great goldsmiths (Claude Ballin, Nicolas Delaunay, Thomas Germain) were all born during Louis XIV's reign, and began their careers at a time when he was showering commissions on goldsmiths. He wished them to create works of art which would add to his glory and renown by surrounding him with an ever grander luxury. Even when the flamboyance of the rococo style was beginning to play an increasingly large part in French art, the influence of these men continued to be felt. Especially in the provinces, craftsmen found it difficult to abandon the lambrequins, the shells, the scale decorations and other ornamental devices used by these great artists. This remained true even when the Louis XV and Louis XVI styles were completely in the ascendant.

A gold or silver object is always to some extent an architectural creation. It must always rest on its base or on feet in the same way, even though the fantasies of a changing fashion may have loaded it with elaborate decoration in relief which gives it something of the appearance of a piece of sculpture.

When the XVIIIth century opened, the repertory of shapes and decorative motifs derived from the Renaissance had been transformed by French taste.

*The dominant influence
of architectural forms*

Plain surfaces began to make their appearance, heightening and setting off a decoration which was confined to the edges and nodal points of the pieces. This decoration derived its essential character from the ornamental elements of architecture. The edges, the moldings, the applied decoration, all derive from architectural cornices, denticulations, columns, etc. The carved heads and caryatids used on buildings in the Renaissance style appear on silver as masks, adapting themselves to the handles of wine coolers, of jugs and other vessels. This close relationship with architecture is particularly striking in the shapes given to the candlesticks, candelabra and the monumental centerpieces of the period.

One of the most important characteristics of late Louis XIV silver is the quality of the chasing and engraving of the surfaces. Not only were ornaments applied in high relief—moldings, animal heads, etc.—on the bodies and on the borders of plates and dishes, but a whole new range of engraved decorative motifs appear. These were generally designed by, or borrowed from the designs of great ornamental draughtsmen like Bérain, Marot or Robert de Cotte. The most frequently used motifs were trellis patterns on a dull ground, or quatrefoils, shells, scrolls, interlacing motifs or lambrequins.

From the beginning of the "Régence" period goldsmiths' work became more and more decorative; sculpture began to play a dominant role in ornamentation.

*The predominant role
of sculpture*

The reaction which set in at the end of the reign of Louis XIV led at first to an excessive use of luxurious decoration. Shapes lost the solemn proportions they had had in the XVIIth century; symmetry was abandoned and gave way to surfaces which intersect, intertwine and interpenetrate, almost like the prolific growth of some tropical weed. This liberation was the first stage in a development which was to produce the purest of all French styles—the Louis XV style.

Parties and entertainments became more intimate; and silver shapes changed accordingly. There were no more heavy decorations, only small delicate pieces which could be comfortably used by the individual.

Dining-room tables which were never removed from the room for which they were designed, appeared at this period.

For the first time the word "couvert" (cutlery) takes on the sense in which we understand it today. That is to say, it embraces, in addition to the spoon, fork and knife, all the other silverware used at the table. Hitherto only the first three of these had been embraced in the meaning of the term; they had come into use when a dining table was only a simple plank of wood resting on trestles and erected wherever required, either in the bedroom or the boudoir.

But the introduction of coffee, chocolate and tea, brought a large number of specialized pieces into being. Coffee was often prepared by the drinker himself and special little mills were devised to grind it. Sometimes these were of the utmost elegance like the one from the Dauphin's service, now in the Louvre. The art of the silversmith played a part in almost all the facets of everyday life. This led to a progressive adaptation of shapes for daily use.

At this period table silver developed the shapes and proportions which are still in use today. The fork was given its definitive form with four prongs; the spoon, which still retains the shape and depth which it was then first given, was strengthened a little at the fore-edge from which food is taken. The sizes, too, became just those that we know today.

Jugs and other vessels ceased to be tall objects perched on elaborate feet. The feet grew smaller and simpler, or they were replaced by simple moldings or disappeared altogether, allowing the body of the piece to rest directly on the table. The sizes in which round or oval plates, bowls, and entrée dishes were then made are still those prevailing today. The most frequently used type of plate at this period had a hollow-molded border, and this is still the model in use in our time.

Nevertheless, there were a certain number of pieces in which the excesses of the rococo style are evident. The pieces of this type which have survived from the period are few. The most characteristic is perhaps a candlestick by Meissonier, now in the Musée des Arts Décoratifs. It is an essential document of the rococo, illustrating this stage in the evolution of forms at its most astonishing moment. Giles Oppenord, the favorite architect of the Régent of Orléans, was the decorator of the Palais Royal, and J.-A. Meissonier was appointed one of the official draughtsmen to the King. Both of these men were foreigners and played a leading role in creating the full rococo style which, in certain respects, was the most profoundly French of all. The character of the

The evolution of typical forms *of jugs and similar vessels during the XVIIIth century is illustrated in the diagrams at right. The jug at the left (A) is still influenced by the classical forms of the Renaissance and dates from the end of the XVIIth century. The same antique shape appears again in the jug dating from the end of the XVIIIth century (E). Between these two extremes the bulbous part of the body (which, at the beginning and end of the century, was usually in the upper part) is found in the lower part of the vessel. The plinth disappears almost completely from some types of jugs during the course of the XVIIIth century. B. Lidded jug of the "Régence" period. C. Lidded jug of the Louis XV period. D. Lidded jug of the Louis XVI period. E. Late Louis XVI jug dating almost from the "Directoire" period.*

A

forms adopted in this phase of XVIIIth century taste is perhaps best described in the well-known phrase taken from a letter written by the Président de Brosses in 1740; it would probably please many contemporary artists: "The Italians complain that much of our silver is convoluted, involuted and supervoluted, as though we had lost all sense of the circle or the square."

After 1750, rococo quieted down. It is at this period that the most perfect pieces of French silver were produced. In fact the great goldsmiths like Thomas Germain had never entirely abandoned their innate preference for classic shapes. They had restrained the more outrageous deviations of the rococo style. Their good taste henceforward exercised a restraining influence on the more daring uses of curves and counter-curves. Architects and designers infused a vital, though often a disordered spirit into the arts of the period, but the skill of the great goldsmiths (like the Germain family, or Besnier, Loir, Roettiers, Chéret, Balzac, etc.) combined with their natural gifts to restore a just balance, limiting the forms of their creations to those best adapted to the techniques and materials in which they worked. Form is always directly dependent on the material it shapes; this is an undeviating law.

In 1755 Cochin's book "Observations on the Antiquities of Herculaneum," appeared. Greek decorative motifs began to be fashionable; Mme. de Pompadour's interest in classic antiquities brought a new force to bear on craftsmen of the day.

Cochin and Soufflot were opposed to the more extreme rococo artists. Mme. de Pompadour, always a friend to new ideas, joined with them in imposing the style known as "the Greek manner," which rapidly became the new fashion.

Architectural forms were once again the vanguard of fashion

In 1755 the Louis XVI style was born. In all its essentials it was to persist right down until the Empire period. In this new phase of taste, the shapes of silver, like those of furniture, became well-proportioned and balanced once again. Their shapes and decorations derived from classical antiquity. Instead of Oppenord and Meissonier, the fashionable decorative designers of the day were Fortin, de Lalonde and Delafosse. Each of them created a personal and individual style, which can easily be distinguished.

Even during Louis XVI's reign, edicts were occasionally issued making it compulsory for certain types of objects of precious metal to be melted down.

The experimental development of certain alloys dates from this period. Luxury objects had hitherto been available only to the wealthy. Towards the end of the century manufacturers began to think of making such things more easily accessible to those with limited purses. This is symptomatic of the rising importance of the new social classes. Louis XVI thought he ought to encourage development of this sort and personally financed a factory for the manufacture of plated ware that he installed in the Hôtel de Pomponne, a name now used to designate its productions ("pomponne").

During the Louis XVI period, the shapes of objects grew more slender and the decoration thinner. They evolved in unexpected directions. Pieces intended solely for the display-case or side-table came into existence: works of art on the smallest scale, such as knick-knacks, "étuis," perfume bottles, snuff-boxes and tiny candlesticks of gold or other precious metals. The favourite decorative motifs in the repertory of this period were flutings, filets, ribbons, laurel pendants and beading—the motifs, in fact, that were found in the carving of architectural cornices and pediments. S-curves were entirely abandoned; the straight line reappeared together with simple scrolls, tripods, hymeneal torches, cupid's bows, and musical instruments. Sometimes pastoral motifs of a refined character were included. The great center-pieces of the past gave place to a wealth of tiny trees or figures of musicians placed about the dining table.

But at the end of the century the quality of the craftmanship tended to grow inferior and the use of impressed patterns was instituted, so that identical pieces could be repeated any number of times. The body of such objects as saltcellars or wine coolers was often merely composed of bands of pierced and chased metal, through which the interior fittings, invariably of blue glass, were allowed to show.

The creative spirit seems to have abandoned goldsmiths who adopted, without adapting, the models provided by designers, not all of whom were equally imaginative. New materials began to come into use and with the first hesitant steps in the direction of industrialization we find ourselves at the opening of the Revolutionary period.

Shapes themselves changed very little during the Directoire period, but there was a completely new repertory of decorative motifs. They derived entirely from the antique, and embraced sphinxes, griffons, tripods, and palmettes; with the result that traditional shapes were transformed into antique monuments. The grace and balance of the XVIIIth century style only revived with the coming of the more austere Empire style.

Boxes

Jewelers did not comprise a separate independent guild; they were included with the rest of the 350 master-craftsmen of the goldsmiths' guild. Only masters of the goldsmiths'

B   C   D   E

guild were allowed to practice as jewelers; it was merely a question of a specialization within a particular craft.

Boxes are so closely linked with goldsmiths' work that they must be mentioned here. Men and women carried a few sweetmeats, pills, face-creams, powder or other small personal necessities with them then, just as they do now. The small box was devised to carry these articles and it became as indispensable an object of apparel as a coat or a pair of shoes. The word "box" is used generically to describe the snuffbox, the sweetmeat box, the patch-box, etc. In addition "étuis" (holders for needles, sealing wax, etc.) and "nécessaires" (miniature holders fitted with equipment for sewing, writing, etc.) also provided a wide range of objects on which the goldsmith lavished all his technical and artistic skill.

The number of pockets worn by both men and women were multiplied in order to allow numerous little boxes of leather, cardboard, ivory, semi-precious stones, shell, "vernis Martin," silver or gold to be carried about. In the XVIIIth century the manipulation of a snuffbox—the knowledge of how to proffer and take a pinch of snuff—was an important part of elegant manners. A man who owned a certain number of boxes famous for their quality would thereby earn a reputation as a man of taste, just as today a collector's reputation is founded on the high quality of his possessions.

The fashion for boxes increased greatly when the King decided to give them as presents to his favorites and to members of the

diplomatic corps. The treasury archives still survive showing the funds assigned especially to this particular purpose. The documents are known as "The List of the King's Presents" and mention a vast number of marvelous little boxes for snuff which were sometimes set with royal portraits. Miniatures had hitherto been used only in the interiors of boxes. Those with royal portraits gave rise to the general custom of adorning the exterior of the lid with one or more miniatures.

The tremendous vogue these boxes enjoyed brought enormous numbers into existence. The Régent of Orléans had a celebrated collection; still more famous was the collection belonging to the Prince de Conti which included no less than 800 different boxes, all of the most lavish workmanship.

The utmost refinements of luxury were lavished on these small objets d'art. Their decoration was often of a symbolic character relating to the arts or sciences; sometimes a more pictorial decoration was adopted: mythological or pastoral scenes in the style of Boucher, peasant scenes in the style of Teniers or even domestic scenes in the manner of Greuze.

The quality of the finish, the care lavished on their construction and the extraordinary mechanical perfection of their hinges and clasps made them great favorites with collectors.

The color of the gold used in these boxes was varied with great ingenuity by alloying it with various base metals and using a combination of colors on the same piece: green gold (gold and silver); red gold (gold and copper); blue gold (gold and iron); and later white gold (gold and platinum).

Towards 1755 boxes of the "en cage" style began to be made; boxes with sides, lid and base made of semi-precious stones held together by a cage of metal—generally gold.

Endless trouble was taken in perfecting their shapes. There are circular, square, rectangular, oval, and shell-shaped boxes, and boxes in the shape of shuttles, coffins, baskets, etc.

Famous artists were sometimes called upon to decorate them. Occasionally Boucher and Fragonard, and more often van Blarenberghe (who painted minute gouaches) did work of this kind, so that their value was enormously increased.

Some figures will give an indication of the luxury lavished on boxes at this period: the snuff-box presented in 1720 to the Marquis de Scott cost 129,800 livres (between six and seven thousand pounds sterling in money of that period). Normally the price of boxes varied between 20,000 and 30,000 livres, though modest ones cost between 2,000 and 6,000 livres.

XVIIIth Century Goldsmiths' and Silversmiths' Work Today

Eighteenth century goldsmiths' work was not merely a traditional art. The greatest claim to fame of the XVIIIth century goldsmith is that the forms which he devised are still used by modern craftsmen, virtually unchanged. The stylistic perfection of XVIIIth century goldsmiths' work allows it to take a place in modern interiors with ease. Indeed, like a precious stone, its beauty is enhanced by its setting. It does not so much appeal to our romantic sense of the past, as it brings an element of harmony and balance into the modern home.

Louis XVI perfume-burner *of agate and bloodstone with mounts and applie decoration in gold. The shape of the cup and its socle are based on antiqu classic forms. Cameos decorating the socle are in the Pompeian style. (Left* **Some Exceptional Pieces of Silver:** *at top left, lidded jug with hand in the form of a siren; decorated with flowers and wreaths in relief (stampe by Charles Spire and dated 1758). The silver coffeepot at the right was mad by F.-T. Germain in 1756 for the Portuguese Court. At the top, in the cente is a sugar sifter and below it a porringer, or covered dish, of silver-gilt mad at Strasbourg: both are very rare pieces dating from the late XVIIth centur Their shape and decoration are characteristic of those still in use at the begi ning of the XVIIIth century. Flanking the covered dish is a pair of oval goble made by Imlin at Strasbourg in 1730. The two desk candlesticks below we made in 1756 by F.-T. Germain. The double salt-cellar in the center, betwee them, is the work of the Parisian master-goldsmith Jacques Trouvé (1721 To the left and right beside the candlesticks are a silver tumbler with applie decoration (1712) and a mustard pot of a very rare form dating from 173 In the foreground a cake slicer and ladle; the latter was made at Paris Charles Spire in 1753. (Color plate at right.)*

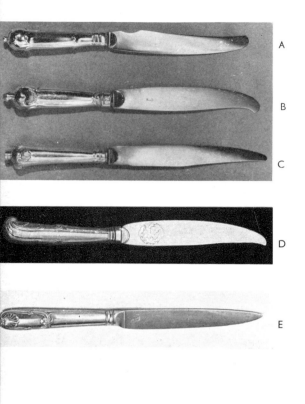

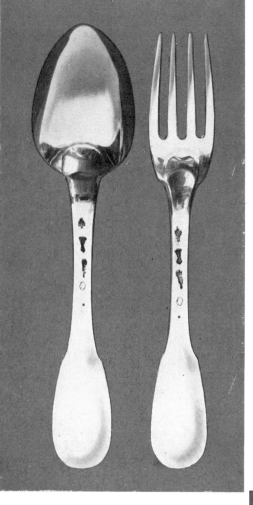

TABLE SILVER was made in a variety of patterns: the undecorated; the raised filet design; the shell motif; and the fiddle-and-shell motif. At left, a plain, undecorated spoon and fork are illustrated. The four marks which usually appear on XVIIIth century silver are clearly visible on the stems. The only decoration is the drop at the junction of the stem with the bowl of the spoon, or the prongs of the fork; this motif appears only towards the end of the century.

KNIFE HANDLES offered a good opportunity for craftsmen to develop originality in the decoration of table silver. A. Type of knife intended to accompany undecorated spoons and forks. B. Type of knife intended to accompany deco-rated spoons and forks bearing a shell, or fiddle-and-shell motif (Paris, 1720). C. This Louis XV knife shows a richer development in decoration (Paris, 1740). D. Knife handle of the type known as "scroll-finished" used in the Louis XV period (the finial at the end of the handle has disappeared). E. Louis XVI knife: the handle has a leaf motif running the length of the handle (Paris, 1780).

THE SPATULATE ENDS of the handles of spoons and forks provide the largest area for decoration. A. This very rich pattern of the fiddle-and-shell type is edged with gadrooning, a relic of the Louis XIV style (Paris, 1733). B. This is a more usual form of the fiddle-and-shell pattern; the shell has two aspects, concave one side and convex on the other (Paris, 1752).

A   B

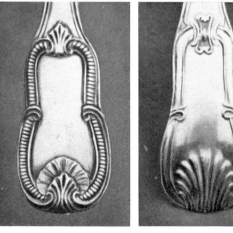

SPOONS WITH PIERCED DECORATION: their shape and size are dictated by the purpose for which they are intended. The pattern of the piercing inva-riably follows the prevailing trend of the style of the period when they were made. A. A spoon for sprinkling sugar, with bowl and stem decorated in the rococo style (Paris, 1750). B. The shell pattern with which the bowl and handle of this olive spoon are pierced, dates from the same period (Paris, 1754).

THIS SUGAR SPOON has a different type of decoration. The shell-design of the end of the handle, the twisted form of the stem, and the pattern of the piercing are all characteristic of the *Régence* style at its best (Paris, 1738).

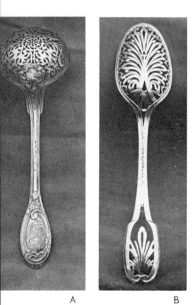

A   B

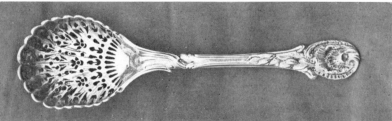

VARIETIES OF TABLE SILVER: from left to right: A. The typical shell design. B. The type with filet decoration. C. This set (1769) is rare for it includes an ice-spoon. It is the work of the well-known Paris goldsmith, E.-P. Balzac.

D. A variant of the shell-and-fiddle pattern, which foreshadows the Louis XVI style. E. Three pieces from a Louis XVI table service: the fiddle design has given way to an elongated handle with a rectilinear pattern (Paris, 1786).

A   B   C   D   E

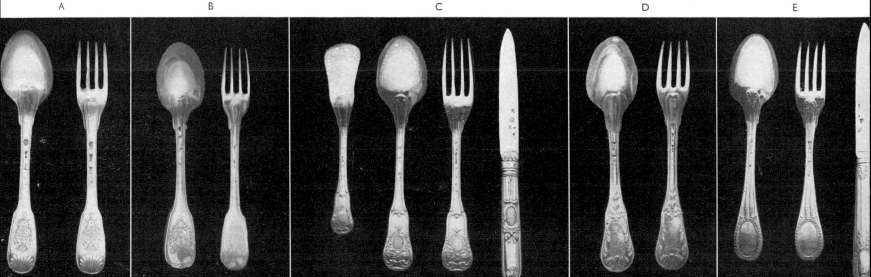

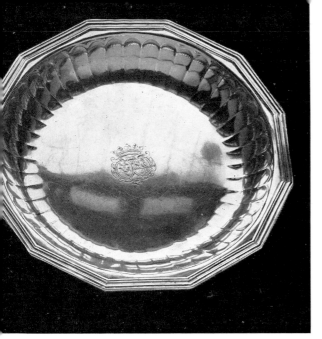

PLATES with polygonal borders came into fashion towards the end of the XVIIth century. They were often supplied with a gadrooned decoration on the molding of the edge, and with fluted sides. A fine example of this form is illustrated at left: a round plate with twelve sides (mark of the Rennes mint, 1705-1734).

THE EDGE and the border enclosed within it both provided an opportunity for decoration of the richest character. The plate illustrated below, executed by Thomas Germain, is a remarkable example of this, and shows one of the greatest XVIIIth century goldsmiths giving a highly personal interpretation of the pre-rococo motifs of the Régence style.

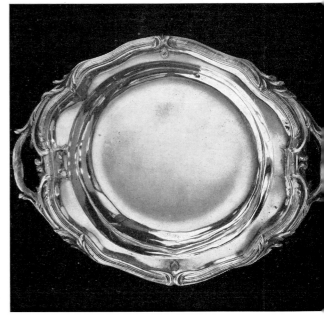

TYPICAL PLATES in use during the XVIIIth century: A. Plates with lobed edges. The molding of the edge is of the typical "à doucine" or hollow-molded type. Usually such plates have five lobes, but sometimes there are six, eight, or even occasionally more. The size of these plates varies between 9-1/2" up to as much as 24 in diameter, and more. B. A similar type of plate, but of oval shape. Plates of this sort were sometimes as long as 40", if they were intended for serving fish. C. The square-shaped serving dish has the same type of edge as the lobed plate, but adapted to its own different form. These dishes were generally made in pairs or in multiples of two. They are a good deal deeper than an ordinary plate, particularly the larger ones which are known as entrée dishes.

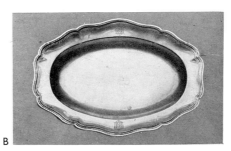
A

B

C

STANDING DISH OR SERVER. This has the same type of shaped border as the plates above, but is supported on a foot. It was intended to hold salt-boxes or spice-boxes, bottles or glasses. The one illustrated bears the marks of the Le Mans mint, 1764.

DISH AND COVER in the typical Louis XVI style: the cover is decorated with broad fluting and is surmounted with a knob in the form of a pineapple resting on a group of acanthus leaves. The ones illustrated were made in 1771 by Jacques-Nicolas Rœttiers.

SIX-LOBED ENTRÉE DISH with handles. The depth of this piece, and its characteristic handles, show that it was intended for foods served in a sauce. Spoons with unusually long handles, known as gravy spoons, were invented for use with dishes of this type.

SHOW PIECES AND LARGE ORNAMENTS such as table decorations, soup-tureens, wine coolers, etc., allowed goldsmiths to give full vent to their imagination and their technical skill. Table decorations were not always made as single compositions. They often took the form of a number of small objects, representing a variety of subjects. These two silver-gilt figures come from a series of sixteen statuettes, all different, made for the Portuguese court in 1757 by the Parisian goldsmith Cousinet. The figures of men and women were arranged in pairs, with couples dressed in characteristic costumes of different countries: China, England, France, Germany, Hungary, Italy, Poland and Spain. Once, they held a garland of fruits and leaves in their hands.

CENTERPIECES

WINE-COOLERS like this one were included only in exceptionally luxurious services: the necessary requirements of their function might be expected to thwart such decorative audacity as is displayed here. Normally their ornamentation follows the general trend of the style of the period in which they were made. The one opposite was executed by Thomas Germain in 1727. Its harmonious silhouette and technical perfection show how a great craftsman could make use of the exuberant rococo style, without abandoning his sense of tradition.

LIDS OF SOUP-TUREENS and pie-dishes were often ᵈated with representations of the principal ingredients ᵏn making a soup, or a game-pie. It is not unusual to ᵗhe lid covered with vegetables, fruit, game, and birds, sometimes spread almost entirely over its surface. ᵏn soup-tureens are called "*pots à oille*" from the ᵗsh word "olla" for a concoction of vegetables and meat ᵈd in oil. The famous soup-tureen illustrated is known "Boar's Head" soup-tureen from the shape of its handles. ᵐed part of a table service made by Thomas Germain ᵗe *Régent* of France. Germain lavished a wealth of the ᵒcoco type of *Régence* ornament on its decoration.

IN THIS WINE-COOLER, architectural motifs have taken the place of the shell, vegetable, and animal elements so dear to rococo artists. Louis XVI decorative motifs are used with particularly happy effect on the plinth or foot of this piece, which was made by Robert-Joseph Auguste (Paris, 1778).

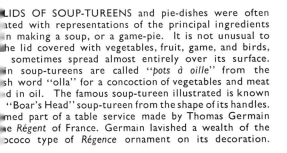

CENTERPIECES played an important part in the decoration of the dinner table during the XVIIIth century. They were often designed to hold various condiments, such as pepper, salt, spices and sauces. Frequently, too, they were supplied with candle holders on movable branches. This *Régence* centerpiece was also intended to hold four oil and vinegar cruets. The central dish was for sauces.

A

B

C

D

E

F

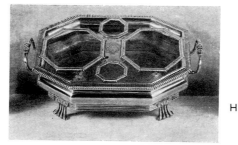

G

H

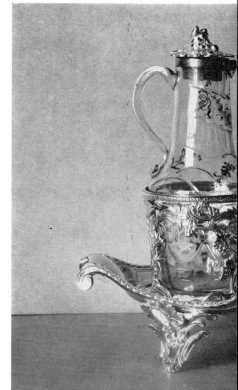

TUMBLERS OR BEAKERS varied very little in shape throughout the XVIIIth century; the form generally adopted was tulip-shaped, with or without a foot. The hallmarks indicate the date when a piece was made, and the decoration (which may be applied, chased, or engraved) usually followed the prevailing decorative trends of the day. The principal types of ornamentation employed were plain or barely decorated surfaces, engraved decoration, and decoration applied in relief, in that order of importance.

A. LIDDED BEAKER in the RÉGENCE style, with plain undecorated sides. Such covered pieces generally formed a part of a traveling service.

B. The lower part of this tumbler has an applied decoration and the neck engraved with an interlacing design on a dull ground; the foot is gadrooned. This is characteristic of the pieces dating from the early years of the century (Paris, 1712).

C. On this tumbler, the decoration takes the form of bullrushes applied in relief and chased; the foot is reeded and decorated with a ribbon motif. It dates from the Louis XVI period (Paris, 1776).

D. The lower half of the body and the neck of this Louis XVI tumbler are engraved; the foot is embossed with ovoli and an interlacing design (1789).

J

K

L

I

SAUCE-BOATS, SALTCELLARS, oil and vinegar cruets, mustard-pots, and egg-cups were all in common use during the XVIIIth century. These pieces provided goldsmiths with an opportunity to create some of their greatest masterpieces, for their small size did not allow them to be overcharged with decoration. Their shape was already fixed by the function that they had to perform, and has remained almost unchanged down to our day.

E. DOUBLE-LIPPED SAUCE-BOAT, with handles. Its molded edge is a sinuous shape. It rests on a gadrooned foot (Paris, 1722).

F. IN THE LATEST PHASES of the rococo style an abuse of ornament tended to destroy the form of object decorated, and this proliferation of decoration caused the reaction which ultimately led to the birth of the Louis XVI style. This sauce-boat was made for Mme. de Pompadour by François Joubert in 1754.

G. BY CONTRAST, the form of this sauce-boat has been greatly purified. The handle is borrowed from classical art, and the general form is that of a Roman lamp. A beading, characteristic of the Louis XVI style at its best, runs around the foot (Paris, 1785).

H. THIS CRUET is typical of the form adopted at the beginning of the XVIIIth century. The cut corners and the gadrooning recall the late XVIIth century style. Two small spaces at each side, between the bottle-holders, are intended for the stoppers.

I. THIS CRUET is a perfect example of the fully developed Louis XV style. It was made by the goldsmith E.-P. Balzac (Paris, 1750).

J. LOUIS XVI MUSTARD-POT and stand with open-work holder intended to hold the glass mustard-pot itself (Paris, 1780).

K. THIS EGG-CUP, with applied decoration on the lower part of the cup and the foot, surrounded by gadroons, is typical of the style at the beginning of the century (Paris, 1712).

L. DOUBLE EGG-CUP (Paris, 1762). The two small cups are united by a central motif in the form of a wheatsheaf.

M. THIS SALTCELLAR, in the form of a barrel carried on a wheelbarrow pushed by a cupid, is an exceptional piece which shows what originality goldsmiths could bring to the creation of an everyday piece. The group is further enlivened by a small greyhound. It was made at Paris in 1753 by A.-S. Durand.

N. LIDDED SALTCELLAR with a curving base and shell-shaped lid. This saltcellar is typical of the Louis XV period; such pieces were sometimes made with a lid, sometimes without.

O. DURING THE LOUIS XVI PERIOD, the interior of saltcellars was often of glass, supported in a silver mount; sometimes composed of garlands and resting on baluster-shaped feet; sometimes of a simple band of pierced metal.

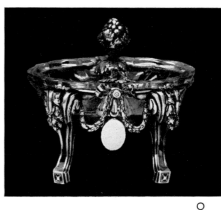

M

N

O

THIS EWER, in the shape of a helmet, is of a type which had remained unchanged ever since the Renaissance. Ewers intended to hold liquids were frequently plated. When they were made of silver, they were usually decorated in the most ornate Louis XIV style and were intended as ornamental pieces rather than for use.

JUGS AND BASINS were designed for use either at the dining or the toilet table. The one illustrated opposite was made in 1758 by F.-T. Germain for the Portuguese court.

THIS TOILET JUG illustrates the most refined type of late XVIIIth century goldsmith's work. The handle is a figure of Narcissus admiring himself in a pool of shell form which serves as a lid for the jug. The main body of the piece is chased with elongated leaves and a frieze of scrolled foliage runs around the shoulders. Made by Chéret in 1784.

THE EARLIEST TEAPOTS originated, for the most part, in the ports such as Bordeaux and Marseilles, where tea was first landed. The pieces made at Paris are generally of remarkably fine quality, as can be seen in the example illustrated above which was made there in 1750 by E.-F. Godin.

CREAM JUGS were usually of a simple form with the lower part of the body bulb-shaped and the top surrounded with a molding. The body was generally left plain, or decorated with twisted flutes. They are rarely more than 3 3/4"-6" high. This one was made in Paris in 1749.

INDIVIDUAL COFFEE or chocolate pots, known as "égoïstes" were made with a straight or curving handle and the lower part bulb-shaped. They were made in great numbers throughout the century. The one illustrated is of silver-gilt, and was made by François-Thomas Germain in 1755. Height, 3". Lip and knob are decorated with motifs suggested by the coffee plant.

COFFEE AND CHOCOLATE POTS with a straight handle and resting on three short feet were made throughout the century. Their shapes vary very little. Decoration is usually confined to the knob of the lid, the lip, and the point of junction of the feet with the body. The importance of the coffeepot varies with the quality of this decoration. The one illustrated here was made in Paris in 1755.

CANDLESTICKS provided the chief source of light in the XVIIIth century, both for rooms and at table. They range from a simple stem with a single light, up to models with a considerable number of candle sockets. In the latter case they are known as candelabra and possess two or more branches, each terminating in a socket. The candelabrum at left is of two lights, supported on a stem, and has a base with cut corners. The decoration with masks and gadrooning is typical of pieces dating from the beginning of the century.

THE LOUIS XV style affected the general design of candlesticks very little. At the most it was reflected in the ornamentation. The pair illustrated here were made in Paris in 1744.

THIS SILVER CANDLESTICK in the full rococo style shows the lengths to which the distortion of form was occasionally carried. But it also displays the skill with which the goldsmiths of the day were able to give a harmonious and balanced effect to such exaggerated shapes. It was made by Claude Duvivier after a design by Meissonier.

THE BRANCHES AND STEM of this candelabrum dating from the Transitional period between the Louis XV and Louis XVI style were made by different craftsmen. This is not uncommon and explains the differences found between the decorations of the arms and the stem.

THIS THREE-LIGHT CANDELABRUM is characteristic of the style of the latter end of the century. The design and decoration are borrowed from engravings made by such great ornamental designers as Lalonde and Delafosse. It is characteristic of the Louis XVI style.

THE SOCKET of this long-handled chamber candlestick rests on a base with a lobed edge, strengthened with a hollow molding. The handles of this type of candlestick were frequently of the same spatulate form as a spoon or fork.

103

LIDDED BOWLS and vegetable dishes were amongst the principal fittings of traveling services. The lidded bowl is perhaps the key piece of such a set: it is often valuable for studying the evolution of the forms and decoration of a goldsmith's work during the XVIIIth century. The one illustrated opposite is amongst the finest examples known. It was made by Thomas Germain in 1733. The handles and the knob are in the form of coiled serpents; the knob rises from a base of radiating gadroons. This piece is of remarkably satisfactory proportions.

LIDDED BOWL AND STAND: the style of the handles and the general decoration of this bowl are characteristic of the *Régence* period. These two pieces were made by Alexis Loir, the most celebrated member of a large family of goldsmiths.

THE GENERAL FORM of this lidded bowl and its dish is typical of the Transitional period between the Louis XV and Louis XVI styles. The decoration and chasing already foreshadow the Louis XVI style (Paris, 1769).

THE HANDLES of this piece are emblazoned with the coat-of-arms of the owner. The knob, in the form of a realistic artichoke, rises from the twisting flutes of the lid. It was made by T. Germain in 1733.

THIS "POT A OILLE", or entrée dish, dates from the beginning of the XVIIIth century. It is decorated in the late Louis XIV style, but its proportions (9-1/2" × 8-1/2") are those of the practical shapes towards which goldsmiths' work was moving.

CIRCULAR SOUP-TUREEN and its "*dormant*" or stand. The so-called "hen shape" of the body is often found in pieces in the Louis XV style. This piece, with its decoration of curves and counter-curves, is very typical of the Louis XV style.

IN THIS OVAL SOUP-TUREEN and its "*dormant*", the form and decoration are strictly architectural and derived from classical models. It was made by the goldsmith Robert-Joseph Auguste in 1780.

THIS OVAL SOUP-TUREEN was executed by François-Thomas Germain about the middle of the XVIIIth century. The lid and the handles in the form of sticks of celery emerge from the body of the piece in remarkably easy and fluent fashion; the knob is in the form of a pomegranate cut open to reveal its interior.

A

B

A VAST NUMBER OF PIECES went to make up a complete toilet service. Certain sets such as those given by the King or the *Régent* included as many as 200 different pieces. The principal ones were mirror frames, face cream and powder jars, jugs and basins, small candlesticks, pots and perfume flasks, shaving bowls and brushes. In traveling sets, all the utensils required for a meal, as well as writing materials, were often added to these. The major pieces on which the goldsmiths lavished their especial skill are now often found separately in museums and important private collections: jugs, basins, powder boxes, and soap holders are most frequently seen. A. Jug and basin from a toilet service (Paris, 1706). B. Three pieces from a traveling toilet set (made at Lille in the first half of the century). At the right and left: two circular powder boxes decorated with simple moldings. In the center: a toilet-tidy intended to hold discarded toilet tissues, etc.; a particularly rare piece, forming part of the same set. C. Some pieces from a very important traveling service made by R.-J. Auguste in 1777 for one of the Duchesses of Oldenburg; it consists of a salver, a stand supporting a pair of perfume containers, an orris-powder box and a knife for taking toilet creams from a jar. D. The sponge holder is a matching piece in the same set.

D

C

A

B

C

E

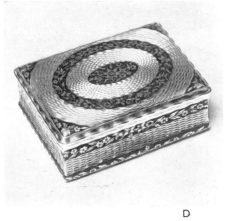

D

GOLD BOXES have survived in greater number than any other type of XVIIIth century goldsmiths' work, for their owners were never legally compelled to melt them down, as they were with so much French gold and silver. A. Rectangular Louis XV agate box, enclosed in a framework of pierced gold of rococo design; the motifs of the lid are scrolled and the corners are chased with roses. B. Louis XV gold and mother-of-pearl box. Such colored materials as mother-of-pearl and semi-precious stones began to be used for boxes about the middle of the century. This type of box is known as the "*en cage*" (caged) type. The style produced some of the most beautiful and most successful boxes. C. Louis XV snuffbox (Paris, 1753). D. Snuffbox of gold of several colors made by the goldsmith Ducrolay in 1740. He was one of the most famous XVIIIth century makers of gold boxes. E. Louis XV gold box of curving outline. The lid is agate, carved with a mythological scene.

NÉCESSAIRES whatever their purpose, whether intended as pin or needle cases, work boxes, or writing cases, are as beautifully wrought as the finest snuffboxes. In the XVIIIth century fashionable people took infinite trouble in choosing the most elegant presents for their friends, as can be seen from the inscriptions on these minute boxes: "A token of my love," "Friendship's offering," "Love unites us," etc.

A. LOUIS XV NÉCESSAIRE, in the form of a coffer of lapis lazuli and chased gold. It contains a large number of utensils, some intended for writing, others for sewing.

B. NÉCESSAIRE fitted with toilet equipment, of gold and moss-agate (mid XVIIIth century).

C. NÉCESSAIRE for scent bottles, decorated in Chinese style in colored enamel (Paris, 1776).

D. NÉCESSAIRE of agate, mounted in gold, for perfume bottles (Paris, Louis XV period).

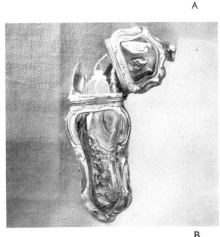

A

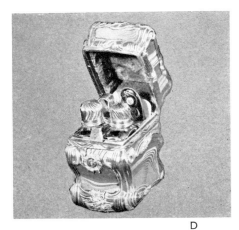

D

B

E. MINIATURE traveling-writing set of gold and enamel, dating from the Louis XV period. It contains three sections of a pen-holder inserted into three of its corners and a pencil in the fourth.

C

E

FINE SPECIMENS OF NÉCESSAIRES and needle-cases showing the range of decoration and skilled workmanship of which the makers of these small boxes were capable. The lid of the writing *nécessaire* (top) is decorated with a clock. The two *nécessaires* fitted for perfume and sewing (center) are of agate and semi-precious stones in chased gold mounts. The other *nécessaire* (bottom of page) is decorated in two ways. The body is covered with a guilloche pattern with a reserve enameled with flowers in the style of Hungarian embroidery, through which the gold ground can be seen.

(Color plate at right.)

THIS BOX is one of the most extraordinary ever made. It is the work of Louis-Nicolas Van Blarenberghe and was made in 1770 for the Duc de Choiseul. It consists of a series of miniature gouache paintings in a gold setting. On the lid of the box the Duc de Choiseul can be seen in his bedchamber. This room is a perfect example of the most elegant type of interior decoration of the Louis XV period. On each side of the wall mirror are paintings by Greuze, one of them, "Blowing a Kiss," is now in an English private collection, while the other, "The Offering to Love," is to be found in the Wallace Collection. On the front the Duc de Choiseul, Louis XV's Foreign Minister, can be seen talking with his secretaries. He is seated at his desk, a masterpiece by Caffiéri. This celebrated piece of furniture belonged subsequently to Talleyrand, and afterwards to Metternich. In the background two paintings by Hubert Robert can be seen. On this box, Blarenberghe's gouaches, which are only just over 3" wide, are painted with such detail that an inventory of the Duc de Choiseul's collection of paintings could be made from them.

A

B

C

D

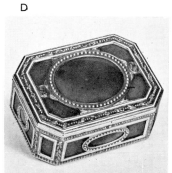

E

F

SOME FINE LOUIS XVI BOXES:

A. Box of chased gold. The lid and sides are inset with enamel miniatures in the style of Greuze.

B. Gold and enameled snuffbox. Improved techniques of hinge-making enabled goldsmiths to make oval and circular boxes during the Louis XVI period.

C. Chased gold box in the Transitional manner between the Louis XV and Louis XVI styles. Louis XV decorative motifs are used here for a composition which has the rectilinear qualities of the Louis XVI style.

D. Gold and cornaline box typical of the "caged" type.

E. Circular box of gold enameled in a variety of colors.

F. Typical examples of late XVIIIth century oval boxes. The watch with two dials set into the lid of the chased gold box at the right is particularly unusual.

A

THIS GOLD WATCH-CASE, made in Paris about 1735, by Étienne Lenoir, is enameled with a scene of Diana at the Bath (at left).

VENUS AND ADONIS — one of the favorite themes in XVIIIth century repertory — are seen here in relief in gold against an enamel background on this watch-case which was made in Paris about 1730 (at right).

CLOCKMAKERS eventually obtained the legal right to work in gold and silver (a privilege hitherto accorded to goldsmiths only). Watches were henceforward as richly decorated as snuff boxes and *nécessaires*. They too were often given as presents and people prized them with the rest of their jewelry. Watch-cases richly decorated with enamel were extremely fashionable during Louis XVI's reign. Their makers vied with one another in devising the most varied and elaborate shapes; indeed, circular watches were much less fashionable than those of more exaggerated design.

THIS GOLD WATCH-CASE, made in Paris about 1750, by Julien Le Roy (at left), is entirely chased with patterns of shell and rococo forms.

A BASKET of flowers in relief set against a background of guilloches, palm fronds and rococo shapes, decorates the case of this gold watch made in Paris in 1765 by Baillon (at right).

B

A. THE DIAL OF THIS GOLD WATCH is set inside a guitar-shaped case enameled reddish-brown over a guilloched ground. The dial is concealed within the body of the instrument.

B. THIS SPHERICAL, BLACK AND GOLD enameled watch-case is inscribed around the center with the dedication: "You are still more wonderful." (« Vous en avez l'éclat. »)

C. THE DIAL of this watch in the form of a lyre of gold and colored enamel is in the center of the instrument. On the back are musical motifs and doves.

C

THIS GOLD WATCH made in Paris in 1770 is decorated in relief with interlacing flowers treated naturalistically, a decoration typical of the Transitional style (above).

THREE MINIATURES ingeniously mounted in a setting of gold and brilliants ornament this Louis XVI watch (right).

A CLASSICAL subject in enamel, surrounded by pearls and colored enamels, and enclosed in a richly embossed framework, decorates this Louis XVI watch-case (left).

PERFUME DISPENSER, made of a powder-blue Chinese porcelain vase, fitted with a tap. The vase is mounted on gilt bronze rock-work. During the first half of the century only Chinese porcelain was considered worthy of being set in fine, highly-chased mounts. Occasionally gilded copper was used instead of gilt bronze.

GILT BRONZE

The Role of Gilt Bronze in the XVIIIth Century

Gilt bronze did not begin to play a really important part in interior decoration until the beginning of the XVIIIth century. Nevertheless it was not unknown at earlier periods. Even in the Middle Ages, craftsmen had used it in combination with semi-precious stones and enamel, as exemplified by numerous surviving reliquaries, chasses, pyxes, coffers and bishop's crosses. Renaissance metal workers, too—particularly in Italy—created a large number of magnificent objects of gilt bronze, set with coral and semi-precious stones.

In the XVIIIth century, however, the decorative function of gilt bronze was enormously extended. During one of the most triumphant periods in the history of French art, it was used to decorate furniture, and lighting equipment. Almost everything, large or small, used in the decoration of the house was either made of or mounted with gilt bronze at one time or another. Earlier centuries had been content to use simple materials in their interior decoration: wood, stone, marble or iron, carved or wrought, elegant or coarse, according to the spirit of the age. Since gold and silver gilt objects were largely forbidden (see p. 91), the new elegance and luxury which came into being in the XVIIIth century found its perfect expression in gilt bronze. It played an essential role in all interior decoration, giving an unusually sumptuous character to the more important pieces of furniture as well as to a wide variety of smaller objects.

The XVIIIth century was the golden age for furniture mounted with gilt bronze. For this material conferred a remarkable richness on furniture and its almost infinite malleability made it admirably suited to the new shapes and types of furniture devised during the period. Cabinetmakers, bronze-founders, sculptors and gilders all collaborated so closely in the production of furniture at this period that it is difficult to separate their individual contributions; each played his part in creating the perfectly harmonious effect of the whole. Bronze mounts continued to perform a utilitarian function, protecting the corners of furniture, strengthening and supporting the legs and weaker points in the construction; but its purpose extended far beyond this. In the previous century, mounts had generally been applied only at certain fixed points such as at corners and edges, or in the center of the front or sides. They were bold in character, as befitted their functions. But, in the course of the XVIIIth century, they gradually became lighter and were used at any or every point on the surface of a piece of furniture just as the craftsman's fancy dictated.

Gilt bronze was used not so much to separate the component parts of a piece of furniture from one another to emphasize their individual character, as it was for its unifying effect. With the latter end in view, it was applied to furniture at an ever increasing number of points; as a gallery round the top, in the form of swags and decorative pendants at the corners,

as drawer handles, as shoes to protect the feet, in the form of ornamental masks, as a decoration for the center of the lower edge, or in the form of astragals and moldings of various types. The effect of this increasing use of gilt bronze on furniture was to produce an elaborate play of light on its surface; it was also an indispensable complement to the finest marquetry.

Gilt bronze was used either to make or to mount an almost infinitely varied range of objects. The surviving advertisements issued by bronze-founders of the period, or by celebrated art dealers like Lazare Duvaux, list the many objects then made of gilt bronze. Chandeliers, chimney lights, cartel clocks, barometers, etc., are only a few of the objects which were generally made wholly or in part of gilt bronze.

Sometimes it was used to replace less precious materials such as copper or iron, that had been employed in earlier periods. Bronze was relatively easily worked and it made it possible for the same model to be repeated an almost indefinite number of times. This greatly facilitated the supply of such objects to the rising middle classes.

Gilt bronze was put to particularly elegant use in mounting objects made of other materials. Up to this time, mounting had been merely used to strengthen an object or make it easier to use. The primary aim of XVIIIth century mounts was to decorate and enrich. Even great decorative artists of the period, such as Oppenord and Meissonier, were willing to provide designs for gilt bronze mounts. Such things were greatly sought after and played an important part in the art collections of the period. In his "Picturesque Tour of Paris," Dargenville wrote: "Painting is not the only ornament of Monsieur Blondel de Gaigny's collection. His house is furnished with a large quantity of the finest pieces of early porcelain, whose beauty is only rivaled by the splendor of the mounts in which they are set." This fashion for mounting objects in gilt bronze was one of the most original contributions of the period to the decorative arts. The mounts were not only beautiful in themselves, but they provided a foil for the objects on which they were applied.

The best bronze-chasers of the period completely transformed many objects with the gilt bronze mounts they gave them. This treatment was carried out in two different ways: sometimes an object (a vase, for instance) was allowed to retain its original form and function, the mount merely providing an added beauty; but sometimes their original purpose was totally altered by the mount. Thus two Chinese lacquer boxes might be transformed into a potpourri vase, or an upright vase into a ewer. The material was even more imaginatively used to combine several different objects on a single base, by providing them with an appropriately decorative setting to create a new and complex composition. An instance of this is the magnificently mounted vase adapted as a perfume dispenser, which is reproduced on page 110.

This method was applied to lighting fixtures with outstanding success. Figures and objects of Dresden or Chinese porcelain were assembled and transformed into candlesticks or candelabra, thereby producing some of the most elegant objets d'art devised during the period.

Indeed it would hardly be an exaggeration to describe the XVIIIth century as a period utterly intoxicated with a love of gilt bronze. In interior decoration, it provided a multiplicity of centers of interest, with its glitter and reflections. It was given the most diversified and complicated forms, sometimes molded into flowers and rock work, sometimes twisted in pierced volutes with denticulated edges. It was made into graceful flower stems, palm-trees, elegant sprays of leaves, etc. Every sort of object was a pretext for a mount; flower pots, small porcelain figures, pieces of fluorspar, rock-crystal or lapis lazuli carvings, vases of porphyry, marble, porcelain or lacquer—all were enriched and enlivened by gilt bronze.

It can certainly be claimed that the great age of mounted objects came to an end with the end of the century itself. Pieces made subsequently, in the XVIIIth century style, do not begin to rival genuine XVIIIth century examples in quality, imaginative character or vitality.

It should be noted that, in spite of its relatively low value, gilt bronze did not entirely escape the same kind of sumptuary edict which had had such a disastrous effect on the silver- and goldsmiths' work of the period. In 1792, during the Revolution, a "Summary List" was drawn up, setting forth the "material suitable to be converted into cash which is to be found in the former Royal residence of Fontainebleau and its dependencies." This list includes an item drawn up in the following terms: "Candlesticks and wall lights of gilt bronze from the various rooms: 4,805 livres, 3 marcs, 4 onces."

Processes, Shapes and Decorations

Bronze (an amalgam of tin, copper and zinc) was particularly well adapted to the manufacture of objets d'art, for its close-grained texture allowed a high finish. Its great strength made it particularly suitable to support and strengthen other more fragile objects. Its color and appearance could be varied almost indefinitely, for it provided an admirable base for gilding, silvering, and a wide variety of patination. In the XVIIIth century, bronze-chasers worked either under the control of an artist-designer or on their own; many of the latter were capable of producing admirable designs. They were particularly skilled in maintaining a unity of effect right through the whole series of very complex processes which led up to the production of a work in gilt bronze. Such an operation was carried out in the following stages:

1. A sketch-model was made in terra-cotta or clay;
2. It was then molded in plaster;
3. The plaster model was worked over once again—that is to say, its surface and its shapes were perfected; a further cast then taken in bronze which was known as the "cast on plaster;"
4. The bronze-chaser then intervened to touch up this bronze "casting model." The surface of this model was finished as smoothly as possible so as to avoid or minimize chasing the subsequent castings;
5. Once this model had been given the necessary finish, it was turned over successively to the following subsidiary craftsmen: first the bronze-caster; then to the chaser ("ciseleur"), who removed imperfections, lumps and other faults due to the casting; it was then handed to the mounter who examined and assembled the various component pieces either by soldering, or riveting or by means of dowels and/or screws; it then passed to the gilder who applied the final coat of pure gold, by the mercury gilding process; lastly it went back again to the mounter who was responsible for the final assembling of the pieces and for fastening them on the object to be mounted.

Such, briefly, were the various operations which had to by performed before a gilt bronze object came into being.

Chasing is the most important of all the various processes which have just been described. It was the operation which gave a piece of bronze its unique character.

In fact, when a piece was handed over by the bronze-caster to the chaser, it resembled the original model only very imperfectly. The casting left scars, lumps and vent holes where the molten metal had been poured into the mold. First the chaser removed the worst of these defects with the aid of an engraver's needle, or "burin." Then he began to burnish and give modeling to the surface with other tools known as "rifloirs" (files) and "matoirs" (riveting hammers). (In England bronze chasing was never carried to anything like the degree of perfection it reached in France, consequently tools of this sort were never used there and there is no precise English name for them.)

It was at this stage that the chaser was really able to display his technical and artistic skill. He was not necessarily concerned that the finished piece conform exactly to the original model, but sometimes allowed his imagination free play, perfecting and improving the work technically and æsthetically.

It was, of course, only the great bronze-chasers who had sufficient genius to work with this independence and freedom; less competent workmen were merely concerned to see that the finished product conformed as closely as possible to the original design, which they had merely copied.

In the XVIIIth century, the best chasers were skilled modelers and draughtsmen as well. It was this command of a variety of artistic techniques which enabled them to achieve so remarkable a mastery of their craft.

The best gilt bronze owes a great deal to the high quality of its gilding. This was carried out in a procedure which is no longer in use today, owing to its harmful effect on the health of the gilders. It was known as the mercury gilding process and consisted, first, of forming an amalgam of gold and mercury according to a special formula. This was then spread on the metal and heated and the mercury was driven off as a vapor. The thin coating of gold, left in an absolutely pure state on the surface of the object, adhered with extraordinary tenacity. Contemporary craftsmen brought this technique to the highest degree of perfection. Among the most celebrated gilders of the earlier part of the century were, for instance, Jacques Cloquemain, and his collaborators, Boulle, Claude Marlau and Josserand. They all gilded in the manner known as "ormolu," a term which is constantly met with in contemporary documents relating to objects in gilt bronze. The term does not indicate any particular quality or purity of the gold, but derives from the fact that the gold ("or") was ground ("moulu") to a powder in order that it could be better amalgamated with the mercury.

The list of gilders gives some idea of the importance of the gilt bronze industry and in particular of that department of the industry concerned with the supply of furniture bronzes. The "Paris Almanac" for 1788 mentions no fewer than 61 gilders, while the names of only 25 cabinetmakers are listed. Some of these gilders were the regular collaborators of individual cabinetmakers of renown; Barthélemy Antin, for instance, was the favorite gilder of the celebrated cabinetmaker Cressent; Galien and Gobert worked for Œben; above all there were the two most famous gilders of the period, Gouthière and Thomire. When F.-Th. Germain went bankrupt, he owed Gouthière 20,000 livres for gilding done on silver which he himself had made. This fact also throws an interesting light on the organization of Parisian craftsmen's guilds. Only master gilders were allowed to gild the silver made by goldsmiths; the craftsman who made the piece was not permitted to do so.

The character of XVIIIth century gilt is due therefore not merely to the artist-designer, who conceived it, nor entirely to the bronze-caster and to the chaser who actually created its forms, but also to the incomparable character of the mercury gilding used at the period, a technique which is almost forgotten today. The shapes of bronze mounts were naturally dictated by those of the objects on which they were to be attached. Only furniture mounts and the gilt bronze mounts of porcelain, lacquer, etc., developed a wide range of forms of their own. But even the shapes of these were natural manifestations of the characteristic stylistic trends of each period, from the rococo of the "Régence" and Louis XV periods down to the neo-classic style in fashion at the end of the century.

The Great Bronze-Workers

There were no particular factories or centers renowned for making fine bronzes such as were famous for the making of furniture or tapestry. Furniture was, in general, made in the neighborhood of the faubourg Saint-Antoine, and tapestry at centers such as Aubusson, Beauvais, etc. As in earlier centuries, the names of very few bronze-workers are known to us. This is partly due to the complexity of the manufactur-

ing processes as a result of which no single craftsman could be said to be wholly responsible for the creation of a bronze. In addition, a patron, when commissioning a chest of drawers from some great cabinetmaker, would never have given a thought to who would make its bronze mounts. The only reason that the names of certain craftsmen like Caffiéri, Gouthière and Thomire are familiar to us today is that their commissions came largely from the Crown or from the upper ranks of society. This has enabled scholars to trace references to them in archives and official documents. Occasionally great artists did their own bronze-founding; for instance, Coysevox submitted a bill for 1,600 livres to the Prince de Conti "for making the model, supplying the wax, modeling all the individual pieces, casting in bronze, finishing, perfecting and setting in place as instructed," a splendid bust of the Prince de Condé. Later Clodion and Marin frequently chose bronze as the most suitable material for reproducing their small sculptures.

Here are the names of some of the greatest artist-craftsmen who worked in bronze: Caffiéri, who worked at the Tuileries, at the Hôtel des Ambassadeurs, at the Château de Choisy, at St. Hubert and at La Muette; Étienne Sauvage, whom the Tzar summoned to Russia in 1716; Gallien, who was commissioned by the Crown to make the magnificent clock now in the "Cabinet du Conseil" at Versailles; Desprez, who worked frequently for Louis XV; Danthiau; Leblanc; the two Varins, father and son, who cast a large number of vases for the royal palaces; Duplessis, who collaborated with Winant and Hervien in making the bronze mounts of the magnificent writing desk that belonged to Louis XV, which is now in the Louvre; and Forestier and Charbonnier, who were the special collaborators of the cabinetmakers Œben and Riesener.

Gouthière

Gouthière may be considered the last great gilt bronze worker of the century, for Thomire is generally regarded as belonging to the XIXth century. Gouthière was born at Troyes in 1740, and began to work for the Crown in 1769. He immediately showed himself to be one of the most remarkable bronze-casters and chasers of his period. He quickly developed a highly individualistic style which can be fairly easily recognized, for it has certain distinctive characteristics: an elaboration of detail, a subtle organization of decorative themes and, particularly, the use of fruit and vegetable forms in his mounts. Owing to the predominant role that Gouthière played in the art of making gilt bronze, it is only natural that his works were frequently imitated and widely reproduced.

Yet few documents survive relating to this master craftsman. For the most part we are dependent solely on a careful study of the high quality and individual character of his works in our attempts to identify them. Only a single one of his pieces is signed: the clock known as "The Avignon Clock" (see p. 119). The group of figures flanking the dial were modeled by the sculptor Boizot. But, while Boizot's contribution to this work is hardly outstanding, Gouthière's interpretation is perfect, and it is a monument to his skill as a bronze-chaser. This clock was presented by the town of Avignon to a member of the Rochechouart family, whose arms are displayed at the top of the piece. The two figures on the base, symbolizing rivers, represent the Rhône and the Durance. Certain works executed by Gouthière for the Duc d'Aumont, his daughter the Duchesse de Mazarin, and for M. de Bondy were said to have been marvels of delicacy and grace. Mme. du Barry was this great artist's most lavish patron. The vast quantity of work which he undertook for her at Louveciennes was the ultimate cause of his ruin.

In 1793, the former favorite of Louis XV owed Gouthière more than 750,000 livres for gilt bronzes.

XVIIIth Century Gilt Bronze in the Modern House

Any decorative scheme in the XVIIIth century manner derived much of its effect from the indispensable presence of gilt bronze. The sumptuous character of the result depended on whether it was used on the furniture alone or in even greater profusion in the form of clocks, wall lights, andirons, etc.

More than any other material, gilt bronze gives an impression of richness. If XVIIIth century bronzes sometimes appear to have become darkened by a patina due to age, they can easily be restored to their original brightness by cleaning. Only then is it possible to get some idea of what the interiors of the period must have looked like, when golds of various colors and finishes competed with one another on the furniture, on the paneling on the walls, and in innumerable bronze objects scattered about the room.

Even nowadays the advantages of gilt bronze for furnishing and decoration are not unappreciated. Although the high cost of manufacture seems to preclude any possibility of producing gilt bronze on a commercial scale today, modern interior decorators know how to make use of it when sufficient means are put at their disposal to enable them do so. Indeed decorators may be said to prefer gilt bronze to any other type of decoration in producing especially rich effects, as can be seen in certain private houses and official residences today. Their preference indicates the importance of the role that gilt bronze can play in a modern interior, if it be used in a reasonable and restrained fashion.

On the other hand, the processes by which XVIIIth century gilt bronze was produced provide a lesson to our times in the way in which different artists used to subordinate their individual personalities and collaborate to produce a unified effect. In the XVIIIth century, of course, gilt bronze was only a relatively inexpensive ornamental accessory; nevertheless it often displayed all the subtlety of the finest goldsmiths' work of the period. As a material, it adapted itself particularly happily to the spirit of fantasy and imagination which inspired the great ornamental designers of the period —artists whose particular skill lay in their ability to adapt current stylistic tendencies to even the humblest objects used in interior decoration.

THREE-BRANCH CANDELABRUM of chased and gilt bronze, dating from the Louis
Quinze period. In the center is a Dresden porcelain lion painted in natural colors,
supporting a shield bearing the arms of the Sulkowski family. In the second half of the
century marble or alabaster objects were often mounted in gilt bronze as candelabra.

A

B

C

D

WALL-CLOCKS, OR "CARTEL" CLOCKS as they were often called in the XVIIIth century, were supported on a bracket attached to the wall and decorated in the same manner as the clock. The lower part of this bracket usually ended in an ornamental knob. Clockmakers lavished their greatest ingenuity on the decoration of wall-clocks, which sometimes seem to combine the richness of the finest furniture made by Cressent or Riesener, with a goldsmith's or jeweler's technical skill.

A. THE LATE XVIIth CENTURY WALL-CLOCK was usually decorated with a veneer of shell inlaid with arabesques in brass in the Boulle style. The same form continued to be made throughout the early years of the XVIIIth century.

B. IN THIS RÉGENCE CLOCK the case is almost entirely overrun by gilt bronze ornament. At this date the numerals were usually painted on small enameled plaques inserted into the gilt bronze dial of the clock (above, left). It was only later that enamelers became sufficiently skilful to make the dial in a single piece. The movement of this clock is by Étienne Baillon.

C. LOUIS XV wall-clock of red Vernis Martin and gilt bronze.

D. THE CASE OF THIS LOUIS XV WALL-CLOCK made by Caffiéri is entirely of gilt bronze, and its form is completely asymmetrical. Nevertheless the richness of the material, the ingenuity of the design, and the carefully composed forms of the curves all combine to invest it with an admirable balance.

LOUIS QUINZE CLOCK mounted on the back of a camel.
During the Louis Quinze and Louis Seize periods, sculptors
often produced small animals of this sort, designed to form
the principal decorative feature of a clock. This particular
piece achieves an agreeable combination of the naturalistic
and the exotic, which adds elegance to the overall effect.

A

B   C

A — THE GOLDSMITH AND THE BRONZE-CHASER have contributed more to the appearance of this clock than the clockmaker himself. The rhinoceros, and the Chinaman, reflect the French love of the exotic. The skill of the bronze-chaser is seen in the exuberant rococo mounts.

B — COLORED SHELL was often used in the decoration of clock cases. This Louis XV wall-clock has a body veneered with green shell, a beautiful color which heightens the effect of the gilt bronze mounts.

C — UNDER LOUIS XV the wall-clock continued to be a more important type than the mantel clock, which was only just beginning to come into fashion. The wall-clock illustrated here is signed by Caffiéri.

CLOCKS AND TIMEPIECES of all sorts were made in great numbers from the beginning of the XVIIIth century. They were masterpieces of craftsmanship and owed their beauty not only to the clockmaker, but to the skill of the decorative sculptor and the jeweler. Frequently, too, an element of surprise and mystery was introduced for mechanical toys were often incorporated into their structure.

D — SMALL BRONZE FIGURES often add greatly to the charm and interest of wall-clocks. In this typical Louis XV clock they are combined with a wealth of scroll work and rococo forms.

E — THE CABINETMAKER was often more responsible than the clockmaker for the beauty of a standing clock. The example illustrated dates from the Louis XV period and is veneered with satin-wood, bordered with mahogany, and mounted in gilt bronze.

E

D

A. THE FIGURES AND ANIMALS with which this clock case is ornamented are typical of the taste for the exotic and the oriental which prevailed at the middle of the XVIIIth century. These elements go admirably with the elaborate rococo forms of the gilt bronze case.

B. IN THIS CLOCK MADE FOR THE PETIT TRIANON and dating from the Transitional period between the Louis XV and the Louis XVI styles, symmetry is beginning to appear once again in the shape of the case. The decoration, deriving from trellis-work, and the medallion of agricultural implements in the center of the front, reflect the love of gardening which had recently become a fashionable hobby in royal circles.

B

C. THE BUST OF A NEGRESS IN GILT AND PATINATED BRONZE is featured in this unusual mantel clock made for the King in 1784. It is fitted with elaborate mechanical devices. By pulling the left earring the pupils of the eyes are made to close and to show the time. Although there are still many traces of the Louis XV taste for the exotic here, the Louis XVI style is evident in the rectilinear design of the body.

D. THE ALLEGORIC FORM of this clock, known as the "Avignon" clock, is typical of the latter part of the XVIIIth century. It is a masterpiece of small-scale sculpture, and is the only work by Gouthière which has a genuine signature on it.

C

D

A

B

D

UNDER LOUIS XVI clocks decorated with a particular theme became more and more fashionable. Subjects sometimes played so important a part in the design of the case as to partially conceal the dial. At the same time, a contrary tendency gave birth to "skeleton clocks," in which the movement was almost entirely exposed and constituted the sole decorative feature.

A. "BIRD-CAGE CLOCKS." This type of clock is extremely rare. It was suspended from the ceiling, like a chandelier, with the dial placed on the underside. When the hour strikes a mechanical arrangement causes the birds in the cage to sing and flap their wings.

B. REVOLVING DIALS could be adapted to an almost infinite variety of uses. This clock was made by Le Pautre for the King's study at Versailles. The marble figures of a mermaid and a merman on the case are examples of the decorative sculpture of the period.

C. THE SO-CALLED "LYRE" CLOCKS combine ingenuity and elegance, for the dial is also the pendulum, and swings to and fro.

D. BALLOONS BECAME POPULAR in 1784 when Montgolfier made the first human ascent in one of them. This clock, which is in the shape of a balloon, is said to commemorate the balloon ascent of the Duke of Orléans at La Muette.

E. THE PENDULUM of this astronomical clock is in the form of a sunburst mounted with Apollo's head. In addition to showing the time it indicates the date as well as the position of the sun and the phases of the moon.

C

E

A

B

CHANDELIERS played an important part in interior décor during the XVIIIth century. The most popular variety was that in which the chandelier was hung with pendants of cut rock-crystal, which reflect light, and increase the rich effect of the traditional gilt bronze frame. The use of porcelain flowers on chandeliers was only a modification of the idea of hanging chandeliers with rock-crystal pendants.

A. THIS ROCK-CRYSTAL CHANDELIER comes from the Palace of Versailles. The cutting of the floral motifs and the elaborate pendants are typical of the Louis XIV style.

B. ON THIS CHANDELIER of chased and gilt bronze the lights are supported on elaborately scrolled rococo arms, on which small figures of cupids are seated. It is an outstanding example of Louis XV style, at its height.

C. THIS GIRANDOLE is an adaptation of the chandelier and is intended to be placed on a side table or in front of a mirror. It is distinguished from a table candelabrum by the elaboration of its decoration, and by the fact that it is hung with rock-crystal pendants.

D. LOUIS XVI CHANDELIER of gilt bronze and rock-crystal. The fashion for rock-crystal chandeliers continued into the Louis XVI period, but bronze no longer plays a supporting role. It is given its own decorative function as a complement to the rock-crystal pendants.

E. THIS LOUIS XVI CHANDELIER of chased and gilt bronze is one of Pierre Gouthière's masterpieces. The main stem is in the form of a fluted column from which scrolled branches emerge, terminating in acanthus leaves. The design, with its emphasis on architectural motifs, is influenced by the work of Delafosse.

E

C

ANDIRONS

ANDIRONS were objects of strictly utilitarian function. It is therefore somewhat surprising to find them ornamented with gilt bronze. But it replaced the silver often used in their decoration at the end of the XVIIth century. Andirons are often ornamented with animals—particularly with dogs—for their original form is said to have been inspired by the position of a dog seated beside the fire.

C

F

B

I

A. THESE RÉGENCE ANDIRONS surmounted by symmetrically arranged urns supporting allegoric figures are reminiscent of the age of Louis XIV. Sometimes urns served as perfume burners, which were filled with unguents that evaporated in the heat from the fire and scented the room.

A

B. FANTASTIC ANIMALS OF VARIOUS KINDS, such as dragons and salamanders, symbolizing fire, were often used in the elaborate decoration of *Régence* andirons.

C. THIS LOUIS XV ANDIRON is signed by F.-Th. Germain. There is a rare perfection of balance between the movement in the details and the quiet, harmonious effect of the whole. Its technical skill reminds us of how close the art of the gilt-bronze worker was to that of the jeweler.

E

D

D — THIS ROCOCO ANDIRON of the Louis XV period is surmounted by a leaping horse. When the same animal appears on a pair of andirons it is generally represented in two different poses.

E — THIS ROCOCO ANDIRON is of foliated and floral form, enlivened by the figure of a bird perched on the summit. Under Louis XVI the chasing of the bronze of andirons was carried to an extraordinary degree of elaboration, for the neo-classic style of decoration allowed a wide variety of effects, ranging from dull to burnished surfaces and from simple draperies to elaborate floral and fruit garlands.

F — ANDIRONS from the Palace of Fontainebleau ornamented with a cupid on a fabulous beast.

G — THE RIGOROUSLY ARCHITECTURAL CHARACTER of the main elements of this Louis XVI andiron give it a solemn aspect.

H and I — ANIMALS were made the principal feature of the decoration of some of the finest Louis XVI andirons. The one surmounted by a stag comes from the pavilion of Louveciennes and was made for Mme. du Barry by Gouthière.

G

F

H

BAROMETERS began to play an important part in the decoration of interiors towards the end of the XVIIth century. In general their construction and decoration are similar to those of contemporary clocks.

A

B. A BAROMETER AND A THERMOMETER are sometimes combined in a single case. The one below dates from the Louis XVI period, and its general form is clearly borrowed from that of a wall-clock.

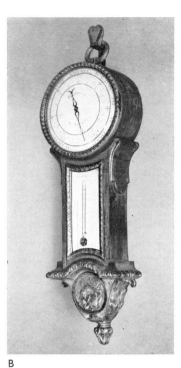

B

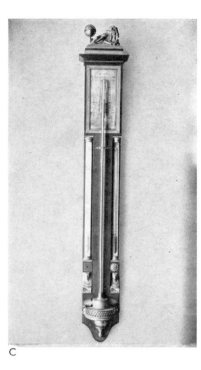

C

A. THIS LOUIS XVI BAROMETER of chased and gilt bronze is in the form of a sheaf of flowers tied by a ribbon bow. This type of barometer almost always formed a pair with a wall-clock of the same shape and size.

C and D. THE PRINCIPLES on which the barometer works dictated its shape. Torricelli's invention required a column of mercury 33-1/2″ high; hence the elongated shape of certain barometers. Above (C) is an example from the end of the XVIIIth century. The one below (D) dates from the Louis XV period. It is singularly decorative, of elongated sinuous form, bordered with pierced gilt bronze rococo mounts.

E and F. BAROMETERS were often of such elaborate form that they were clearly intended for decoration rather than for scientific purposes. Such pieces are often ornamented with a wealth of allegoric figures such as Father Time and Venus and Cupid, as are found on the cartel-shaped example illustrated (E). The main body of this fine *Régence* barometer (F) is of wood; gilt bronze is used merely around the dial, the edges and the base.

D

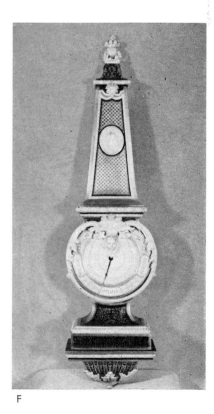

F

S CLOCK, in the form of a lazuli obelisk, dates from the s XV period, and is decorated with oric figures representing Ceres the Sun in gilt bronze. Its comon piece is a barometer of similar truction decorated with figures of une and Rain. *(Color plate opposite.)*

E

125

B

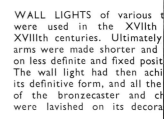

WALL LIGHTS of various t
were used in the XVIIth
XVIIIth centuries. Ultimately
arms were made shorter and
on less definite and fixed posit
The wall light had then achi
its definitive form, and all the
of the bronzecaster and cl
were lavished on its decora

A. EARLY LOUIS XV W
LIGHTS of gilt bronze were
enlivened by figures of mon
for animals were then very fas
able as a form of decoration.
arms are of the most elabo
sinuous, and anti-symmetrical f
It should also be noted that
candle socket is of different de

B and C. THE TWISTED FOLIAGE of these wall lights shows the
rococo style at its fullest development in the Louis XV period.

A

D and E. In these two wall lights, dating
from about the middle of the XVIIIth century,
the forms are considerably less distorted and
the foliage is given a more naturalistic character, which foreshadowed the Louis XVI style.

D

E

C

WALL LIGHTS

LIGHTING BY MEANS OF WALL LIGHTS played an increasing part in the decoration of rooms during the reign of Louis XVI. They tended to become smaller in order that they might be suitable for the smaller living-rooms and boudoirs which were then fashionable. The neo-classical and geometrical forms in fashion tended to give them a symmetrical character which was increased by the fact that they were always arranged on the wall in pairs.

F. THIS FINE LOUIS XVI WALL LIGHT from the Petit Trianon at Versailles is based on the design of a hunting horn, a motif greatly in favor in the latter part of the XVIIIth century. It continued to be used during the Directoire and the Empire periods.

G. THE CENTRAL STEM of this two-branched wall light, in the form of a flaming torch, is a motif derived from Pompeii. Its elegance and the refinement of its finish suggests that it may possibly be a work by Pierre Gouthière.

A

F

G

I. THIS ELEGANT LYRE-SHAPED WALL LIGHT dates from the Louis XVI period, and was probably intended for a music room.

J. THIS TYPE OF WALL LIGHT, with a single branch, was usually intended for a boudoir. The one illustrated is in the form of a pair of intertwined serpents attached to the wall by a ribbon bow. Both are motifs frequently used during the Louis XVI period.

H. THIS THREE BRANCH WALL LIGHT with scrolled and foliated branches still owes much to the Louis XV style, but the symmetrical character of the style of the following period is already beginning to become apparent.

H

I

J

B

A. THE GREAT BRONZE-WORKERS of the Louis XVI period created wall lights which are real masterpieces. This one was ordered by Queen Marie-Antoinette for her dressing-room at Saint-Cloud. It is in the form of a central torch to which are attached three branches of myrtle, terminating in drip-pans loaded with fruit. Pearl garlands hang between these while the central branch is surmounted by a cupid clasping a flaming heart.

B. ONE OF THE MOST GRACEFUL of Louis XVI designs, this wall light is in the form of a caryatid whose arms terminate in scrolls on which the candle sockets are supported.

C. A WALL LIGHT OF CANNON DESIGN. The stem is in the form of a culverin of patinated bronze ornamented with the arms of the Royal House of France. The two branches are oak sprays of gilt bronze, terminating in sockets wich are concealed within leafy cups.

C

A

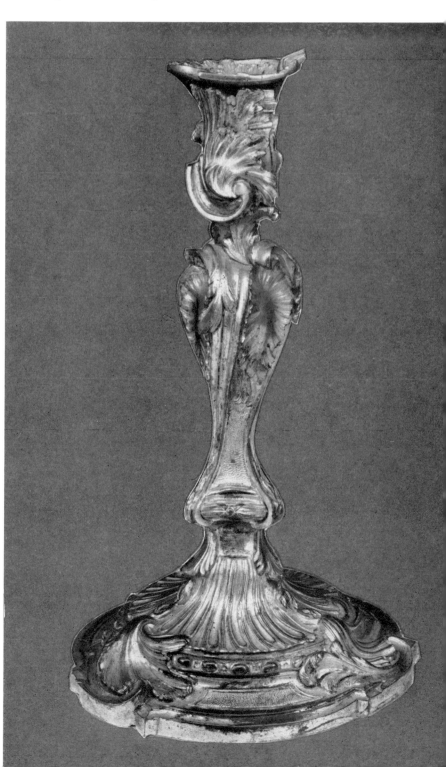

B. THE ROCOCO decoration of the base and the stem of this early Louis XV candelabrum of two lights show how well rococo forms and the material of gilt bronze blend together.

THE SHAPES OF CANDLE-STICKS, candelabra and girandoles of gilt bronze are generally copied from those of gold and silver. Many of them, however, are modified to take the greatest possible advantage of the inherent properties of the material, and the wide range of form of which it is capable.

A. THIS RÉGENCE CANDLE-STICK illustrates how the most audacious and exuberant designs in the rococo style can be better carried out in chased and gilt bronze than in silver or gold, for the character of the metal is more appropriate to casting and chasing than to hammering.

C. THIS LOUIS XV CANDELABRUM of three lights was directly inspired by a model in silver.

D and E. TWO CANDLE-STICKS of gilt bronze which show the Louis XV style in its early and late stages; both equally typical of the gilt bronze work of the period.

F. THE EXTRAORDINARILY SINUOUS forms of this three-light candelabrum of gilt bronze are of greater interest than the chasing. The design is typical of the Louis XV period.

CANDLESTICKS AND CANDELABRA

A. CANDLESTICK, decorated with lions, masks and claws, the burnished ornament standing out in relief against backgrounds which are recessed and given a dull finish.

LATE XVIIIth CENTURY BRONZE-WORKERS made great use of the available repertory of designs, particularly those invented by such engravers as Delafosse and Lalonde. The architectural character of these designs was particularly well-suited to the construction of candlesticks and candelabra. The finest effects of gilt bronze at this period are due to the high quality of the chasing and to the use of dull and burnished gilding, which allowed diversified surface effects in the same piece.

B

A

B and C. DELAFOSSE INSPIRED the design of these two fine candelabra. The first has three branches and rests on goats' feet; a candle-socket surmounts the central stem. The second, with two branches, has a foot of a markedly architectural character, in the form of three spreading feet terminating in a Greek key. This is a departure from the traditional circular base.

D

D. LOUIS XVI CANDELABRUM of gilt bronze with three branches. The decorative motifs consist of flutings, chandelles and acanthus leaves.

E. THIS GILT BRONZE CANDLESTICK in the form of a caryatid for the stem, and resting on a circular base decorated with beading and garlands, dates from the end of the XVIIIth century, though it anticipates the style of the beginning of the XIXth.

E

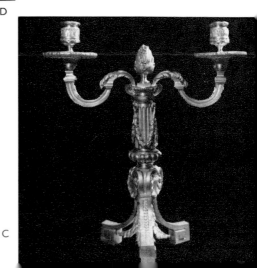

C

A

B

THE FASHION FOR MOUNTING OBJECTS of porcelain and pottery in gilt bronze produced some of the most characteristic works of art of the XVIIIth century. Figures and objects of the finest soft-paste porcelain, both French and imported, were mounted in gilt bronze to form table-lamps and decorative pieces.

A. PSEUDO-CHINESE dwarf figure of Mennecy porcelain, mounted in gilt bronze, dating from the Louis XV period.

B. A DRESDEN PORCELAIN FIGURE AND FLOWERS are mounted on this Louis XV chandelier, which is provided with a lamp shade made in a contemporary design.

C. THE PERFECTION OF THE MOUNTING very often surpasses in value and importance that of the object mounted. An example is this small Chinese figure set in an elaborate gilt bronze mount of the Louis XV period.

C

D

E

D. THE FIGURES AND FLOWERS on this three-branched candelabrum dating from the Louis XV period are of Dresden porcelain.

E. THE TASTE FOR CHINESE OBJECTS coincided with the fashion for mounting objects in gilt bronze and inspired innumerable pieces of the character of this elaborate three-branched Louis XV candelabrum.

F. THE DISORDERLY ARRAY of the bullrushes of chased gilt bronze which surround the Dresden porcelain swan on this candelabrum are the only elements which relate to the Louis XV style. The form of the gilt bronze branches, the laurel garlands, the Greek-key feet and the base are in the neo-classic style, and are typical of the Louis XVI period.

F

A

B

C

WHEN THE FASHION FOR MOUNTING PORCELAIN IN GILT BRONZE grew widespread during the reign of Louis XIV, almost anything provided an excuse for using elaborate gilt bronze mounts: flower pots and porcelain figures, pieces of fluorspar, rock crystal, lapis lazuli, porphyry vases, marble, etc. Before gilt bronze came into fashion, such objects had occasionally been mounted in silver, so the earliest gilt bronze mounts naturally follow the style of this contemporary silversmith work.

A. THIS CONICAL CHINESE PORCELAIN WINE-COOLER of the K'ang-H'si period is bronze-mounted in the *Régence* style. Similar mounts in silver are known.

B. THE GILT BRONZE MOUNT of this pot-pourri vase made of a Chinese lacquer box is in the purest Louis XV style, and has been attributed to Thomas Germain.

C. THIS CHINESE LACQUER pot-pourri vase was probably mounted in gilt bronze by Lazare Duvaux. The rich effect of the lacquer is heightened by the gilt bronze setting.

D. THE GILT BRONZE MOUNTS of this lacquered vase are the work of the famous Louis XV gilt bronze worker, Duplessis. They convert an upright vase into a jug.

E. THIS PEAR-SHAPED CHINESE PORCELAIN VESSEL was richly mounted in gilt bronze in the style of Caffiéri during the early Louis XVI period.

D

E

F

A

B

A. THIS VASE OF CHINESE CELADON PORCELAIN has been converted into a jug by its Louis XV gilt bronze mounts. The piece is remarkable both for the elegance of the form of the mounts, and for the rare quality of their chasing.

B. THIS LACQUER FLOWER-POT came from the Château de Bellevue and was made especially for Mme. de Pompadour. The bronzes are stamped with the crowned "C," which is the control mark for the years 1745-1749.

C. A SÈVRES PORCELAIN VASE, dating from the Louis XVI period, has been converted into a candelabrum with three lights, by means of gilt bronze mounts.

AT THE END OF THE REIGN of Louis XVI not only were small objects like vases, perfume burners, etc., mounted in order to increase their richness or modify their purpose, but a number of larger pieces (specially created for ornamental purposes alone and usually made of marble) were also mounted in the richest style. The three examples illustrated here were all made by the celebrated bronze founder, Gouthière; one of the two vases of serpentine marble below (D and E) is mounted with a wood nymph and a naiad, and the other with two goats' heads; the third example is a perfume burner (F, p. 132) of agate, resting on a tripod whose legs are each surmounted by the head of a faun crowned with rushes.

D

E

133

WOOD PANELING

Wall Paneling in XVIIIth Century Decoration

Wall paneling was brought to the highest degree of refinement in the XVIIIth century. It was one of the main factors making for the comfort and beauty of the interiors of the period which, as the century advanced, became ever more luxurious and intimate in character. Throughout the period it played a leading role in the decoration of rooms.

There was an ever increasing demand for comfort in rooms where the daily life of society was spent. The nobility had given up moving from one château to another; they now lived in fixed residences where they cultivated the art of good living. In the XVIIIth century wall paneling or "boiserie" (this word which is commonly used today to describe wall paneling of all sorts derives from the French word "bois" for "wood") performed the role which tapestry had generally played in the past. Nevertheless, paneling was not unknown at earlier periods. In certain châteaux there are rooms where wood is used not only to cover the walls but the ceilings as well. In the XVIIIth century the paneling or wainscot usually ran all the way up to the cornice or picture molding ("lambris de hauteur"); later on it sometimes ran up only waist high ("lambris d'appui"). This wall paneling provided a protection against cold and damp and, as it was specially designed for the particular room in which it was used, it was completely effective in these respects.

The decorative function of wall paneling grew ever more important as the century progressed. Its character and carved decorations followed the general stylistic trends of the period. Woodwork, used to cover the undressed stones of a wall, had always been decorated in some way or other from the very earliest periods. Basically, this decoration had been intended to hide the joints in the paneling, but in the XVIIIth century it became far more important. The huge tapestries used in the past to cover entire walls were relegated to attics or provincial châteaux. Their place was taken by wall paneling running right up to the ceiling in a series of rectangular panels, invariably of carefully chosen proportions and usually richly decorated.

At the same time the coffering and the beams of the ceiling tended to give way to a simpler, flatter type of treatment.

The substitution of wall paneling for large tapestries completely changed the atmosphere of the interior of houses. The paneling was seldom left in the natural color of the wood, for that was considered too somber; usually it was painted white, pale yellow, lilac or pale green. The carved decorations of the panels were usually painted a paler tone of the color used on the rest of the wall, or sometimes they were gilded.

Architects designed the wall paneling of their rooms in the same general style as the rest of the interior decoration; it was carved with decorative motifs appropriate to the prevailing style of the period. Paneling used in the great state apartments or reception rooms was conceived on entirely different lines from that used in smaller, more intimate rooms. In the same way, the forms of the decoration were adapted to the scale and purpose for which the room was intended. Tapestry, when it was used at all, played a purely subordinate and decorative role, often being framed in the paneling itself, while the new developments of glass-making enabled mirrors to take an ever more important part in decoration. When François-Bernard Perrot discovered that mirrors could be made by blowing glass instead of merely by pouring it into molds, it became possible to produce much larger mirrors. These were soon widely employed; architects designed carefully proportioned areas in the wall paneling for large mirrors, that were to be framed into the woodwork. Thenceforward the mirror played an important role in interior decoration.

The taste for wall paneling persisted right through the century; only the style of the decoration differed from period to period. So important was the wall paneling that no really elegant person would have dreamed of installing Louis XV furniture in a room with paneling of the Louis XIV period.

Repertory of Decorative Motifs and Various Styles of Wall Paneling

The repertory of ornamental motifs available for the decoration of wall paneling was devised by the ornamental designers and craftsmen of the period; it differed in no respect from the general character of prevailing styles.

The ornamental designer

The drawings and engraved designs of ornamental designers merely codified the prevailing trends of taste and fashion. Their designs, whether for paneling, furniture or other decorative objects, were executed by craftsmen of the appropriate

...is wall paneling illustrates the richness of effect sometimes achieved in ...eriors of the "Régence" period. The larger panels are inset with Chinese ...ck and gold lacquer and the narrow flanking panels, painted white, are ...ightened with gilding on the carved decoration which is of the utmost richness ...d refinement. The carving of the panels (which are 16' high) is as rich as the ...coration of the lacquer itself and it is interesting to note how the Chinese ...ures of the lacquer reappear as carved decorative motifs at the top and ...ttom of the panels. Such a sumptuous setting must be furnished with equal ...lendor and quality. The frames of the "Régence" sofa and armchairs as ...ll as the table and the "torchère" in the background are as richly carved ...the paneling, while the elegant gilt bronze mounts of the chest of drawers by ...essent conform perfectly with the decorative scheme. (Color plate left.)

craftsmen's guilds. As a result there was a remarkable unity between the wall paneling and the objects it housed. The "lambrisseurs,"* as the craftsmen who made the wall paneling were called, adopted the current ornamental motifs of the period. The evolution of the decoration of wall paneling followed almost exactly the same lines of development as did wood sculpture during the same period.

The crossette, a favorite motif in carved wall paneling, came into existence then. At first it was merely a flat form of decoration. Little by little it was given greater relief and ultimately developed into the true crossette with reliefs and hollows, and with scrolls emerging around it. In the same way the shape of the legs of furniture, which were straight under Louis XIV, began to bend slightly during the "Régence" period, and became of marked cabriole design under Louis XV. Under Louis XVI they became straight once again.

The egg-and-tongue type of molding in its various forms had been a basic feature of the decorative repertory of the Renaissance, but it disappeared almost completely under Louis XIV, during the "Régence" period and under Louis XV. Its place was taken by the water leaf or acanthus leaf. Under Louis XVI the acanthus leaf was often displaced by the laurel leaf which plays as important a part in the decoration of wood paneling as it does in other fields of decoration at this period.

Shell motifs, too, were important during the earlier part of the century. They had been known and used under Louis XIII; under Louis XIV they were given a thicker shape. They became far more exuberant under Louis XV, the center was deeper-cut and scrolls emerged from around the edges. Then, in reaction to this profuseness, the scrolls disappeared, and the purer form of the Louis XVI shell appeared.

The craftsmen

It was the ornamental designer who provided the repertory of shapes and decorative motifs used, but it was the craftsmen who translated these into material form and it was their tools which gave these forms life and vitality. In this way, the woodcarvers, while interpreting the schemes of the ornamental designers and architects, still played a really creative role of their own. It is to them that we owe the refinements of detail, the perfect technical mastery, which gives life to the material. They were accustomed to produce small models after the architect's designs, which they submitted for their clients' approval; these small objects were masterpieces of craftsmanship and it is impossible to regard the woodcarvers who produced them as simple workmen slavishly following the ideas of others.

Great thought was given to harmonizing the decoration of the wall paneling with that of the furnishings of the room. The size of a panel or the prominence of a particular ornamental motif was not a matter of chance or fancy, but arose from the necessity of keeping the decoration of the paneling carefully proportionate to that of the rest of the furnishings.

What is commonly called a style is in fact due to a collaboration of designer and craftsman. It was these two who decided the form of the "Régence" style, in which vestigial traces of the Louis XIV style survive, but which had a much more elegant character. It was they, too, who invented the Louis XV style full of fancy and imagination, grace and delicacy. Symmetrical lines gave way to pleasant curves and conceits; Louis XV wall paneling was delicately carved with flowers, foliage, etc., in an exuberance appropriate to the rococo style; figures and animals were gradually added to the ornamental repertory and sometimes decorative trophies as well, whose character often made some oblique allusion to the householders themselves.

*Neither "sculpteurs du bois" (wood carvers) nor "boiserie" (wood paneling) were words then in current use.

These diagrams *illustrate the types of carving used on wall paneling at different periods during the XVIIIth century. As the wood was only rarely left in its natural color, the sculptor had to take account not only of the play of light and shade but of the contrast of colors in which his carving would ultimately appear: in a light color against a stronger background, in a darker color or in gold on a white or light colored background. These four examples are taken from the narrow side panels ("parcloses") of contemporary woodwork.*

A. **Something of the symmetry** *of the last years of the reign of Louis XIV still survives in this "Régence" panel, although the sinuous lines of certain of the curves foreshadow elements which were to be emphasized in later styles.* B. *Under Louis XV the exuberant S-curves and scrolls reach their fullest development: symmetry has completely disappeared from the individual motifs, though a perfect sense of balance remains.* C. *Towards the end of the Louis XV period naturalistic motifs begin to take the place of the rococo forms of the previous period.* D. *Under Louis XVI the taste for the antique emerges in the form of acanthus scrolls, urns, vases filled with flowers, etc., all in the severe linear manner which was characteristic of the last years of the century.*

There can be no doubt that certain individuals, such as the King's favorites, exercised a very important influence on the style of the period. Of these the most potent was certainly Mme. de Pompadour, who played a considerable part in the later stages in the development of the Louis XV style, when towards the end of the reign, calmer, less tormented lines began to replace the contortions and exuberances of the early rococo. This later development of the Louis XV style was known as the Transitional style; it was a forerunner of the Louis XVI style whose early development was much influenced by Mme. de Pompadour's brother, the Marquis de Marigny, Superintendant of the Royal Palaces, as well as by his mentors, the architects Gabriel and Soufflot.

Amongst the ornamental decorators who contributed to the evolution of the style of wall paneling during the XVIIIth century, two are particularly worthy of mention: Charles Delafosse, who played a considerable role in the evolution of the Louis XVI style; and the amazingly exuberant Nicolas Pineau, who provided a wealth of Louis XV designs for the wood carvers and furniture makers of the period.

The Louis XVI style, although inspired by the somewhat severe Graeco-Roman forms of antiquity, developed particularly graceful and characteristically French designs for wall paneling. The moldings of the panel became rectilinear once again and the decorative ornaments derived their beauty from a close observation of natural forms; indeed, in one of its aspects, the Louis XVI style might be described as particularly concerned with verisimilitude in the representation of purely ornamental motifs.

Furniture of Carved and Gilt Wood

The same ornamental repertory of scrolls, garlands, trophies, etc., which was appearing on the carved paneling of the walls, was also used on the carved and gilt wood frames of contemporary furniture. In this way a unique ornamental repertory ran all through a fashionable XVIIIth century room, giving it a remarkably unified effect.

During the "Régence" period the same ornamental motifs found on the wall paneling also occur on the furniture. Under Louis XV the motifs of the delicately carved friezes appear, in modified form on the wall paneling, as long twisted moldings of sinuous outline from which floral motifs and ribbons emerge. The legs of chairs follow exactly the same line of development; by the end of the Louis XV period, it is impossible to find a straight line anywhere in furniture; everything followed the prevailing S-curve of the cabriole leg. Under Louis XVI, carved wood furniture was predominantly decorated with straight lines and flutings; the same flutings appear in the wall paneling of the period in combination with plain moldings devoid of decoration.

All through the XVIIIth century the popularity of furniture of carved and gilded wood ran parallel to the fashion for the splendidly veneered furniture of the period; the one type did not compete with the other in any way. There were no interiors where the furniture was entirely of carved wood or entirely veneered. This mixture of these two materials of quite contrasting character produced some of the most harmonious interiors of the times.

Objects of carved wood affixed to the wall

An even closer relationship united the carved paneling of the wall with the objects of carved and gilt wood which were applied to it or fixed upon it. The first of these, the "trumeau" or panel, was indeed almost part of the wall paneling itself; it is really only a wall panel treated in a particularly imaginative way. It was generally placed over the chimneypiece and often enclosed a painting at the top; sometimes it would be completed by being inset with a mirror accompanied by a pier-table below. The effect of the mirror was to give depth to the wall and increase the apparent size of the room.

The decorations of the "trumeau" (or "pier") were almost identical with those of the wall paneling itself. Its "parcloses" (that is to say the small side panels which flanked a central panel) were decorated in precisely the same manner as the larger panels of the wall.

Panels of mirror inserted into "trumeaux" and framed in moldings of carved and gilded wood gave rise to the idea of mirrors which could be hung independently on the wall paneling; this however was a later development. Such mirrors were ornamental objects which, like paintings, required their own frame. The mirror or picture frame is closely related to carved wall paneling in the XVIIIth century and follows exactly the same course of development. In the more restricted area of the frame, all the decorative elements appropriate to contemporary styles appear. The form of the frame itself resembles in some respects the wall panels which surmounted the doors of the period; the same shapes were adopted and the same type of ornament was used in the cresting. A considerable variety of decorative objects such as mirrors and picture frames, cartel clocks (often in the form of a sunburst), and wall lights, all of carved and gilt wood, were fixed to the wall paneling.

Before the bronze-founders began to create their miraculously cast and chased wall lights, these objects were generally made of carved wood. The original name was "bras de lumière" (arm-light), so called because they took the form of a human arm holding out one or more lights from the wall. This type continued to be made and admired throughout the entire century; it was never entirely eliminated by the richer, more sophisticated designs developed for gilt bronze wall lights.

When fixed to the wall paneling, these carved-wood wall lights formed an integral part of the carved decoration of the paneling itself. They were generally placed on each side of a panel of mirror in order to allow a spectator to see himself more clearly; thus they were generally given the same stylistic character as the carved "parcloses" which stood on either side of the mirror panel.

Furniture of carved and gilt wood, not fixed to the wall

The side-table or pier-table, although not fixed to the wall, was invariably placed against it; gradually however a type of table evolved from it which was entirely independent of the wall and became a sideboard or a "table à gibier" (game table—so called because game, brought back from shooting, was laid on it). The evolution of the side-table runs parallel to that of all other types of furniture supported on legs; as the century advanced the cross stretcher joining the legs gradually disappeared. As a result, it became very necessary to strengthen the molding supporting the top, in order to give the piece greater solidity; the decoration of either type of table was very similar.

The "torchère" (or pedestal light) of carved and gilt wood stands on the floor and is entirely independent of the wall. It thus allows the candelabrum or girandole standing on it to cast its light farther into the room than could the fixed wall lights.

Portable candlesticks, too, were sometimes made of carved and gilt wood, occasionally in the form of small urns.

Clockcases of carved and gilt wood follow the same evolutionary development as do other forms of gilt wood. All the decorative motifs used in the carving of wall paneling, chairs, etc., are also found, on an appropriate scale, on these clock-cases. Such were the permanent decorative elements of the period; they are differentiated only by the quality and refinement of their workmanship.

The importance of gildin

The forms of objects created in carved and gilt wood, whether large or small, follow the general stylistic trends of the period. It was the gilding of carved wood which conferred a special and individual quality on the material. The sharp transitions from the parts in relief to the hollows was smoothed over by many coats of gesso. For gesso, a mixture of white plaster and fish glue was used as a base for gilding. The application of this preliminary coat was the work of the "repareur" who was a specialist in "finishing" the carving, giving emphasis to the details of certain of the scrolls, etc., which could be attenuated and given greater vitality of form by this extra layer of material. In fact the "repareur" played the same role in relation to carved wood as the bronze-chaser did in the finishing of a bronze casting. The work demanded a real creative effort and the success of the final result was largely dependent on this craftsman.

The work of the "repareur" was followed by that of the gilder. The technique of gilding hardly changed at all throughout the century. More than thirty different stages and processes were used between the application of the gesso ground and the final burnishing. It is this final precious envelope of gesso and gold which gives XVIIIth century carved wood its true beauty.

XVIIIth Century Carved Wood in Modern Interiors

Carved and gilt wood first began to be a sign of luxury and wealth in the XVIIth century; it epitomized all the grandeur of the age of Louis XIV. Under Louis XV it developed a more elegant and more refined character. Under Louis XVI it adapted itself to the fragile forms of neo-classical decoration: bows, arrows, ribbons, etc. Today XVIIIth century gilt wood enjoys a favor which is in complete contrast to its neglect in the years preceding the war. The large, bare, uniform surfaces of modern walls set off and heighten its beauty and it provides an admirably unifying element between various pieces of old and modern furniture. This function is particularly apparent when it is used for framing pictures. Contemporary paintings take their place in XVIIIth century frames without any loss of effect; indeed, they sometimes seem to harmonize more closely, thereafter, with the traditional furniture and wall paneling of the great styles of the past.

In order to create a sumptuous but bright drawing room, *the interio decorator M. Grellou has covered the walls with white and gold Régenc paneling, and laid a long Aubusson carpet on the floor. The armchairs ar upholstered with Gobelin tapestry. A comfortable modern sofa and armchair have been put into the room, so that the ensemble should not be at all conven tional or stiff. Their soft color, and the stronger color of the materia draped over the gueridon table, harmonize with the carpet and heighten th beauty of the wall paneling. The subdued gilding of the paneling emphasize panels of Chinese paintings on silk. To lighten the room, instead of a singl central chandelier which might have seemed too heavy, two delicate crysta chandeliers have been chosen, which do not cut across the perspectives of th room. M. and Mme. A. who are great collectors, have arranged some piece of Chinese coral-colored porcelain on the top of the sideboard which ca be seen against the far wall. Above the sideboard, on a panel of materia hang two Fragonard canvases, surmounted by a picture by Aubry. Anothe panel of material above the sofa shows off a portrait by Nattier to advantage (Color plate opposite.)*

WALL PANELING

WALL PANELING OF CARVED WOOD reached its full development in the XVIIIth century. Sculptors, painters, and lacquerers all combined to transform its originally utilitarian character into a really rich pictorial background for furniture. An astonishing variety of wood paneling is known. No two pieces are carved with the same design, though it is not unusual to find identical chairs, clock-cases and other pieces of furniture. The reason for this is that wood paneling had to be conceived anew for each room, its shapes being governed by the numbers of openings in the wall, the size of the room, and the degree of richness required in its decoration.

MIRRORS in the forms of overmantels, or mirrors set into the paneling facing one another as part of the decoration of a room, exercised a profound influence on the particular character of wall paneling all through the century.

GENERALLY XVIIIth CENTURY PANELING was painted, sometimes in two colors, occasionally in several. They were also painted with decorative scenes, generally lacquered in gold. Wood was rarely left its natural color, though this was done in the case of the justly famous paneling at the Château de Rambouillet.

B

A

WALL PANELING

A. ELEMENTS of both the Louis XIV and the Louis XV style are found on this example of wall paneling, on the main panels as well as on the smaller ones (carved circa 1730). Characteristic motifs of the two styles, however, are merely juxtaposed and no attempt is made to blend them into a new style, as was the case in the Transitional period between the Louis XV and the Louis XVI styles.

B. THE LOUIS XV STYLE is seen in its fullest development in this overmantel panel (circa 1750). A trophy of musical instruments is framed within a richly carved rococo scrolling.

C. THE SMALL FIGURE IN THE MANNER OF HUET carved in the center of the main panel, and the asymmetrical shape of the subsidiary ones, are both remarkably elegant. The small size of these Louis XV panels shows that they were intended for use in one of the small rooms characteristic of the period. The fact that the lower panels are devoid of carving should be noted. When the skirting board is richly decorated, it is almost always of provincial or foreign origin and is very rarely of the same high quality as Parisian paneling.

D. A PROFUSION OF DELICATELY CARVED SCROLLS and floral elements fills the lower part of the two adjacent panels illustrated, dating from the beginning of the Transitional period between the Louis XV and Louis XVI styles.

E. IN THIS NARROW PANEL, dating from the end of the *Régence* period, the ovolo decoration of the borders, the rococo cartouche, and the elaborate scrolls which emerge from it, all foreshadow the early Louis XV style (compare with the paneling in plate A).

C

E

141

CARVED WOOD PANELING

A. TROPHIES of all sorts were particularly suitable for the decoration of carved wall paneling. They were usually placed at the top of panels intended to be inset with a mirror or a painting, or sometimes enclosed within the curve surmounting an arch. The one illustrated here surmounts the top of a door and is enclosed by the recessed door frame. It is a fine example of its type and dates from about 1740. In rooms which were not paneled with wood, the stone or marble frame of the doors was sometimes treated in the same way.

B. CHINESE LACQUER was occasionally used in the decoration of wall paneling. Lacquer panels taken from screens were sometimes inserted into the woodwork, but lacquer was also specially made for this purpose as is the case with the paneling illustrated. Carving is hardly used so as to allow the *chinoiserie* decoration in gold on a black ground to tell with full effect. The molded frame is marbled a tortoiseshell color (about 1750).

C. PAINTERS were sometimes called in where a particularly rich effect was desired. They were often highly skilful in adapting their compositions to the style of the carving of the panels, as can be seen from this example with its Turkish subject painted by Lancret (circa 1730).

A

B

C

A

A. GILDING was generally applied only on the moldings or on medallions carved in relief with figure subjects. In that event, the background was generally light colored, as in the *Régence* panel illustrated above (dating from about 1725).

B. THIS DETAIL of a narrow length of Louis XV paneling shows Nicolas Pineau's remarkable technical skill. His carving is characterized by an elaborate play of beautifully balanced scrolls usually arranged around a central motif — perhaps a foliated cross or a rococo cartouche.

C. THE SHELL FORMS found in the Louis XV period gradually grew flatter and simpler as the Transitional style between the Louis XV and the Louis XVI styles developed. This is clearly illustrated by this small panel intended to fill the space above a side table. As the Louis XVI period approached, decorative motifs gradually took on an increasingly architectural character.

C

B

B

A

A. IN THE LOUIS XVI PERIOD the panel above a mirror was generally carved with one of the favorite ornamental motifs of the times, such as hunting trophies, sprays of oak or laurel, antique urns, or foliated garlands.

B. THIS LOUIS XVI WALL PANELING is of the finest quality. The chimney-piece is of blue-turquin marble enriched with gilt bronze. Above is a round-topped mirror, the frame skilfully carved to give an effect of depth and perspective. Between it and the door is a narrow upright panel left entirely uncarved. The double door itself is surmounted by a plaster overdoor in high relief. The decoration of Louis XVI wall paneling is characterized by a return to the decorative elements in favor during the Renaissance. This is illustrated in the elaborate form taken by the cornice, with its acanthus-leaf modillions, its denticulations and its brackets carved with an acanthus leaf motif.

A

B

B. THE CARVING OF THE FRAME of a screen is very often influenced by the type of material which it is intended to enclose. A room whose walls are hung with Beauvais tapestries was often furnished with a fire-screen mounted with a panel of the same material. In the one illustrated here the scrolled forms surrounding the central figure are echoed in the carved wood frame.

SCREENS intended as fire screens or as protection against draught were generally given an ornamental character matching the general design of the room for which they were intended.

A. THE SYMMETRICAL character of Louis XIV furniture still persists in this fire screen dating from the *Régence* period. The top rail of its gilt frame is carved with motifs similar to the backs of the armchairs of the period.

C

C. THE DESIGN OF THE FRAMES of fire screens is often inspired by the carving of picture frames, as can be seen in this oval example framing a piece of Aubusson tapestry of the Louis XVI period.

D. THIS LOUIS XV SCREEN shows how closely the carved frames adhere to the forms of the woodwork of chairs. Even the feet seem to derive from the arm supports of an armchair.

D

E

E. THE CARVING OF THE FRAME of this Louis XVI screen could easily be found repeated almost exactly on the back of a chair of the same period.

A

B

AN EXTRAORDINARY

WEALTH of carving and gilding was
lavished on the frames of pictures as well
as on mirrors, in the XVIIIth century.   Although
picture frames were occasionally cast in gilt bronze,
the finest ones were invariably of carved and gilt wood
and, like the carving of the contemporary wall paneling,
show the remarkable technical skill of wood carvers of
the period. The basic design of the great majority of
picture frames is a kind of hollow molding which sets
the picture somewhat deeper than the carving of the frame.

A and B. DIFFERENT, CONTRASTING TYPES of treatment of
the gilt ground were often used on carved wood frames. This
technique which had already come into existence during the
Louis XIV period consists in engraving a pattern of small
motifs, generally of guilloche or trellis work, on those parts
of the frame which have been left free of carving. This
treatment can be seen in the example illustrated in A.

C and H. THE TOP OF THE PICTURE FRAME is often
carved with some symbolic or pictorial device, such as a
lion, musical instruments, a Maltese cross, a chain, etc.
Sometimes a smaller motif is adopted as in the case
of frame C, dating from the *Régence* period,
where the top is carved with an ornamental
motif which hints at the exuberance of
rococo decoration which was soon
to come into widespread use.

C

D - E

I

THE SHAPE AND
size of the frame is dictated
by the dimensions of the pic
ture or mirror it is to enclose.
The top is usually surmounted by a
cresting incorporating one of the characteristic motifs of the period. Sometimes these are replaced by a shield on
which an inscription, or the initials of the
owner, can be placed. The lower edge is
often carved with a cartouche intended to
bear the title of the work and the name of the
artist (frames D and E: Louis XV; F and G:
Louis XVI). MIRRORS came into increasing use
during the XVIIIth century as the technique
of making them was mastered. Hanging mirrors then came into existence, and often
replaced the earlier mirrors inserted in
the wall paneling itself. The frames
of hanging mirrors were generally
strengthened and enriched with
decoration as in the Louis XV
frame (I) and the Louis XVI
example (J) below.

H

F - G

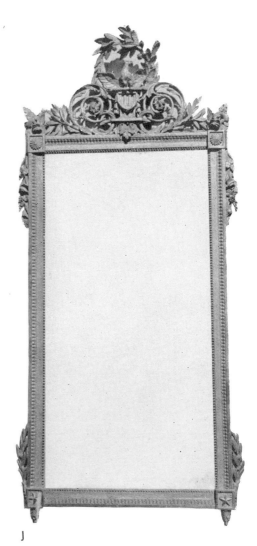

J

147

A

THE SIDE TABLE, or the console table as it is sometimes called, began to grow less architectural in form and became more sculptural soon after the beginning of the XVIIIth century. Its position naturally depended on the arrangement of the room in which it was to stand; normally, side tables are either placed between two windows or between two doors. Above, there was usually a panel either of mirror or carved wood. It will thus be seen that the side table is rather a part of the interior decoration of a room than a piece of furniture; it is in fact a sort of projection of the wall paneling itself. It was the responsibility of the architect to choose the themes with which these tables were to be decorated, so that they would harmonize with the rest of the wall decoration, though they were generally far more elaborately carved.

A. THE TYPICAL SIDE TABLE of the earlier part of the century rests on two legs, whose double curved shape determined the silhouette of the piece. A medallion, sometimes carved with a portrait in relief, may sometimes appear in the center of the frieze. The XVIIIth century side table is given a rather more sinuous shape than the true Louis XIV console, which gradually developed into the pre-rococo style of the *Régence* period.

B. IMPORTANT SIDE TABLES are sometimes supported on four legs instead of two. All are generally of cabriole form though the inner sides of the back ones are usually flat to enable the table to stand close against the wall. *Régence* side tables generally retain the rectangular frieze of an earlier period, but the lambrequin decoration in its center gradually becomes richer, the carving pierced, and scrolled forms appear, as in the example illustrated.

C. WOOD CARVERS displayed a remarkable technical virtuosity in the carving of side tables. The one illustrated below shows an extraordinarily elaborate interplay of scrolled and floral forms in the design of the lambrequin, legs and the stretcher. The marble tops which were usually of rectilinear shape at the beginning of the century and during the *Régence* period now conform to the sinuous shape of the carved wood under-structure.

C

B

D. DURING THE REIGN OF LOUIS XV, the four-legged console table was not generally intended to stand against the wall. It was a richly carved piece of furniture and usually had some prominent trophy at the crossing of the stretcher. The one illustrated opposite has a military trophy of almost monumental character sculptured on the cross-stretcher between the legs.

D

A

A. THE LEGS in the form of caryatids on this XVIIIth century side table are survivals of the Louis XIV style.

B. THE ORNAMENTAL DESIGNS OF DELAFOSSE have inspired the design of this small Louis XVI side table, supported on three elegant curved legs.

C. UNDER LOUIS XVI the search for neo-classic forms gave rise to side tables resting on eight feet, not entirely dissimilar from the architectural type of side table made in Louis XIV's reign.

D. THE CARVING of this side table is particularly lavish. It is by G. Jacob, one of the few Louis XVI chairmakers who both designed and carved side tables.

E. THE SINGLE central foot on which this late XVIIIth century side table rests is in the form of a vase. It recalls the designs of the engraver Salembier.

B

C

E

D

A

B

PEDESTALS, OR TORCHÈRES, as they are sometimes called, stood entirely free of the wall, and were intended to support large candelabra. When Louis XIV began his economy campaign he forbade the making of pedestals in precious metals. Nevertheless gilt wood, which henceforward replaced the use of metal, allowed craftsmen great opportunities for the display of their technical skill, as can be seen from this Louis XV pedestal (A).

C

THE XVIIIth CENTURY is the great period for the purely ornamental torchère (C and D). The garlands of roses and dolphins such as are found on this torchère disappeared towards the end of the century and were replaced by classical figures as for example winged victories and sphinxes.

THESE TWO TORCHÈRES (B), in the form of a pair of negresses or Indians, support short pedestals on their heads on which candelabra were intended to stand. They are typical examples of the taste for exoticism which prevailed in the XVIIIth century and were perhaps inspired by Rousseau's doctrine of the "noble savage."

SOME OF THE GREATEST classical sculptors of the day did not disdain to create torchères of a monumental character worthy to take their place in the finest architectural settings (E). The monumental pedestal at the right (9′ 10-1/2″ high) was made by Falconet for the Château of Versailles.

E

D

THE SUNBURST IS A DECORATIVE MOTIF particularly characteristic of the reign of Louis XIV, but it is still found throughout the
XVIIIth century either adopted as a mirror frame or as a barometer case.

CARVED GILT WOOD barometer cases often take the same form
as gilt bronze barometers. Thus a barometer was often paired with
a wall clock, or a thermometer and a barometer were combined in one case.

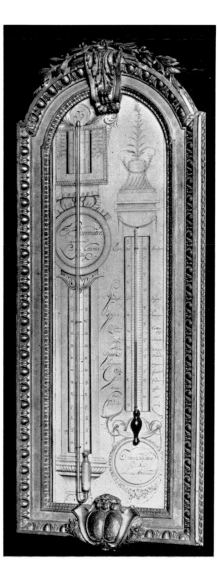

THE SHAPE OF A BAROMETER CASE
varies according to the type of instrument it encloses. The most common
form, in which readings are inscribed
on a circular dial, gives opportunities
for varied decorative motifs. The ones
in which the barometer takes the form
of a tube of mercury are generally
of a more or less rectilinear design.

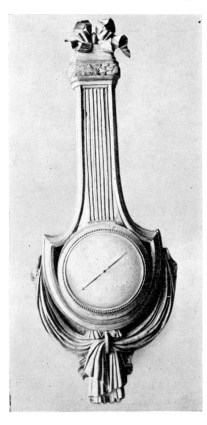

B

PROVINCIAL influences are clearly to be seen in this bird cage (B) supported on an elaborately carved and pierced bracket. The cage (C) below is of a more Italianate character. Such cages were also produced at Turin where the wood carvers were almost as skilful as their French colleagues.

A

C

THESE TWO LOUIS XVI
WALL CLOCKS (D and E)
of gilt wood clearly show the
influence of similar types
made of gilt bronze.

WOOD CARVERS sometimes took pleasure in imitating objects really intended to be made of metal. Occasionally it seems as though they deliberately tried to show their versatility.

THE MODELS for elaborate objects ultimately intended to be executed in gilt bronze were sometimes made of carved wood (they were also, of course, made of wax or terra cotta). Such working models are naturally very rare to-day; they are greatly sought after, and sometimes are of very great value. This centerpiece (A), for instance, is of a type which was not infrequently found in gold or silver.

WOOD CARVERS were sufficiently skilful to translate into terms of their own material even such wildly exuberant forms as this *Régence* wall light (F), in which figures, animals, flowers and palm sprays are mingled in a prodigiously elaborate display of fantasy.

CARPETS, TAPESTRIES AND TEXTILES

The Character of XVIIIth Century Tapestry

Tapestries no longer had a truly utilitarian function in the XVIIIth century; they were used for decoration alone. The great XVIIth century tapestries, that covered entire walls, were intended to provide protection against cold and damp as well as to convey a sense of luxury. In the XVIIIth century, tapestries were made solely for ornamental purposes; they became smaller and, at the same time, the subjects began to imitate painting closely.

Tapestries became smaller because their former function as a wall-protection was largely taken over by paneling. Tapestry now became only one of the elements in the decorative scheme of a room, and, like mirrors and paintings, was inserted into the wall paneling in positions specially designed for it, or was hung directly on the paneling itself. Sometimes, in the provinces, tapestry was still used to cover the entire surface of the walls in the old-fashioned way. It then provided a background for furniture, which was usually of carved and unstained wood. But, in the more elegant town-houses of the period, tapestry was principally employed to break up the monotony of large panels of carved wood. It then performed the role of a kind of mobile fresco, adding its bright colors to the decorative scheme of the room. It was used not only on the wall-paneling but also in the smaller panels above the doors; sometimes, towards the end of the century, it was even used around the windows and the door embrasures. Such tapestry was generally designed to imitate curtains or hangings and was intended to exclude draughts.

Their subject matter developed along the same lines taken by all the arts; that is to say, from pompous and solemn Louis XIV subjects to the pleasing and graceful Louis XV style. But this change in subject matter took place slowly. It was only towards the end of the "Régence" period that designs no longer used the imposing subjects drawn from sacred or secular history, which had added so much to the solemnity of decoration in the previous century. The new subjects were pastoral, or scenes of hunting, mythology, or gallantry; sometimes exotic themes were employed. These were better adapted to the restricted wall-space now available for tapestry.

Tapestry tended increasingly to imitate painting. This trend began circa 1715, when the former artistic independence of the tapestry-weaver began to be forfeited to the artists who designed tapestry cartoons. Taste and fashion demanded that the weavers should carefully follow the designs provided by painters. Such slavish copying allowed no opportunity for personal interpretation. In order to achieve an exact reproduction of a painting the range of colors used by the weavers had to be considerably extended. These changes were not brought about without some resistance on the part of the tapestry weavers, who saw that the unique character of their art was threatened. In the provinces, especially at Aubusson, the weavers continued to interpret their models as freely as before, and often chose their own color schemes. But elsewhere, and especially at the Gobelin and Beauvais factories, the influence of painting became paramount during the "Régence" period and during the early years of Louis XV's reign. This was largely due to the controlling hand of the painter Oudry, who provided a great number of the tapestry cartoons at this period and personally supervised their execution.

The Factories

Sets of tapestry

The widespread fashion for sets of a series of tapestries, linked by a single theme, played an important part in the development of tapestry weaving in the XVIIIth century. When a series met with particular success it was often repeated several times, sometimes at more than one factory.

The series of "Grotesques" by Bérain and Monnoyer were woven on a number of occasions at Beauvais, between 1690 and 1730. At the Gobelin factory the "Don Quixote" series designed by Coypel was repeated no less than nine times between 1714 and 1789. Sets produced from the same cartoons at the various factories often differed considerably. They thus provide an opportunity to study the special characteristics of the individual factories. These stylistic differences can be seen particularly clearly when a tapestry woven at the Gobelin or Beauvais factory is compared with a replica made at Aubusson. The set known as "Louis XV's Hunts," designed by Oudry, was woven at the Gobelin factory under the personal supervision of the painter, who insisted on as close a reproduction of his cartoons as possible and compelled the weavers to use a particularly wide range of colors. These included a number of half-tones which are always very liable to fade. As a result only the basic colors have retained their original brightness. But when the same

The luxurious décor of the earlier years of the century is very well illustrated by this tapestry woven at the Gobelin factory under the direction of Philippe de Behagle. Its subject is: "The Triumph of Aphrodite." It forms part of a set of four marine subjects commissioned in 1690 by Mme. de Montespan after designs by Bérain, a late XVIIth century artist, who created a large number of decorative schemes for interiors, wall paneling, etc., which foreshadowed the general trends of XVIIIth century decoration. It was he who first devised the purely decorative type of tapestry which eventually displaced the great tapestries with figure subjects, which had been fashionable in the age of Louis XIV. Some 250 tapestries were produced after his designs and engravings. (Color plate at left.)

set was woven at Aubusson, brighter colors were used, without any half-tones; the result is that the Aubusson versions are much better preserved today.

The sets were always woven with figure subjects, and were generally used in the principal living rooms only. The so-called "verdure" tapestries (landscape subjects sometimes enlivened with animals and birds) were intended for the decoration of rooms of secondary importance. The Gobelin factory never made any "verdure" tapestries at all; at Beauvais, however, a number were woven in the earlier part of the century when Behagle was director. Behagle was a Fleming, the inventor of the so-called "Flemish style". It was his work which inspired Oudry to design the cartoons of his "verdures fines" which were woven in 1735 and were repeated several times between then and 1769.

"Verdure" tapestries were chiefly woven at Aubusson and Beauvais under Louis XIV. The Gobelin factory, under Louis XV, specialized in the type of tapestry known as "chancelleries" because the King intended them for use in the offices of high legal officials. Several series of these tapestries survive, woven with the emblems of the monarchy. The arms of the leading magistrates and the judges who received these presents from the King were often woven in the borders. Tapestries of this sort were woven from about 1700 onwards on the low-warp looms of the Gobelin factory. These "chancelleries," however, have become very rare, for most of them were burnt during the Revolution.

The Gobelin factory

Both low-warp and high-warp weaving was practiced at the Gobelin factory, but the great reputation of this Royal factory was due to the pieces executed in the high-warp workshops.

At the beginning of the century the traditions and styles created by Lebrun dominated the work of the factory. As a result many religious and mythological subjects continued to be woven in the solemn, noble and somewhat pompous manner for which he had been responsible during his term as director of the factory from its creation in 1662 up to his death in 1690. Tapestries with subjects of the Lebrun type carry on the Louis XIV tradition well into the early years of the reign of Louis XV.

But from the beginning of the century there was another source of inspiration at the Gobelin factory. This derived from the art of the theatre and grew increasingly important up to the middle of Louis XV's reign. From the reopening of the Gobelin factory in 1699 (after it had been closed for five years) the style devised by Bérain was adopted; soon afterwards Mansart, the new director, ordered a series of "Grotesque Months" from Audran.

During the "Régence" period the prevailing taste for the oriental caused a number of tapestries to be woven with exotic subject-matter. This style reached its highest point in the cartoons with Chinese themes designed by Boucher. This fashion for "chinoiseries" and "turqueries" persisted over a long period, for the series known as "Turkish Costumes," woven after Van Loo's designs, was executed as late as 1777, at the beginning of the reign of Louis XVI.

The Beauvais factory

Unlike the Gobelin factory which worked for the King alone, the directors of the Beauvais factory filled private orders, though the factory received large subsidies from the King. Beauvais had a considerable number of private clients for whom work was carried out in addition to such pieces as the King chose to order. Superb tapestries like the set known as the "Marine Deities" date from this period. These were woven after cartoons by Bérain, who had also executed designs for a series of "Grotesques" for the factory. In its early years the Beauvais factory was not always financially successful and passed through some difficult periods. However, this ended in 1726 when Jean-Baptiste Oudry was appointed as "painter charged with providing cartoons and superintending weaving." Eight years later the painter was given the entire direction of the factory, and it was then that he began to compel the weavers to make a literal transcript of his painted cartoons.

It was at this same period that the Beauvais factory produced its greatest series: "The History of Don Quixote" after designs by Natoire, and the "Fables of La Fontaine" after Oudry. While he was director, Oudry often brought in Boucher to design cartoons, and this extraordinarily fertile artist produced no fewer than 45 designs for Beauvais in twenty years: these included great mythological series, such as "The Loves of the Gods" as well as sets of an exotic character, such as the set of "Chinese Tapestries." It must be noted however that Boucher only made the small oil sketches for this last series; the full-size cartoons were enlarged from them by Jean-Joseph Du Mons, who succeeded Oudry as the artistic director of the factory in 1755.

During the final period of the factory's existence François Casanova provided it with a large number of cartoons.

The Aubusson factory

At Aubusson only low-warp looms were used. Aubusson was not a single factory as were Gobelin or Beauvais, but consisted of separate independent workshops, all of which had been granted the right, in 1655, to call themselves the "Royal Manufactory of Aubusson." It was stated in the patent that this title should always be woven on the narrow outer border of each tapestry produced in the factory. This border was blue at Aubusson and brown at the nearby tapestry-weaving center of Felletin, where the workshops were accorded the same privileges as those at Aubusson. Nevertheless Felletin tapestries are of markedly inferior quality and are much less sought-after than those woven at Aubusson. In their turn, Aubusson tapestries are themselves inferior to those of the Beauvais or Gobelin factories. The differences between them are especially noticeable in the range of colors. Where Aubusson used three colors, the Beauvais factory used seven, eight, or even more; on the other hand, the bright colors of Aubusson are much better preserved than those of Beauvais. Nevertheless certain workshops at Aubusson were capable of producing tapestry which could bear comparison with those made at Beauvais or even at the Gobelin factories, but only if the client who commissioned the tapestry paid a high price for it.

In 1685 the Revocation of the Edict of Nantes dealt a severe blow to Aubusson, which was a Protestant center, for many of the weavers emigrated to foreign countries. But the factory was reorganized in 1732, with excellent results, and the most brilliant works of the factory date from that time. Skilled painters like Jean-Joseph Du Mons, who had worked for the Beauvais factory, came to work at Aubusson and undertook the education of the tapestry weavers of the district, for whom a special art school had just been founded. In addition, cartoons painted by some of the greatest artists for the Gobelin and Beauvais factories were lent to Aubusson. It is worth noticing that red was used at Aubusson only after 1731, when a dyer from the Gobelin factory came to work in the neighborhood of the Aubusson workshops.

At this period the great sets which had already been made at the Gobelin and Beauvais factories began to be woven on the Aubusson looms also: the "Chinese Tapestries" after Boucher, the "Fables of La Fontaine" after Oudry, "Don Quixote" after Coypel's designs, are only three famous sets of the many woven there.

The Aubusson weavers, however, were little inclined to copy their cartoons in a servile manner and made little attempt to imitate paintings. They were fond of weaving subjects taken directly from popular engravings of the period, interpreting them with freshness and vigor and adapting them to their own techniques. If a tapestry woven at Aubusson, using a pastoral scene after an engraving by Huet, is compared with the original print, it will be seen that considerable changes have been introduced in order to make the subject suitable for the tapestry looms.

In addition to weaving tapestries with figure subjects, Aubusson also produced a number of tapestries woven with landscapes inspired by the paintings of Pillement or the cartoons of Oudry. These "verdures" were still used on the looms during the Louis XVI period. Boucher's pastoral subjects were still being woven at this period, as well as seascapes after Vernet, though the old borders in the style of carved Louis XV frames were replaced by borders more in accordance with the Louis XVI style. At the same time charming decorative tapestries with floral themes in the Louis XVI style were being woven in considerable numbers: the principal decorative types had a plain ground either strewn with small separate flowers, or patterned with lozenges or bunches of flowers. This type of tapestry was a survival of the "mille-fleurs" tradition of the Middle Ages and the XVIth century.

e Felletin
d Lille factories

Although the figure tapestries and innumerable "verdures" produced at Felletin are somewhat coarsely woven, they are nevertheless remarkable for their bright, gay coloring. On the other hand, the tapestries made at the small factory at Lille, although rather crudely designed and woven, have a much more subtle range of color. The narrow outer border of Lille tapestries is always woven with a fleur-de-lys on a red shield enclosed with interlaced L's, the King's monogram. Lille tapestries were generally woven with mythological subjects, but a certain number of "verdure" tapestries were made there also in the style known as "le jardin à la française" ("Formal Gardens.")

The tapestries woven at these secondary centers are almost entirely lacking in depth and perspective; this fault is particularly noticeable in the big sets, such as the "Don Quixote" series.

Upholstery Tapestry

The custom of upholstering furniture with tapestry seems to date from the "Régence" period. It was at this period that armchairs with backs entirely covered with tapestry, generally of a poppy design, first made their appearance. This same type of poppy decoration continued under Louis XV, but usually as a pattern surrounding a central reserve woven with a landscape, a bird, or an animal, against a background of foliage. On certain types of smaller chairs, tapestry woven solely with a floral decoration began to appear at this period. These two types of decoration were very frequently repeated, but tapestry for chairs, etc., was also woven with figure and animal subjects such as the "Fables of La Fontaine" set, based on the designs by Oudry. Figure subjects were generally used on the backs of the chairs while animals and landscapes were considered more suitable for the seat.

In order to produce a harmonious effect, the tapestry on the furniture was generally woven with the same or at least a similar design to those used on the wall panels. Thus Chinese motifs would appear on the sofas and armchairs of a suite for a room whose walls were to be hung with a set of tapestries in the "chinoiserie" style. At Aubusson, especially during the Louis XVI period, wall tapestries decorated with drapery swags or medallions of a particularly charming character were specially made to go with sets of the above-mentioned type of upholstery tapestry, decorated with similar motifs.

Although Aubusson was particularly active as a center for the production of upholstery tapestries with the most varied subjects, the Gobelin factory also made them. This type of upholstery was never greatly favored at Versailles; nevertheless the Regent of Orléans was one of the first to order tapestries from the Gobelin factory to upholster the chairs of his great gallery at the Palais Royal. Later Mme. de Pompadour, who possessed a number of suites of furniture upholstered with tapestry, ordered Boucher to make special designs for such work. Beauvais enjoyed even greater success than did the Gobelin factory with its upholstery tapestry.

The fashion for covering furniture with needlework in the manner of tapestry (i.e. gros-point or petit-point) had been very much in fashion during the reign of Louis XIV; although less frequently used in the XVIIIth century, it was still occasionally practiced. Chairs, and more particularly both small and large screens, were also sometimes covered with Savonnerie tapestry (that is to say, tapestry made in the carpet technique). The subjects of these were almost invariably the same: the "Fables of La Fontaine" and "Indian Scenes."

Carpets

At the beginning of the century the Savonnerie factory (installed in an old soap — "savon" — works at Chaillot) was passing through a very difficult period. It was only in 1711 that the factory obtained a commission to supply tapestries for the chapel at Versailles. In the following year, after some reorganization, it became the "Royal Factory for the Manufacture of Carpets in the Persian and Near Eastern Styles."

Nevertheless the appearance of the deep velvet pile carpets known as "Savonneries" is essentially different from that of Oriental carpets, although the texture of both types had certain marked resemblances. Savonnerie was woven on a loom which looked very much like the high-warp tapestry loom, but the technique itself was entirely different. Carpets in the French technique are distinguished by their particular softness and by the variety of the colors used, by the skill with which effects of perspective were achieved, by the correctness of the drawing and the harmonious composition of the whole. In comparison with Oriental carpets, Savonnerie carpets had the advantage of merging with Western conceptions of decoration and harmonizing with the decorative elements of rooms. Oriental carpets, on the other hand, are conceived as entirely self-sufficient works of art. Savonnerie carpets, described in the factory's patent as being "in the Near Eastern fashion," had really no Oriental characteristics at all. They followed the general stylistic trends of XVIIIth century decoration: large acanthus-leaf scrolls, medallions decorated in monochrome surrounded with flowers, or reserves enclosing such motifs as trophies or various Royal emblems.

The XVIIIth century was the most successful period of the Savonnerie factory's existence, but the type of carpet on which its fame was based was also made at Beauvais. The greatest success, however, was achieved by the Aubusson factories, where a type of smooth, pileless carpet was produced under the name of "Savonnerie." Nowadays this type of carpet is referred to as "Aubusson" in contrast to the pile carpets in the Persian style which are more properly called "Savonneries." The Aubusson carpets were in fact much less expensive than those produced at the Savonnerie factory.

Aubusson carpets were woven on a low-warp loom in exactly the same method as was tapestry itself. In fact this type of carpet is merely a tapestry on which one may walk.

The very fact that they could adapt their tapestry looms for carpet-weaving allowed the Aubusson workers to produce a smooth carpet which had the double advantage of using considerably less wool and taking much less time to produce than a pile carpet.

In spite of the basic differences between the two methods of weaving, the same type of decorative motifs were used at Aubusson as at the Savonnerie factory, though the smooth surface of Aubusson carpets allowed a clearer and more precise design to be produced while the Savonnerie designs were much less exact owing to the deep pile which prevented any clearly defined outlines from emerging. The technique adopted by the Aubusson weavers was quite definitely designed to imitate the rich effects of deep pile carpets. They were able to give a surprising effect of relief to their designs by a careful use of contrasting colors and shadowing, techniques which they adapted from those used for tapestry weaving. The Aubusson style can be recognized by the general simplification of the decorative motifs, although of course these follow the general stylistic trends of the century. During the "Régence" period the patterns tend to be elaborate, somewhat heavy and woven in an all-over design. On the rare specimens surviving from this period the most notable features are the decorations of the corners and the elaborately composed central motifs. Later, flowers, leaves and rococo forms appear, and little by little displace the trophies and sunbursts associated with the Louis XIV style.

During the Louis XV period the borders became narrower, the ground began to take on greater importance in the design, and patterns of flowers strewn regularly over the background appear with greater frequency. During the transitional period between the Louis XV and the Louis XVI styles, there is a distinct preference for floral designs and at the same time the lines of the design, which had hitherto been markedly sinuous, begin to grow straighter.

Textiles

It is not possible to treat upholstery fabrics entirely apart from dress materials. The rigorous distinction between the two types of material which exists today did not hold true in the XVIIIth century. Only the character of the material itself gives an indication of the purpose for which it was intended; it is not infrequent to find the same design appearing on both upholstery fabrics and dress materials. The differences between the two types are merely confined to certain technical differences in the manufacture and to the rather different range of color used for upholstery fabrics and dress materials.

The technique of stamping a design on velvet and other materials was invented by a Parisian braid-maker, circa 1680. Later it was imported into Holland where it became known as Utrecht velvet. It was enormously popular throughout the XVIIIth century. Finally French technicians came into their own again when Amiens became the center for this type of stuff, which was thenceforward known as Amiens velvet. Towards the end of the century, Oberkampf established a factory at Jouy-en-Josas for the production of printed cottons under the name of "toile de Jouy," a material which quickly obtained world-wide celebrity for the freshness and brilliance of its patterns.

The designs of such costly materials as damasks, brocades, embroidered materials, silk velvet and Utrecht velvet, as well as those of more modest stuffs, like cotton and spun-silks, followed the general trends of XVIIIth century design and changed according to the fashions of the period.

In the earlier part of the century, materials intended as wall-hangings were generally woven with somewhat solemn designs, but subsequently the scale of patterns tended to grow smaller and to adapt to the more modest proportions of the smaller rooms of the period. The huge fruit and flowers of the earlier type of decoration gradually decreased in size and tended to become more normally proportioned. Designs became gayer and more imaginative, reflecting the increasing influence of women on the life of the period. This appears particularly clearly in the designs of Pillement and Huet. Ribbons, braiding, shells, cupids and landscapes, sinuous lines and a generally lighter type of decoration made their appearance on textiles in the Louis XVI style. All-over patterns of flowers and striped designs were then particularly fashionable. The most important name connected with textiles in the Louis XV style, indeed one of the most important in the entire history of textiles, is that of Philippe de La Salle, who designed some of the most outstandingly beautiful designs used at the Lyons silk factories. Philippe de La Salle was not only a brilliant ornamental designer, but he was thoroughly familiar with all the technical processes of weaving. This enabled him to transpose his own decorative compositions into the form of textiles with a hitherto undreamed-of success.

XVIIIth Century Tapestries, Carpets and Textiles in the Modern Home

Eighteenth century tapestries are very much sought after at the present time and are once again being used in the decoration of modern interiors. They bring a warm and decorative note into the interiors of both town and country houses. Sometimes they provide the keynote on which the entire decoration of a room is based. The large, bare walls of modern apartments are particularly well suited to set off an XVIIIth century tapestry that will not only introduce a note of light and color but will also provide a focal point in the room. "Verdures," and "chinoiserie" tapestries in the style of Pillement are the most popular designs today.

Similarly, XVIIIth century carpets are more and more in demand and increasingly tend to displace Oriental carpets in general esteem.

Original XVIIIth century textiles, insofar as their present state of preservation allows, are kept as documents to be copied at the Lyons silk factories. They are greatly sought after by all textile manufacturers whose staple products are still based on the traditional designs of Louis XV and Louis XVI materials of every variety. The elegant character of XVIIIth century textiles accords particularly well with the trends of modern taste.

The taste for the exotic, so dear to the XVIIIth century, generally took the form of "Chinoiseries." These compositions were often woven after paintings—either paintings which had been actually executed as designs for tapestry, or, occasionally, after wall-paintings. The detail illustrated here comes from an Aubusson tapestry entitled "The Cup of Tea," which was woven after a cartoon by Boucher. The colors of Aubusson tapestry are much better preserved than those woven at the Gobelin and Beauvais factories; they are brighter, clearer and do not make use of those half-tones which were so impermanent and have today almost all faded, due to the effects of exposure to light. At Aubusson a thick black line around the edges of the various parts of the design took the place of half-tones. (Color plate at right

A

THE AUBUSSON FACTORY specialized in imitating the type of tapestry made at the Gobelin and Savonnerie factories. Its productions never attained the high quality of its two great rivals, for they were much cheaper and intended for a less affluent public.

THIS *VERDURE*, in the Chinese mode (A), dates from the mid-Louis XV period and is in the style of Pillement. It includes a number of exotic elements then in fashion, such as Chinese pagodas and multicolored oriental birds. The border is an excellent example of its type, and is copied from a carved and gilt wood picture-frame.

THIS GENRE SCENE "A Game of Blind Man's Buff" (B) is attributed to J.-B. Huet, who played an important part in the revival of weaving at Aubusson, which began in 1731 under the direction of J.-J.du Mons.

MUCH DECORATIVE TAPESTRY (C) of this type was produced at the Aubusson factory during the later years of the century. The central medallion is woven with a theme taken from one of the "Fables" of La Fontaine; the overall pattern is in the style of Ranson.

B

C

A

TAPESTRY produced at the beginning of the XVIIIth century at the Royal Gobelin factory was influenced by paintings in the Grand Manner —the work of those Louis XIV artists who had been employed in the factory, such as Charles Le Brun, Van der Meulen, Martin (the "Battle Painter") and Mignard; subsequently Oudry and Boucher both played similar roles in relation to the later work of the factory. Three of these painters, Le Brun, Mignard and Oudry, were directors of the factory.

THE INFLUENCE of the XVIIth century is discernible in this tapestry designed by Parrocel (A) which represents "The Turkish Ambassador Mohammed Effendi Entering the Tuileries Gardens." It was woven in 1734.

THE TECHNICAL RESOURCES available at the Gobelin factory greatly increased towards the middle of the XVIIIth century, allowing weavers to make tapestries closely resembling the paintings from which they were copied. This gave rise to a controversy between the painters who designed tapestries and the directors of the factory as to whether this was appropriate to the form. This Gobelin tapestry "Flora and Zephyr" (B) is an excellent example of the close imitation of a painting.

TYPICAL LOUIS XVI ORNAMENTAL motifs are to be seen in the surround of the central medallion of this tapestry (C) representing "The Loves of Neptune and Amymone" designed by François Boucher. It is an example of the attempt made by Neilson, Cozette and Houdron, towards the end of the century, to return to a style of weaving less imitative of painting. The border still imitates the style of contemporary picture frames.

B

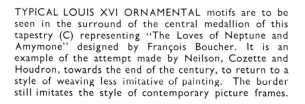

C

LILLE TAPESTRIES are colorful, but their subjects, often borrowed from Téniers as in the example illustrated, are usually of inferior design with very little sense of modeling. The one at right (D) known as "The Card Party" bears the mark of the workshop of the widow Werniers. The border is an exact copy of a picture frame.

SAVONNERIE TAPESTRIES are extraordinarily rare, but those which exist are of a remarkably high quality. The one illustrated here (E) is part of a series of four tapestries ordered by Louis XIV in 1713. It is characteristic of the decorative style prevailing in France in the early years of the XVIIIth century.

THE GOBELIN factory earned a particularly high reputation for tapestries made as seat covers (i'). Sets of these were often woven after subjects taken from the "Fables" of La Fontaine, and are perhaps the most celebrated type produced at the factory. An example is seen on the back of this *Régence* armchair.

(Captions for page 163.)

THE BEAUVAIS FACTORY maintained the highest standards of tapestry weaving throughout the XVIIIth century. Although a number of subjects taken from Gobelin tapestries were woven there, Beauvais specialized in "verdure" tapestries, landscapes and scenes with shepherds and shepherdesses (A).

A

SOME OF THE BEST PAINTERS of the century worked for the Beauvais factory with great success. This tapestry (C) known as "The Dance" reflects the taste for a theatrical type of exoticism which became fashionable during the Louis XVI period. It forms part of a set designed by Leprince, executed between 1770 and 1793, under the title "Russian Games."

THE INTRODUCTION OF PURELY ANECDOTAL SUBJECTS (B) and a taste for imitating paintings too exactly hampered the art of tapestry weaving towards the middle of the century. This can be seen in the example illustrated below after a design by François Casanova. It is one of a set of eight pieces known as "Country Amusements" woven at Beauvais between 1780 and 1793.

C

B

D

F

E

A

WHEN A SET OF TAPESTRY DESIGNS achieved great success at the factory where it was first woven it was not only repeated there, but was frequently imitated elsewhere. Thus the famous set of "Don Quixote" tapestries was woven in different forms at the Gobelin factory throughout the century, and was also used at Aubusson and at Beauvais. These different series of the same subjects are of great interest for they allow the evolution of style of the various factories to be studied and compared.

THE AUBUSSON factory (A). "Don Quixote Consulting the Enchanted Head in Don Antonio Mereno's House." The composition of this tapestry is heavy and the contrast of colors is crude, showing the difficulty workers at the Aubusson factory had in reproducing a complicated subject.

THE GOBELIN factory (B). One of the panels from a set of fifteen of the *Régence* period and woven about 1717 after cartoons designed by Charles Coypel. The ornamental cartouches, surrounds and borders were designed by Belin de Fontenay and Claude Audran. The scene shows Don Quixote protecting Basilio as he is about to marry Quiterie by a ruse.

THE BEAUVAIS factory (C). This is a detail from "Sancho Panza's Meal" designed by Natoire. In contrast to Coypel's treatment of the subject, Natoire has spread the composition over the entire surface of the panel.

B

C

THE VARIOUS WAYS in which different types of themes have been treated by different factories also allows of interesting comparisons not only of the style but also of the techniques of these factories. The fashion for exoticism allowed both weavers and cartoon designers free play for their imagination in the creation of an imaginary orientalism. Designs of this type were provided by a number of great artists, notably Boucher, Pillement and Van Loo.

THE SET OF CHINESE SUBJECTS (A) designed by François Boucher for the Aubusson factory in the Louis XV period continued to be repeated in the Louis XVI period, though the borders were then of a more neo-classic type as can be seen from the example here where ovoli and floral sprays have replaced the scrolls which would have appeared earlier in the century.

INDIAN SUBJECTS (B) were used at the Gobelin factory throughout the century. The design and character of the set illustrated here, which was woven in the Louis XVI period, have not been changed since it was originally designed by Desportes in 1736.

THE "CHINESE DANCE" (C), designed by Boucher for the Beauvais factory, is a detail rom a fine set, worthy of the Gobelin weavers.

A

B

C

B

ALLEGORIC MOTIFS dear to Louis XIV, such as the sun, the sunflower, etc., continued to be employed as decorative features for upholstery during the early years of the century. This early *Régence* armchair (A) is covered with celebrated Utrecht velvet.

TYPICAL RÉGENCE DAMASK (B) usually consists of a pattern in two different colors standing out against a dark red ground. This sort of material was used for wall hangings, curtains, and chair covers. The same type of pattern was also found on materials used for dresses. It is only the quality of the tissue itself which gives any indication of the purpose for which it is made: these two fragments of stuff (opposite at the right) taken from contemporary dresses which were made in the ample style known as the "pleated Watteau" type illustrate this point.

STRAW-COLORED SATIN woven in *Régence* design is strewn with large tulips embroidered in natural colors (C). This type of decoration with flowers in natural colors is very unusual.

CREAM-COLORED SATIN (D) in the Louis XV style has an embroidered floral design arranged in elegant sinuous curves. It was particularly well-adapted to the wide-skirted dresses of the period.

AN INCREDIBLE VARIETY of decorative motifs was used in XVIIIth century materials. This silk upholstery was designed by Philippe de La Salle for the Empress Catherine II. It incorporates a Russian eagle trampling on a trophy of Turkish arms, with a background of blue drapery swags. (*Color plate opposite.*)

C

D

167

C

A

B

UNDER LOUIS XV, and later under Louis XVI, simple types of materials with a pattern in natural colors were produced at the same time as the more grandiose designs prepared by Philippe de La Salle. The two Louis XV materials illustrated here are typical of the fashions then in vogue.

THE LIGHT AND GRACEFUL PATTERN of this material with its floral motifs in old silver on a lavender-blue ground (A) makes it equally suitable for the covering of a chair or for a woman's dress.

THIS VERY RICH AND HIGHLY COLORED SILK is embroidered with bunches of flowers in silk and chenille on a blue ribbed ground (B).

UNDER LOUIS XVI, PATTERNS INSPIRED BY the wall paintings at Pompeii began to appear in woven textiles. An example is this damask woven in two colors on a golden yellow ground (C). This type of large-scale design was intended to be used for wall hangings, curtains, or for the hangings of a canopied bed.

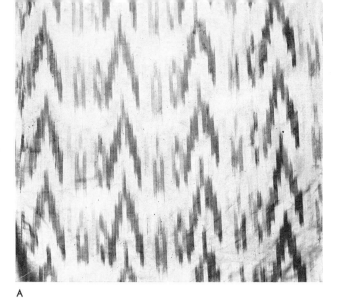

A

A TECHNIQUE which has been forgotten today was devised in the Louis XVI period, by means of which taffeta (A) could be woven in the style known as "chiné à la branche" (Bargello work), a type of decoration in pink, yellow, blue and green, resembling Hungarian embroidery. This thin material was suitable for women's dresses.

EMBROIDERED MATERIALS intended as upholstery were similar to tapestries woven for the same purpose. This example designed for use on the seat of a Louis XVI armchair (B) is taken from a design by Philippe de La Salle known as "The Gardener." The pattern is embroidered in various colors on a beige-colored satin medallion, sewn down on a background of pale blue satin; the border is embroidered with a colorful floral pattern on a beige satin ground. The subject on the back of the chair is entirely different, and represents a young girl gardening.

B

STRIPED PATTERNS came into fashion towards the end of the Louis XVI period. This taffeta (C) is woven with narrow, ribbed stripes of periwinkle blue and white, alternating with stripes embroidered with trails of flowers on a white ground. This silk taffeta, supple and strong, was especially made for dresses.

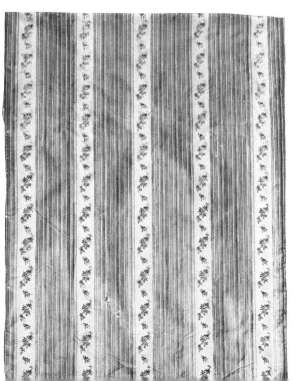

C

A

THIS AUBUSSON CARPET in the *Régence* style was woven after a design by Robert de Cotte, one of Louis XIV's architects and a vice-protector of the Académie Royale de Peinture et de Sculpture. Aubusson carpets were woven on the same looms as tapestry. This procedure allowed them to be made more cheaply than by knotting, and had the additional advantage of allowing more detail to be introduced into the design. *(Color plate opposite.)*

THE TASTE FOR INDIAN AND PERSIAN printed cottons was introduced into France by the Compagnie des Indes (East India Company). It was the attempt to imitate materials of this sort which gave rise to the celebrated *toiles de Jouy* (printed cottons) which enjoyed such an enormous success in the second half of the XVIIIth century. Designs were inspired both by the Oriental patterns of the early printed cottons imported into France, and also by the compositions of certain outstanding contemporary painters.

THE FLORAL ARABESQUE PATTERN of this cretonne (A) was inspired by Oriental designs. The pastoral theme of the other cretonne (B) was designed by Jean-Baptiste Huet, who made many patterns for the Jouy factory. In this case the background is of a small diapered design. An infinite variety of colors and backgrounds were used for the patterns printed at the Jouy factory. They included all-over designs of small dots, large dots, squares, diapers, trellises, etc. The ground, however, was always white or a pale brown.

B

B

FRENCH CARPETS naturally derived their general character from the setting, the furniture, the paneling, and the style of the room in which they were destined to be placed. The decorative motifs were those in fashion at the time the carpet was made.

All three French carpet factories, Aubusson, Savonnerie, and Gobelin, produced carpets of two clearly defined types: the smooth pileless carpets, and deep pile carpets in the Turkish style. The smooth pileless carpet was first created at the Aubusson factory and even when it is made elsewhere, as it often was later, it is still known as an Aubusson carpet.

Although Aubusson also made carpets with a deep pile (knotted carpets in imitation of Turkish and Persian models) Savonnerie, with its monopoly of royal commissions, took the lead in the manufacture of carpets of this type. All the finest examples of this type of carpet surviving today were made at the Savonnerie factory.

AT THE BEGINNING OF THE CENTURY decorative motifs occupied almost the entire surface of Aubusson carpets; the ground was hardly allowed to show but was covered, right up to the corners, with scrolls, foliated motifs and shells. The same general tendency is also to be seen in the two pile carpets illustrated here: (A) a Gobelin carpet woven in the Savonnerie knotted style, dating from the beginning of the century (repaired). (B) Gobelin carpet of the Savonnerie type dating from the *Régence* period.

A

A

DURING THE RÉGENCE PERIOD the designs of carpets became even richer. The borders were wide, and treated as though they were in relief. Patterns continued to occupy almost the entire surface of the carpet, but floral and foliated motifs as well as rococo forms gradually began to appear, and little by little replaced the trophies and sunbursts of the earlier age. There is a greater freedom in the type of design towards the end of the period, as the Louis XV style begins to assert itself. (A) Aubusson carpet in the knotted Savonnerie style. (B) Savonnerie carpet (detail).

B

A

UNDER LOUIS XV the background began to take on an importance of its own. The center was generally occupied by a single large decorative feature of more or less homogenous character. It usually is of sinuous outline and the ground around it is strewn with floral sprays. Generally the border is narrower than in the *Régence* period. Few rectilinear motifs are used. Even the borders themselves are sometimes given a sinuous outline. (A) Aubusson pile carpet in the Savonnerie style. (B) Smooth surface Aubusson carpet with a pale green ground and a light border. (C) Aubusson pile carpet in the Savonnerie style, dating from the end of the Louis XV period.

B

C

A

B

UNDER LOUIS XVI the design of carpets grew lighter. Straight lines began to reappear; flowers, garlands, and ribbons made their appearance as did trophies of gardening tools, a motif made very popular by the engravings of the ornamental designer Salembier. (A) Fragment of a Louis XVI Aubusson carpet, the pattern of lozenges, squares and circles is arranged in quincunx form; the individual motifs are enclosed by floral garlands and rosettes in a design typical of the period. (B) Savonnerie pile carpet made at the Gobelin factory. The design is formed by a long interlacing garland of roses; in the center is a bunch of blue convolvulus from which trails of leaves and flowers emerge to occupy the interstices of the design; the entire background is brown. The beading and the wave motif which ornament the border are in golden yellow on a green ground.

CARPETS

C

AT THE END OF THE LOUIS XVI PERIOD the decorative motifs themselves no longer spread all over the ground, but were enclosed within geometrical shapes. The background was generally plain; and the delicate forms of the floral garlands and ribbons stood out against the complicated interplay of rectilinear borders. In general the character of the design was inspired by antique art, such as the frescoes of Pompeii, but the emphasis was on rectilinear lines and geometrical shapes.

A. Louis XVI Aubusson carpet.
B. Late Louis XVI Aubusson carpet.
C. Aubusson pile carpet in the Savonnerie style.

A

B

AUBUSSON PILE CARPET in the Savonnerie style. Its pattern is based on a design by Salembier and is characteristic of this period, when late Louis XVI forms were beginning to evolve towards the Directoire style.

PLASTER BUST OF A CHILD by Jean-Antoine Houdon, who specialized in portrait-
busts and became the most famous portrait-sculptor in Europe. His sitters were
generally literary figures or artists, but he was also extremely successful in achieving
in his children's portraits a natural intimacy and charm which is altogether inimitable.

SCULPTURE

The Position of Sculpture in the XVIIIth Century

During the XVIIIth century sculpture began to depart from traditional forms and subjects. Both its patrons and its artistic purpose changed radically during the course of the century, and at the same time it developed many new techniques and methods.

Sculptors turned more and more towards new sources of patronage as the generous support which the Court had extended in the previous century began to decrease. During the reign of Louis XIV, artists had devoted their talents largely to the glorification of the sovereign; now they were more and more frequently employed in satisfying the tastes of the public. Collectors and art patrons were much more numerous than they had been in the previous century, and provided sculptors with far greater opportunities to sell their work. This new development permitted sculptors to free themselves from the somewhat oppressive tutelage of the Court and to shake off the limiting authority exercised by painters in the "Académie Royale de Peinture et de Sculpture."

Within the ranks of the Académie there had always been struggles between the different members as to the privileges to which they were entitled. The battle between the painters and sculptors was particularly bitter. The painters regarded themselves as the natural leaders of the Academy and controlled it completely. Sculptors saw themselves progressively deprived of the honors due them, as well as of the employment which was so lavishly extended to their more fortunate painter-colleagues. Pigalle was the first sculptor to protest against the unfavorable position in which he and his colleagues found themselves toward the middle of the century. According to the account given by Bachaumont in his "Mémoires Secrets," he was offended because the Order of Saint-Michel was conferred on famous painters only, and never on sculptors; so he set himself the task of obtaining this distinction, not for reasons of vanity, but rather so as to counter what he regarded as a slight on the art he practiced. Pigalle insisted "on sharing the large number of official posts open to artists on a level of equality with painters." He proposed that "there should be a Royal sculptor just as there was a Royal painter, and a Sculptor Director of the French Academy at Rome as well." The results of this rivalry exercised a marked influence on the development of sculpture during the period.

The artistic role of sculpture also changed as a consequence of still more important causes.

The development of sculpture had always been closely linked with the great state building programs. Sculptors played a particularly important role in the construction of new Royal palaces and châteaux, and especially in the decoration of their gardens. In their plans for Royal residences, architects always included designs for hedge walks and gardens, carefully arranging them with views, vistas and perspectives which were to be decorated with many pieces of sculpture. The equestrian groups decorating the gardens of Louis XIV's country palace at Marly, for instance, brought widespread fame to their sculptors Coysevox and Coustou, and this is only a single example among many, illustrating the considerable fame many sculptors enjoyed during the latter part of the XVIIth century.

During the course of his reign Louis XIV had developed a positive passion for building, but with his death the great period of building Royal palaces came to an end.

Architects soon saw that what had once been their chief employment had now vanished almost completely. New developments were taking place in French social life and, taking advantage of these, architects turned their talents towards the design and building of private houses on a smaller scale.

But the arrangement of the interiors of these new dwellings, with their limited interior space, left little opportunity for the display of monumental sculpture. Sculptors, like painters, found themselves driven to take account of these new physical conditions. Like painters, too, they turned their attention to works on a smaller scale, and to themes more suitable for these smaller interiors. Sculpture was essentially a decorative art; in the XVIIIth century it abandoned the solemn themes and treatment which had been demanded of it in the previous century, and so it turned for new inspiration to nature and to man.

Sculpture developed new techniques and adopted new subjects. The so-called "sculpture d'édition" made its appearance at this period. This was sculpture intended to be reproduced in a considerable number of copies. It usually consisted of small groups or figures on a reduced scale. Sculptors turned from the monumental to the decorative and the ornamental. This meant undertaking work which in the past would have been regarded as of a secondary character. A striking example of this is to be found at Versailles where Caffiéri was equally prepared to carve doors and even picture frames or to model busts and statues.

Clodion deliberately chose terra-cotta as his favorite material so that numerous reproductions of his small-scale figure sculptures could be reproduced. J.-B. Lemoyne, Bouchardon, Falconet, Pigalle, Pajou, Clodion, Houdon, Julien and Caffiéri all undertook sculpture of a decorative character. In addition to this, some of them worked both for the Sèvres porcelain factory and for the great bronze-casters, not merely as artist-sculptors but also as ornamental designers.

The great variety of the work produced by sculptors during this century can be divided into three main divisions: statuary, decorative sculpture and sculpture intended as an integral part of the overall architectural decoration.

This decorative design for a fountain by Bouchardon shows the central feature surrounded by an elaborate group of figures in movement. Contemporary sculptors would have had no difficulty in creating it in marble, stone or bronze, as required. Bouchardon had a particular gift for sculptured groups embodying the pastoral themes which were so fashionable in the XVIIIth century.

The Evolution of Sculpture During Three Reigns.

Towards the end of the reign of Louis XIV, the leading stylistic conflict of the XVIIIth century—that between the rococo and the antique—had already begun to emerge. "Rocaille" in an incipient form, was to be found in Coysevox's sculptures at Marly, which works were done during the reign of Louis XIV himself. During the "Régence" period this style was perpetuated by his few pupils, hardly numerous enough to be regarded as forming a school. The chief of these were Nicolas and Guillaume Coustou, his nephews. Nicolas, the elder, undertook a great deal of carving of different sorts for the Crown, and Guillaume created magnificent decorative works like the "Marly Horses" which were intended

to replace those which Coysevox had made for the same palace. He also left one of the best portraits of the Queen, in his bust of "Marie Leczinska."

Although the traditions of the previous century, based on Renaissance classicism, passed out of fashion, they never completely died out. All through the century, running parallel to the rococo style, there was an undercurrent of classicism. It is to this source that certain of the more severe and more monumental types of XVIIIth century sculpture are to be traced. Nevertheless an impulse towards a more expressive style in sculpture remained predominant. J.-B. Lemoyne, L.-S. Adam and P.-A. Slodtz were all concerned with the expression of emotion, movement and vitality, even at a time when the work of their contemporary, Bouchardon, was already foreshadowing a return to the antique, in the neo-classic style. But the evolution of sculpture is always much slower than that of painting and its divergent stylistic tendencies are much less clearly marked than painting styles.

In XVIIIth century sculpture there is a dichotomy between the general trend of fashion and the work of a number of academic artists whose traditionalism amounted to no more than the survival into one period of the style of the previous age. For this reason, it is not always easy to distinguish between a piece of sculpture produced during the "Régence" period and one made during the Louis XV period.

Portrait Busts, the Great Achievement of the XVIIIth Century

In his portrait sculpture, Jean-Baptiste Lemoyne succeeded in giving permanent form to fleeting expressions, to nuances of feeling and character, which had been entirely ignored by the portrait sculpture of the XVIIIth century.

Lemoyne strove for a realistic presentation of his subject, and his care for truthful representation sometimes carried him almost to the point of brutality, as can be seen in his famous bust of Louis XV as an old man. The extraordinary subtlety and technical skill with which he manipulated his medium enabled him to give permanent and precise form to his sensitive perceptions and to impart a remarkable intensity of life to his marbles and terra-cottas. The fleeting smile which figures on a number of his busts is particularly characteristic of his manner.

Lemoyne enjoyed the favour of the King and especially of his minister the Comte d'Angiviller. As a result he received commissions for the major part of the series of official statues of the great men of France ordered by the Crown.

He produced a large number of portrait busts. Sometimes his models are represented in modern dress, sometimes in antique classical drapery. The choice of costume was left to his sitter, and the sculptor was thereby able to take advantage of whichever of the two conflicting fashions of the day—the realistic or the neo-classic—a particular patron favored.

Guillaume Coustou was most skilful in giving his busts a sense of movement and in portraying his sitters with remarkable truthfulness. In addition he combined the requirements of contemporary academicism with an admiration for the "antique style."

Pigalle displays a remarkable realism in his busts and in his portrait studies, as well as in his delightful series of figures of children. They are of an exactly opposite character to his great academic pieces which were conceived in cold idealistic terms; for his portrait busts are both moving and true. His children are real children, neither angels nor devils; they are carefully observed and treated as an end in themselves; they are never given the allegoric significance which so many other sculptors attempted in their portraits of children. His large groups and allegoric pieces have an idealized character which is in strong contrast to the realism of his portraits.

But Pigalle's sculptures were never completely "idealized" as were Falconet's, nor in the way that the convention was understood by Diderot. This idealism of the mid-XVIIIth century was compounded of elegance, taste, wit, delicacy, gentleness and grace. Nevertheless Falconet's portrait sculpture is often given an allegoric rather than a realistic character. An example is his "Music" in which Mme. de Pompadour, the favorite of Louis XV and the outstanding woman of the age, is represented in allegoric form.

Mme. de Pompadour's influence can be felt in sculpture just as in the other arts. After her death the simplified forms of the neo-classical style gained in strength and power. Mme. du Barry extended her protection to two sculptors who were responsible for introducing a new spirit into the art of the portrait bust: Felix Lecomte and her especial favorite, Augustin Pajou. He made no fewer than a dozen portraits of her. Eventually he became the official sculptor to Louis XVI. He also executed busts for less grandiose sitters: his parents, his friends and a whole gallery of women.

Pajou also made an important group of busts of the "great men of France." This was in a series similar in scope to the one for which Clodion made one of his few examples of sculpture on a life-sized scale. His "Montesquieu" has some claim to originality, owing to the fact that the sitter is portrayed in classical costume rather than in the costume of the period. This cult of "the great men of France" was extremely fashionable during the Louis XVI period. It provided artists with an opportunity for work on a life-sized scale. For most of the time, the majority of sculptors were required to execute only small decorative pieces. Such was the case not only with Clodion but also with Julien, who made a life-sized statue of "La Fontaine" as part of the same series.

Caffiéri was another who left his mark on this series of portraits of great men with a statue of "Molière," executed with remarkable vigor. This artist's work was largely based on somewhat dramatic concepts of the baroque and, as a result of this, he has left us a remarkably lively series of portraits of the actors and actresses of the "Comédie-Française."

Ornamental designers *provided sculptors with innumerable designs for figures intended to be adapted to the symmetrical lines of decorative vases in the Louis XVI style, like the one illustrated below.*

With Houdon, portrait sculpture rises above fashion and the turmoil of style and influences; it becomes art of the highest sort. For Houdon, more than any sculptor of his time, had the ability to impart a real sense of life to his marble and terra-cotta. His sitters were often literary figures or artists living in Paris. Diderot was among the first of them, and his bust was exhibited at the "Salon" in 1771. He made a number of busts of Voltaire, but the most celebrated of all representations of this great man is the full length statue in which Houdon shows him dressed in the antique style.

Houdon's fame as a sculptor was widespread. He was perhaps even more appreciated in foreign countries than at the French court, possibly because his portraits penetrate a little too deeply into the true character of the sitters. His greatest successes are his portraits of women and children, where his psychological understanding is seen in its most pleasing form. He had a perfect technical mastery of his material and the wide variety of his portrait busts make him the greatest portraitist of the last years of the French monarchy. His allegoric sculpture is of less interest, but his busts strike an extraordinary balance between classical severity and realism.

His strength is partly due to his profound knowledge of the human body, a far deeper knowledge than that of any other artist of the period. He spent much time in the dissecting rooms of the medical schools. His great knowledge of anatomy played an important part in enabling him to seize the very lineaments of character and sensibility in the faces of his sitters. His portraits are documents of an almost scientific sincerity as can be seen from the pock-marked face of his bust of Mirabeau. No better idea of the spirit of the age can be gained than by studying the remarkable series of busts in which he gave permanent form to the features of his contemporaries: Voltaire, Washington, Rousseau, Buffon, Diderot, Mirabeau.

In Houdon's works, the student of XVIIIth century sculpture can study the evolution of an art which is in the very act of developing and changing. They are so numerous that every stage in this evolution can be followed. In addition to his numerous marbles, he made a large number of busts of terra-cotta, of plaster and of bronze. In every technique he succeeded in imparting a sense of life to his material. It is this vitality which gives his portraits of women and children such an astonishing sense of inner harmony. This characteristic of his art is unique and found in the work of no other sculptor.

Small Sculpture and Decorative Sculpture

Small or "drawing room" sculpture, as it is sometimes called, came into existence as the result of the changing social conditions of the XVIIIth century. The fortunes of private collectors were much more modest than those of the Court and rooms were much smaller. The spontaneity of first efforts and sketches, especially as seen in sculptors' waxes and terra-cottas, was admired then just as it is today. All these factors contributed to the success of small-scale sculpture. Figures in Sèvres biscuit porcelain enjoyed a remarkable success; initially this was due to Mme. de Pompadour's personal interest in the form. This type of sculpture was particularly favored by Falconet, who directed the modeling room of the Sèvres factory from 1757 to 1766.

During this period, Falconet created nearly a hundred models for porcelain figures. Their subjects were sometimes taken from designs by Boucher (another artist protected by Mme. de Pompadour), and were sometimes the creations of his own imagination. The celebrated "Falconet Children" show his subjects engaged in the various occupations of the town and the country. They are works which are still attract-

ive today. After Falconet left the factory, Pigalle came to work at Sèvres, and the series known as the "Pigalle Children" are just as highly esteemed as those of his predecessor. Clodion also worked at the Sèvres factory, but he owes his reputation rather to his independent works of decorative sculpture.

Although Pajou worked under the direction of architects with remarkable success and provided admirable sculptural decoration for the halls and staircases of the period, it is Clodion who is really the most representative artist of this type of sculpture. He was a master in the art of modeling cupids, nymphs and bacchantes, all inspired with a deliciously youthful and spiritual sensuality. They either take the form of individual free-standing figures or are part of the bas-reliefs which he produced in such great numbers.

It is on account of works of this type that Clodion has sometimes been called the Fragonard of sculpture. Undoubtedly Fragonard was the most potent influence on Clodion's art, and he learned a great deal from Fragonard's Italianate drawings of Bacchic scenes. He even copied one famous work by the painter as a piece of sculpture: "La Gimblette." Clodion chose his subject matter largely from antiquity. His nymphs pursued by Pan, and other pagan themes were inspired not so much because of any passionate attachment to the classical past, as because they were particularly in key with the taste of the period for a certain type of amiable sensuality. Clodion even made some contribution to the evolution of furniture styles. He provided designs for "torchères," for the figure subjects of clock-cases, for candelabra and vases of antique design; moreover some of his bas-reliefs were executed in gilt-bronze and used as furniture mounts by artist-craftsmen like Gouthière. In addition Clodion employed a considerable workshop which was engaged in casting a number of his terra-cottas in bronze.

Clodion did little in the way of large-scale sculpture, and what he did produce does not cause any regret that he spent so little time on this type of work. His specialty was mythological subjects of a peculiarly elegant and refined type; he excelled in sculptures intended to play their part in the fashionable interiors of the day, decorated in the Pompeian style. These took the form of small statuettes and of bas-reliefs let into the wall decoration itself. If Pigalle can be said to represent the XVIIIth century in sculpture in its most emotional and romantic mood, Falconet in its ideal and spiritual aspect, and Houdon in its understanding of psychological truth, then Clodion is the perfect representative of the amorous and gallant aspects of the last years of the monarchy.

XVIIIth Century Sculpture in Modern Interiors

Small sculpture plays the same part in the furnishing of a modern interior as it did in the XVIIIth century; it provides a work of art which can be looked at from all sides. By providing an element of relief in the decoration it breaks the monotony of plain surfaces and, by its solid and tangible presence, emphasizes the architectural character of a room. For this reason it is very important that the original balance between sculpture and architecture should be maintained in an interior of the period. XVIIIth century sculpture takes its place naturally in our modern interiors for it was precisely in order to be able to play a part in the decoration of the smaller rooms which were then coming into fashion, that sculptors progressively reduced the size of their work. As sculpture formed an integral part of the decoration of a room of the period, it is indispensable today, if a real XVIIIth century atmosphere is to be recreated. In a room whose walls are paneled and carved, or where they are of a pronouncedly architectural character, sculpture creates a focus of interest; thus a piece of sculpture placed in a niche provides just the appropriate element of relief to enliven the wall.

"A SACRIFICE TO PAN, THE GOD OF GARDENS", terra-cotta by Clodion (1738-1814). One of the finest groups created by this artist, who specialized in terra-cottas and has been called the Fragonard of sculpture. He succeeded almost perfectly in imparting the "sensibility" of his period to such pieces as this.

A

B

A COMPARISON of these four busts clearly illustrates the differences in style of four outstanding sculptors of the XVIIIth century.

LEMOINE continues to adhere to the traditional classic mode.

PAJOU is predominantly interested in achieving a successful likeness of his sitter. DEFERNEX perhaps accentuates the individual character of his sitter a little too much.

HOUDON, while still aiming at a naturalistic effect, gives his subject an extraordinary feeling of life and personality.

A. "Portrait of the Marquis de La Fayette as a Young Man," by Defernex.

B. "Portrait of a Young Woman," by Pajou.

C. "Portrait of Jean-François d'Orléans," terra-cotta by Lemoine.

D. "Portrait of Mme. Blaise Guillaume," by Jean-Antoine Houdon.

C

D

B

C

TWO TYPES OF SCULPTURE, utterly different from one another, persist throughout the century. A comparison of the statue of La Fontaine by JULIEN and the bust of Mirabeau by HOUDON illustrates the characteristics of these styles very clearly. Houdon is concerned with the personal character of a living, sentient being; this is clearly visible in Mirabeau's mobile face. Julien, on the other hand, is drawn to the anecdotal aspect of his model: the fox and the volume of La Fontaine's "Fables" which he has placed at the poet's feet symbolize the man but do not succeed in giving life to the monument.

A. "Statue of La Fontaine," by Julien.

B. "Bust of Mirabeau," by Houdon.

C. "Bust of Louise Brongniart as a Child," terra-cotta by Houdon. For his terra-cottas Houdon employed a clay from Lorraine which shrank less than any other when baked. As a result he is able to retain the spontaneous effect of his first sketches.

A

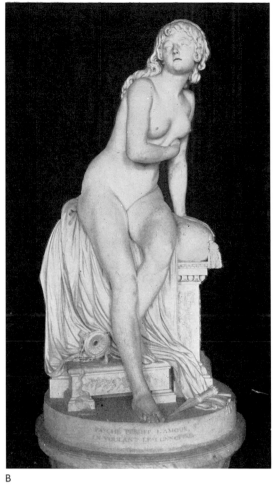

B

C

D

E

THE MIDDLE CLASSES played an increasingly important role as patrons of the arts during the XVIIIth century. To meet the taste of this section of their public, artists began to create small sculptures known as "*sculptures d'édition*" intended to be reproduced in considerable numbers either in terra-cotta, marble, bronze or biscuit porcelain. Even great artists like Houdon and Pajou did not disdain to meet this demand.

A. BOUCHARDON: "Winter," marble. One of a set of the Four Seasons, from the mid-Louis XV period.

B. PAJOU: "Psyche." The close relationship between this statue and classical sculpture is quite obvious. A considerable part of Pajou's output dates from the latter part of the XVIIIth century.

C. HOUDON: "Summer." This great sculptor rarely produced works of an allegoric character.

D. CLODION: Small terracotta dog. One of this artist's innumerable terra-cottas intended for reproduction in considerable numbers.

E. BOIZOT worked particularly for the Sèvres porcelain factory and specialized in allegoric subjects like this "Apollo as Leader of the Muses." Biscuit porcelain allowed almost any number of reproductions to be made.

G

F

F. CLODION: "Bacchante with a Bunch of Grapes," bronze.
G. FALCONET: "Pygmalion and Galatea," Sèvres.
H. CLODION: "The Spring" ("La Source"), terracotta. This is one of the best-known sculptures by this artist. His fame is largely due to the numerous pieces of this type which he modeled for reproduction.

H

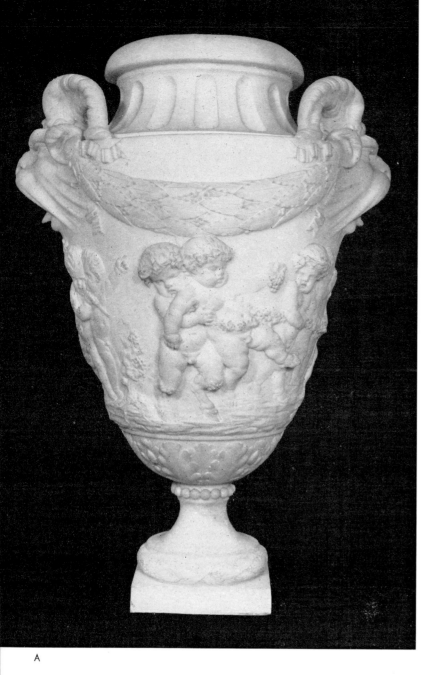

A

B

C

VASES were frequently produced in the XVIIIth century purely as decorations. Sometimes they were filled with floral bouquets either of wrought and gilt iron or mounted in gilt bronze. These subsidiary decorative elements were occasionally the work of the original sculptor himself, but more often they were supplied by anonymous bronze workers. Especially during the Louis XVI period, a wide variety of materials was employed: including marbles (verde-antico, turquoise-blue marble, brecchiated Aleppo marble, etc.), fluorspars, richly veined alabasters and agates.

A. CLODION: The body of this Louis XVI white marble vase is carved with cupids, in relief.

B. LOUIS XVI MARBLE VASE. The handles are formed by figures of a nymph and faun in gilt bronze.

C. CLODION: Terra-cotta vase decorated with a garland of roses. The neck is encircled with a pattern of interlacing design. The entire decoration exemplifies the Louis XVI style in its purest form.

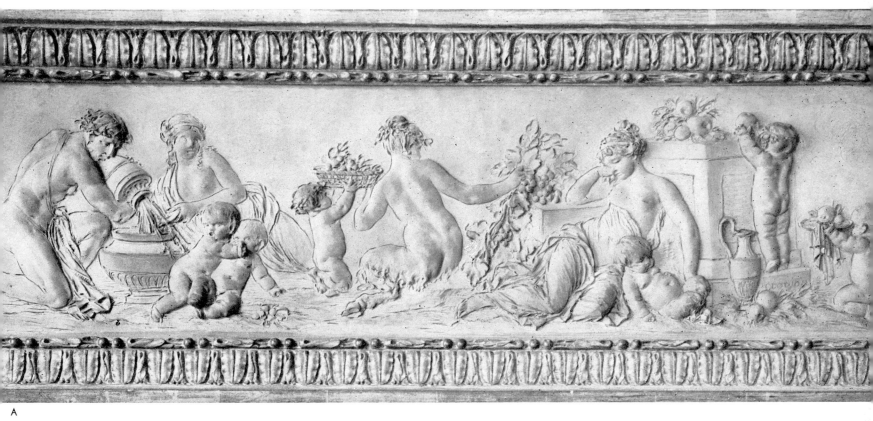

A

BAS-RELIEF is preeminently a decorative type of sculpture, and provided the lesser sculptors of the XVIIIth century with one of their finest mediums of expression. Two contrasting types, by different artists, are illustrated here.

A. CLODION: This bas-relief illustrates the sculptor's technique particularly well. The work is partly in relief and partly engraved in the terra-cotta, a process earning him great fame.

B. ADAM: An elaborate composition representing the "Martyrdom of St. Victor," carved for the chapel at Versailles. The subject is treated in the same grandiloquent style as was used for mythological paintings during the early years of the XVIIIth century.

B

A

C

THE MANTELPIECE played a very important role in interior decoration in the XVIIIth century. The imposing over-mantel compositions which were in favor for the grander chimneypieces of the XVIth and XVIIth centuries were replaced either by a painting or a mirror. Sculpture or bas-reliefs were used only on the architrave or the uprights of mantelpieces, though they were occasionally used above the mirror, for, owing to the difficulty in obtaining mirrors of sufficient size, a space was often left above, to be filled either by a painting or a carved relief.

ALL THE CHARACTERISTICS OF THE *Régence*, or early Louis XV chimneypiece, are to be seen in the one illustrated here (A): a mirror of two separate panels of glass, enclosed in a frame of gilt wood carved with rococo forms, whose style is repeated in the carving of the marble architrave. In the small fashionable rooms of the period, small andirons replaced the vast andirons usual in the monumental chimneypieces of the earlier age.

CHIMNEYPIECES are really only a projecting section of the wall decoration of the room; marble chimneypieces were often carved with decorative motifs similar to those of the wall paneling of the room in which they were placed. The one illustrated here (B) in marble in the Louis XV style comes from the State Apartments at Versailles and is carved with motifs exactly similar to those used on the wall paneling against which it is set.

B

MANTELPIECES

THIS LOUIS XVI MANTELPIECE from the Château de Maisons-Laffitte (E) is a return to the monumental style in fashion two hundred years earlier. The carved group surmounting it is a piece of monumental sculpture rather than an interior decoration. It is by the sculptor Lhuillier, who has here recreated something of the sumptuous effect of the grandiose chimneypieces used in the grand reception rooms of the Renaissance period.

GILT BRONZE was used to enrich chimneypieces just as it was used to decorate the finest furniture of the period. The gilt bronze caryatid set against the upright of this Louis XV chimneypiece (C) is of similar character to the corner mounts of a chest of drawers by Cressent, just as the rococo motifs in the center of its architrave recall the decoration of the lambrequin in the center of the lower edge of a sumptuous piece of furniture of the same type.

CARYATIDS play a natural role in the sculptural decoration of mantelpieces. The pair which support this Louis XVI chimneypiece (D) from the royal library at Bagatelle are in the purest late Louis XVI style, as are the other decorative motifs of the piece: thyrses, laurel wreaths, floral pendants and pastoral trophies.

E

D

DECORATIVE SCULPTURE is seen at its finest in this chimney piece (F) dating from the Louis XVI period, in the Palace of Fontainebleau. The caryatids were carved by Boizot and their gilt bronze decoration is fine enough to have been the work of some great bronzeworker like Gouthière. A last trace of XVIIIth century grace lingers in these late products of the *Ancien Régime*; such things were soon to be replaced by the chilly sphinxes and nude gods of antiquity which came into fashion at the beginning of the Empire period.

F

191

DECORATIVE SCULPTURE received what were perhaps its greatest opportunities in the ornamentation of panels carved in low relief enclosed within the tops of door frames; in the cresting of mirrors; and in the friezes of rooms, which were often carved with scrolls. Play of light and shade was needed to obtain the best effects, and the sculptor had to calculate matters very nicely, taking into consideration not only position and the degree of relief required, but also the way the light would fall from the adjacent windows in the room.

THIS "GYPSERIE," or plaster work in relief, from a house in Provence, is a perfect example of the type of sculpture intended to achieve its effect by the play of light and shade. It also manages to provide a unifying element linking the paneling of the walls to the moldings of the ceiling. Although rather late in date, this relief is in fact a return to the Louis XV manner. Its pastoral style derives from Boucher's paintings and is enclosed in scrolls and rococo forms typical of the mid-XVIIIth century.

THE FOUR SEASONS were often chosen for the decoration of carved over-doors, for there were usually exactly four doors in a room. In the one illustrated here, the allegoric figure representing "Summer" is in fairly high relief so that it is picked out by the light from the window. The artist has treated the other allegoric figure in very low relief, so as not to distract attention from the principal figure. The composition is in perfect accord with the rest of the room's Louis XVI décor.

THIS RELIEF HAS BEEN INSPIRED entirely by the contemporary taste for Pompeian decoration. The draped figures bear amphoræ and classic torches. The extremely low relief employed here makes this panel look very much like painted wall decorations of the period. Paintings, using "trompe-l'œil" effects, were often placed in the archways over doors, and rendered in monotones imitating the different textures of marble, stone or stucco.

DECORATIVE SCULPTURE

SCULPTURE has always been an integral feature in interior decoration. Careful architects always planned rooms, halls and staircases with their ultimate sculptural decoration in mind, often designing niches especially proportioned to the statues, vases, urns, fountains and stoves they were destined to house.

THE CAREFUL DESIGN of this hallway, with its staircase of matched white stone, admirably sets off the delicate arabesques of the iron balustrade. The sculptured pieces—Sigisbert Adam's XVIIIth century statue at the foot of the stairs, and the carved urn in the vestibule niche—complete the effect.

THE DECORATIVE STYLE of the Louis XVI period is seen at its best and most typical in the walls of the dining room at the Château du Marais. Stone, marble, bronze, porphyry and lead are each employed for this purpose and harmonize admirably with one another. Within a niche, a figure of the goddess Pomona is standing on a faience stove decorated in relief with cupids sacrificing at a classical altar. There are medallions enclosed in the oak panels over the doors and similar ones enclosed within pendant laurel swags at the top of each of the wall panels. An extremely beautiful wall cistern of gilt lead stands beside the door.

INTERIOR DECORATION

The Interior Decoration in the XVIIIth Century

The "appartement" *, which consisted of a series of rooms grouped together in part of a dwelling house, made its first appearance in the XVIIIth century.

Up to then, architectural ideas were generally based on concepts of symmetry. The center of a house was always given over to the staircase. Grouping rooms into separate suites became possible only when it became customary to place the staircase at one end of the building.

The changes in social life which took place during the XVIIIth century made the "appartement" ever more of a necessity. First and foremost among these was the new demand for comfort. The creation of the "appartement" was therefore a primary problem for architects of the period.

At the very beginning of the century, reports of the "Académie Royale d'Architecture" mention that "there is no proper place for beds in rooms as they are designed today; the position generally allocated to them is not sufficient to accommodate a bed comfortably." The same care for comfort

*The word "appartement" is not quite the equivalent of the modern word "apartment." "Suite" comes closer to the meaning.

is found again in relation to the other rooms: the drawing-room, the ante-chamber, the small dressing-rooms, cabinets and studies. For the first time care is taken to place the chimney in the position best suited to heat the room efficiently. Another of the reports of a session of the "Académie" reads : "The Company (that is to say the architect members) judges that it is at least as necessary that care should be taken in the internal arrangement of rooms as in the decoration of exteriors of houses."

Sometimes ten or twenty different suites existed in a single château. At Versailles it was customary to give them special names: the gaming rooms were called "Africa," those of the King "Europe," Madame's were known as "Asia," those of Mme. de Maintenon, "America." At the beginning of the century the "appartement" was merely a living room, a place in which to rest in privacy, hence the common expression: "withdrawing into one's own apartments."

The "appartement" was neither so complete nor so self-contained as a modern flat, although it had a very well-defined purpose. The "appartement de parade," which corresponds to what we call today the reception rooms, included the finest rooms in the house. The service suite included the kitchen, etc., then there was the bathroom suite and suites for husband and wife. All formed a part of a grouping of rooms which in time became customary. In his "Turkish Letters" Sainte-Foix wrote, "Husband and wife have their

In this Louis XVI dining room the woodwork is the chief factor determining the style of the room and the arrangement of the furniture. Panels over the doors are decorated with carved fish, vegetables, fruit and game. The rectilinear lines of the Louis XVI furnishings are emphasized by the geometric pattern of the tile flooring.

[Th]is large salon is a triumph of interior deco[ra]tion. Its painted panels are the work of Chris[top]he Huet, who used a combination of birds and [chi]noiseries as his decorative motifs. The chairs [ar]e covered with Beauvais tapestries, patterned [wi]th subjects from La Fontaine's "Fables." [Th]e fire screen is shaped exactly like the backs [of] the chairs, and is also covered with tapestry. (Color plate opposite.)

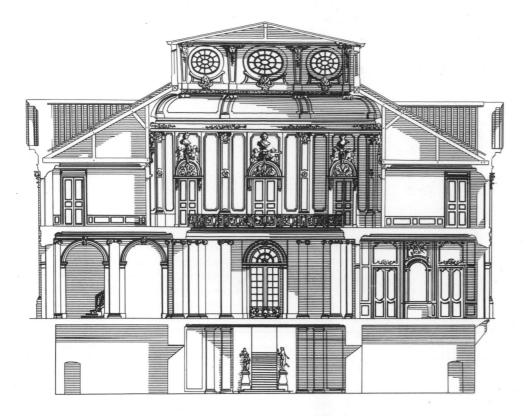

This cross-section of an XVIIIth century house *shows the arrangement of various rooms in relation to the central axis. A considerable area is occupied by the stair-well, both on the ground floor in the entrance hall, and in the gallery on the first floor. This is due to the necessity for lighting both from the roof. As a consequence, the living rooms are very much reduced in size, and the arrangements for passing from one to another are anything but convenient. If the staircase had been built at one end of the house it would have allowed for a very much more satisfactory arrangement of rooms.*

separate suites. It is in Madame's rooms that company is received and games are played, and it is there that one laughs and amuses oneself. The tenants are received in the 'appartement' of the husband, and it is there that business is transacted with creditors or money is borrowed from money lenders. In fact it is there that the endless intrigues and agitations are carried on in order to raise enough money to allow the owners to go on living in this luxurious fashion.''

The social life of the period naturally dictated the development of contemporary decoration and brought into existence the type of room well-adapted to the new social tendencies which arose almost immediately after the death of Louis XIV: the love of luxury, intimacy and pleasure. In just the same way the lavish character of living arrangements in the previous reign had been an emanation of the personality of the King himself. Now, a wider society dictated fashion; decoration became more graceful, more homely, and more pleasing.

The custom of receiving guests in the bedroom went out of fashion. Small rooms, like the boudoir, the study or the rest room, made their appearance. Chimneypieces surmounted by mirrors replaced the monumental constructions of an earlier age; the carved wood paneling of the walls left spaces which were filled with paintings of a gallant character, or with pastoral themes, or scenes of daily life; but paintings that always reflected a happy and carefree mode of existence.

The desire to build pleasant houses and pavilions where the owners could escape from the burdens of daily life, and do exactly as they pleased, represents quite a new phase in social life. Similarly, the rooms where they spent their daily life were supplied with new refinements of comfort and elegance.

Architects vied with one another to devise new forms and settings which would appeal to a society continually demanding more and more refinement.

There was no distinction such as exists today between the painters and sculptors as artists, and their colleagues, the decorators. Both thought of themselves as craftsmen. It seemed quite natural that great painters like Boucher or Huet should paint doors, or that an artist like Lancret should decorate the wall paneling of a room.

Naturally, there were those who still lived an unfashionable life in unfashionable houses, a life linked with the traditions of the age of Louis XIV. These, like their equivalents today, deplored the "decadence" of modern architecture, complaining

that architects were no longer interested in building palaces and only thought "how to arrange a group of small rooms gracefully or how to decorate the wall paneling of a dining-room or a cabinet."

The rooms comprised in a suite remain much the same in our day as they were in the XVIIIth century. The drawing-room, the dining-room, the bedroom, the boudoir, only differ today in the fact that their sizes have changed and their style of decoration has altered. They still preserve much the same arrangement as in the XVIIIth century when the "appartement" comprised reception and living rooms.

Reception rooms:
The Drawing-Room

The drawing-room appeared as a completely new creation in the XVIIIth century with only a distant relationship to the state room of the XVIIth century, whose purpose and arrangement was based on those of Italian palaces.

In the previous century this room had usually been situated on the second floor. It was symmetrical on all sides and included a coved ceiling which was decorated with architectural ornaments and usually painted.

It was a cold and formal room with the furniture arranged in a row along the wall, flanking imposing side-tables of gilt wood. The center of the room was usually left free, though occasionally a small game table ("table à gibier"), as it was called, or a large marble-topped center table on a gilt wood base stood there. This drawing-room was used only for parties and public receptions: friends were generally received in the bedroom. In the XVIIIth century there were sometimes two drawing-rooms in a house, one for summer and one for winter use; later the great and the little drawing-rooms made their appearance. Under Louis XV the size of the drawing-room grew smaller and its comfort increased: its walls were covered with paneling, the chimneypieces, no longer the monumental constructions of the past, were generally only of elbow height or even lower and were surmounted by large wall mirrors. A great variety of different sorts of furniture was used in the drawing-room: chairs, sofas, game tables, and chests of drawers were all very much in vogue at the period. In these rooms the emphasis was on hospitality: Mme. de

Pompadour held her receptions at Bellevue in a drawing-room known as the "Salon de Compagnie."

Under Louis XVI this "Salon de Compagnie" became still more intimate and was often of a very luxurious and distinctive character. There would be a profusion of mirrors, the paneling would be decorated with gilding and richly chased gilt bronze wall lights would be affixed to the walls. More time was spent in rooms of this sort as the century proceeded and their furnishings became richer and more elaborate.

The Dining-Room

Under Louis XIV and Louis XV there was no room to which the function of a dining-room was definitely assigned. The table was laid either in the bed-chamber or in the ante-chamber.

The custom of taking one's meals in the ante-chamber continued for a long period; numerous advertisements of "appartements" for sale or to let have survived. These frequently mention amongst the rooms to let "an ante-chamber, suitable for use as a dining-room."

The dining-room proper, provided with permanent furniture for dining, made its appearance about 1750 and by the time that Louis XVI came to the throne it had grown customary for each suite of rooms to include one intended as a dining-room.

Certain decorative innovations accompanied the invention of this type of room; the walls were often veneered with marble and marble side-tables were an essential feature, serving as sideboards. In addition a fixed position would generally be assigned to a water-fountain or cistern and almost invariably another position, usually a niche, arranged for one of the faience stoves of the period (see p. 193 and 212). These stoves provided an opportunity for elaborate decoration and carving, etc., generally in the form of allegoric figures and usually concealing or disguising their utilitarian purpose. The ventilating chimney of the stove was often concealed within an obelisk or a pyramid; sometimes it took the form of a vase or a tree, while the body of the stove itself was frequently made to resemble a chest of drawers or a "chiffonnier." The water cistern or fountain was often placed in a niche which was generally opposite the one occupied by the stove. These fountains were of terra-cotta, marble or wood and were usually decorated with figures or marine animals. Their basin was generally in the form of a large shell supported by dolphins, rock work or foliage.

Dining-rooms were often circular or oval; the most luxurious had ceilings of cupola form. Curiously enough, the furniture of these dining-rooms was not at all as rich as the fixed decoration of the walls. This was probably because of the earlier tradition of using a simple plank of wood, set on trestles, as a dining-table. Just such a table would certainly have been set up in the ante-chamber or in the bedroom a few years earlier. As the table was always spread with a cloth, cabinet-makers took little trouble about its decoration which would, in any case, have been concealed by the folds of the tablecloth, which hung to the ground. Dining-room chairs were also very simple, often with the back and seat caned and frequently provided merely with a loose cushion covered with some strong material, usually leather.

This type of furniture suffered more than any other from regular use and was therefore constructed with greater solidity than the ordinary chair, giving it a certain simple, rustic character. Usually its frame was painted, the carved molding being emphasized by a deeper tone of the same color. The caning was also painted sometimes with a geometrical pattern or even more curiously with a landscape (see p. 60, B).

The Bedroom

Under Louis XIV, the bedroom was huge, and entirely lacking in intimacy. It was provided with a balustrade around the bed. It was a survival of the great parade-room of the past where the noblemen granted audiences. The bed was concealed behind curtains providing a space to undress.

Regularity and symmetry were a primary consideration in the design of the interiors of a house at the beginning of the XVIIIth century. This section of a house, taken through the staircase and the entrance hall, is a typical example of the arrangement of these two parts of a private house of the period. They lead to the ante-chamber and the rooms on the first floor. The wall paneling rises right up to the cornices without interruption and follows closely around any openings such as doors, etc. This project was designed by Robert de Cotte, First Architect to the King until 1733. He was one of the architects who did most to continue the influence of the XVIIth century well on into the XVIIIth.

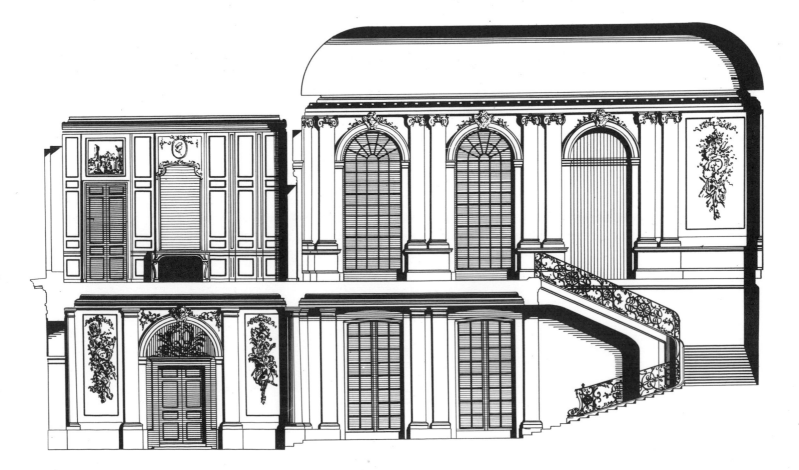

Under Louis XV the curtained bed gave place to the alcove. This consisted of a space cut out of one end of the room by means of two wooden partitions, one on each side of the bed, behind which were small cabinets or dressing-rooms. The bedroom itself became considerably smaller as a result of several little rooms being sub-divided out of it by means of partitions: the cabinet, the ante-chamber, the bathroom, the lavatory, etc. The bed was always left free from the wall on three sides, the foot invariably facing the window. When the bed was arranged parallel to the wall and set in an alcove exactly made to fit it, the room was described as a "chambre en niche" (bedroom with a niche).

More than in any other XVIIIth century room, the furniture of the bedroom depended on the skill and resource of the upholsterer. The bed itself naturally required a large quantity of upholstery of all sorts either in tapestry, silk or damask. The armchairs were thickly padded and more comfortable, as were the stools, seats and sofa. Crimson was the most fashionable color and was almost always edged with braiding and gold fringes. Towards the end of the century, green became the favorite color for the bedroom. Occasionally, a lady with fair coloring might prefer to have her bedroom decorated in blue. Under Louis XVI, the custom of receiving guests in the bedroom was abandoned. A new piece of furniture was added to the room; this was the "secrétaire," which allowed the owner to attend to correspondence or to work in the bedroom. Bedroom furniture became more and more important as time passed. Some idea of its richness may be gathered from the inventory of the objects seized in the bedroom of Mme. de Lafayette at the end of the century: "A bed, a chest of drawers, a bookcase with about two hundred volumes, eight small armchairs, two 'bergère' armchairs with cushions, three large armchairs, two window-curtains, a card-table, a tric-trac table, a mahogany table, a walnut table, six pictures, a panel of mirrors, a clock, two chimney lights, two wall-lights, two candlesticks."

Intimacy *is the note the owner has struck in the decoration of this library. The windows are glazed with old glass, whose colors vary from pane to pane. The 2,000 first editions in modern bindings in the bookcase are only one feature of the decoration. Elsewhere a variety of works of art have been disposed about the room including bronze horses, gold boxes and precious stones mounted in gold.*

The cheerful atmosphere *of this drawing-room owes much to the variety of carefully chosen colors used in its decoration. The walls are hung with silk bordered with blue and yellow braid; the festooned curtains and the firescreen contrast with the upholstery of the chairs. The whole forms a luminous, gay setting which softens the severe lines of the late XVIIIth century furniture.*

The Bathroom

Although Louis XIV was quite content to "clean his face with a cotton handkerchief soaked in spirits of wine," he installed a bathroom suite at Versailles which consisted of a combined bedroom and drawing-room, and the bathroom itself was supplied with two marble baths fitted with bronze taps.

In spite of this royal example, bathrooms, or indeed washing facilities of any sort, seldom went beyond a portable tin basin filled with spirits of wine. Nevertheless certain wealthy nobles did introduce similar arrangements into their private palaces.

At the beginning of the reign of Louis XV it was not customary to reserve a special room for the bath. A portable hip-bath was brought into the bedroom. The heavy wooden tubs lined with lead used at an earlier period were gradually replaced by lighter baths of beaten copper, an invention of

French coppersmiths and the ancestor of our modern bath.

In spite of these technical improvements, bathrooms remained rare; occasionally under Louis XVI the more luxurious town houses included a bathroom in which the walls were painted with aquatic scenes or decorated with carved paneling. In exceptional instances, the walls were covered with mirrors, which were then thought the height of luxury. The floor was generally of parquet, the bath itself shaped like a shell, a shoe or a sofa, and made of wood or marble or copper.

Decoration

The decoration of rooms comprised:

1. The fixed ornamentation, consisting of the wall paneling, the ceiling, the chimneypieces, the side-tables and the floor,

2. The mobile decoration, which consisted of the furniture and objets d'art. These included chairs, large pieces of furniture, bronzes, clocks, wall-hangings, curtains, etc.

The great care taken to harmonize the different elements of a room one with another at this period was due to another characteristic feeling of the times,—the love of a comfortable

The decoration of the walls *was regarded as a very important part of interior decoration in the XVIIIth century as can be seen from the three engravings reproduced here. They show the way in which the different parts of a single room were designed to harmonize one with another. From the "Régence" period onward, decorative motifs became curving and twisted. The carving of the chairs, sofas, tables, etc., placed against the wall was always similar to that of the paneling itself. The curving outline of the sofa, for instance, is echoed by that of the monumental wall mirror.*

Wall panels *between windows are symmetrical and match one another. A pier-table of gilt wood stands against each and is surmounted by a large wall mirror with a pair of wall lights with three branches affixed to the frame at each side. The window in the center is shown with its shutters half-open: these are decorated with carving intended to be seen from outside the house when the shutters are closed.*

An over-mantel mirror *replaced the great chimney-pieces surmounted by carved bas-reliefs used in earlier centuries. The mantelshelf itself was set somewhat lower in order to allow the mirror to be used as a looking-glass; this low mantelshelf soon began to be decorated with clocks, candlesticks, etc. Paintings were inserted into the panels over the doors in frames which match those of the mirrors and the panels between the windows. In addition to the fixed furnishings illustrated here, there was a great profusion of furniture and "objets d'art." Decorators of the period considered it indispensable that both types of decoration, fixed and mobile, should be of the same style and harmonize with one another.*

atmosphere. In the XVIIIth century it was thought indispensable, not only that the different elements of a single room should harmonize one with another, but that there should be harmony between the different rooms of a single house. Under Louis XV, house owners either destroyed their Louis XIV furniture or stored it in the attic. It would have seemed unthinkable to have objects dating from several different centuries side by side in the same room. (The taste for the "antique" is quite modern by comparison.)

It was because the Louis XV style borrowed nothing from the styles of the past, because it knew how to imprint its own individual personality on the artists of the Louis XV and the "Régence" period, that it is the most purely French of all styles. When the Louis XVI style appeared, its borrowings from the past were manifest, even though their interpretation remained sufficiently French to be considered a distinct style.

The Louis XVI style asserted the importance of the ornamental motif over the forms decorated, and this was a sign that the great epoch of the true French style had already ended. Still later, the fauns, thyrses, and classical masks of the Louis XVI style became nothing more than the components of a decorative repertory which had nothing specifically French about it.

The Walls

Under Louis XIV, walls were hung with various materials which not only concealed their coarsely finished surfaces but helped to keep the larger rooms warm. Tapestries were often used, and sometimes leather hangings of the type known as "Cordova," after the Spanish town of that name, although they were really of French manufacture; stamped velvet and damask were also used as wall hangings.

Under Louis XV, wall hangings of Louis XIV character passed out of fashion, to be replaced by wooden paneling carved with moldings and decorative sculpture, usually in natural unstained oak, or in painted and gilded beechwood. Although wooden paneling enjoyed a great vogue as a wall decoration in itself, it was sometimes enriched with paintings by Boucher, Oudry, Watteau or Huet, and occasionally the paneling was inset with panels of Chinese lacquer or its French substitute, "vernis Martin." At about the same time, the earliest painted wallpapers began to be imported from China, though they were not actually made of paper at all but of painted parchment. Bedrooms, especially in the provincial châteaux, had their walls hung with various textiles, usually either with Lyons silk or printed Indian cottons; the pattern invariably matched that of the bed hangings and window curtains. Finally, in the south of France, under Italian influence, stucco or "gypseries" in relief were often used on the walls. Leather hangings were generally used only in ante-chambers.

During the Louis XVI period, walls generally continued to be treated in much the same manner as in the previous reign. Towards the end of the century, however, the first pictorial wallpapers of European make began to appear. They were generally decorated with scenes containing figures or animals.

Ceilings

Under Louis XIV, ceilings were generally coffered and decorated with figure scenes in the Italian manner. Later, a single composition, usually of historical or mythological character, covered the whole surface. Decoration in the ornamental style originated by Audran or Bérain, or sometimes inspired by the work of greater men like Gillot, Watteau or Boucher, was often used in private houses in place of the mythological or historical compositions more appropriate to palaces.

Ceilings were generally white during Louis XV's reign and bordered by gilded or carved cornices; the only decoration was the central rose, from which a chandelier could be hung.

Under Louis XVI, the ceiling was even more simple. It rested directly on the cornice along the top of the paneling.

Throughout the century parquet flooring, consisting of sections of waxed oak assembled in various different patterns, was in use. The parquets of the palace of Versailles were justly celebrated and provided the inspiration for those elsewhere. Towards the end of the century additional imbricated patterns in mahogany were sometimes introduced into these parquets. Rugs and carpets, either from the East, or made in one of the French factories, such as the Savonnerie or the Gobelin factory, were spread on the floors. Parquet was invariably used for the floors of the reception rooms; floors of ante-chambers were flagged or paved with marble.

Under Louis XIV, tapestries, stamped velvets and damasks were the materials principally in use for the upholstery of chairs and for curtains. Upholstery was attached to the chairs with gilt-headed nails.

Under Louis XV, richly embroidered materials of all sorts were used, as well as tapestries or cut velvet, and sometimes leather upholstery was employed for desk chairs.

Under Louis XVI, silks, either plain, striped or with a pattern of floral sprays, were very much in fashion as were Aubusson tapestries. Caning or leather was usually employed on dining-room chairs. The upholstery on the majority of Louis XV and Louis XVI chairs was mounted on detachable frames which could be removed and replaced with an alternative upholstery for winter or summer use. Window curtains generally matched the upholstery of the chairs.

Under Louis XIV, a good deal of gilding and silvering was employed on the walls and furniture. This contrasted well with the bright colors of the furnishing materials, which were usually blue, red or golden yellow.

Under Louis XV, pastel colors were used for the walls: pale green, blue-gray, gray and cream. The wall paneling was almost always painted in two colors and often the moldings were gilded; green and lilac, pink and white, yellow and silver, blue and white, green and blue, green and gold were the favorite combinations. The colors of furnishing fabrics were generally rather stronger, red being specially favored in bedrooms but very little used in the living rooms.

Color was much less often employed under Louis XVI than it had been under Louis XV; the walls were generally of a sober character and usually painted white and gold, the hangings being of crimson, yellow or, sometimes, green. Sky-blue became very fashionable circa 1785.

The fireplace, the sole means of heating rooms for many centuries, was decorated in the style appropriate to its particular period.

At the beginning of the century the monumental chimneys of the XVIIth century began to be abandoned. Nevertheless, chimneypieces continued to be richly decorated and were often of marble mounted with gilt bronze in a manner similar to the finest furniture of the period. Some of them were decorated at their ends, with two caryatids holding up the branches of a candelabrum. An important characteristic of these chimneypieces was the absence of the immense hoods used in the past, and the fact that the fireplace itself grew smaller and smaller. Thus the chimneypiece came to form an integral part of the wall paneling and was frequently carved in the same style as the surrounding wall. The inside of the fireplace was usually lined with pink brick, of faience tiles, or cast-iron plaques. In addition to marble and stone, terracotta was sometimes used in the decoration of chimneypieces with particularly delicate and elegant effects.

The mantelshelf was made lower to permit a panel of

mirror to be placed above it. Decorative objects were placed on the mantelshelf in the XVIIIth century, much in the manner of those used today, the normal furnishing consisting of a clock, flanked by a pair of candelabra or vases of some sort.

An important improvement was made in the mechanism of the chimney itself. The possibility of closing the chimney opening when there was no fire had been explored in the past in order to prevent the unpleasant draughts that this huge opening caused. All sorts of means had been employed and it is known that at the end of the XVIIth century the custom of closing the chimney opening in the summer with painted panels was largely abandoned; instead they were replaced with perspectives painted on canvas or with rocks on which flowers and vegetation were allowed to grow. Traps intended to close the chimney were invented in 1745. In that year a model was demonstrated by which sheets of metal could be raised or lowered across the chimney opening.

Lighting

All the different means of lighting available in the XVIIth century employed candles. They consisted, of wall-lights, sconces, etc., affixed to the wall, chandeliers hanging from the ceiling or portable lighting fitments: candlesticks, etc.

These were made of gilded wood, or of gilt bronze. This last material was invariably used for the finest wall-lights. Elaborate candelabra or "girandoles" with rock-crystal drops which reflected the light, stood on fixed or mobile "torchères."

Chandeliers of bronze or rock crystal were fitted with a large number of lights; the multiplicity of these greatly enriched the effect of a reception or a supper party. Candelabra, portable candlesticks, and chamber candlesticks were naturally used in workrooms or bedrooms. In order to move from one room to the other a candlestick whose light was protected by a glass shade was generally used; this is the type which is generally known today as a garden candlestick.

Goldsmiths played an important part in the manufacture of lighting fittings. Their skill resulted in the production of splendid candelabra, candlesticks, wall-lights, etc. In these too, the cut and polished surfaces of the metal and the chasing of the relief decoration were deliberately designed to amplify the effect of the light by multiplying reflections and sparkle.

The XVIIIth Century Style of Decoration in the Present

The esteem in which the XVIIIth century is now held is evident from the large number of attempts which have been made to recreate XVIIIth century interiors in modern houses. The fact that interior decorators and art lovers select this style is not due to an arbitrary choice; they tend to make use of the furniture and decoration of the XVIIIth century because the remarkable qualities of its material blend particularly well with modern settings. The proportions of the rooms, the furniture and especially of the chairs, remain just as utilitarian today as they were then, because they were devised for a mode of living which allowed "the pleasures of life" ("douceur de vivre") to be enjoyed around the family hearth and in conditions of privacy, which have not changed in essentials since then. The stylistic preferences of an individual owner can be seen in the manner in which he has adapted the XVIIIth century idiom to his own surroundings. It is only in exceptionally costly modern reconstructions that a true picture of the luxury which predominated all through the XVIIIth century can really be obtained.

Modern decoration can easily be based on XVIIIth century styles. A wealth of contemporary documents about the period has survived plus a considerable number of the material artifacts of the decoration, as well as much furniture.

It is still quite possible to create a harmonious interior by adopting some of the elements of XVIIIth century decoration in a modern interior.

The unusually bright colors of this bedroom are exactly in the taste of the Louis XV period, although the fact may appear surprising today. The bed with its canopy in the style known as "à la polonaise" is entirely hung with contemporary cherry-red silk, a color which stands out against the bright blue of the wall paneling into which large panels of printed Indian cotton have been inserted. The pattern of these cottons consists of branches of foliage and flowers.

An alcove gives this bedroom its highly individual character. It is hung with a cream damask patterned in green, dating from the "Régence" period; a day-bed with two ends is set into it. The color of the damask contrasts strongly with the all-over blue of the wall paneling and the yellow of the curtains. Although this bedroom is large, the effect of the contrast of colors is to convey an atmosphere of intimacy. In the foreground is a lady's small writing table which was made by the master cabinetmaker Peridiez. *(Color plate at right.)*

IN THE XVIIIth CENTURY the great drawing-room was never used as a living-room. It was intended for formal receptions only. It is often treated almost as though it were a theatrical setting. The veined marble pilasters and the round over-doors in the room illustrated above both foreshadow the taste for antique art.

PAINTED PANELING gave an atmosphere of luxury and intimacy to the small boudoirs of Louis XV houses. Those illustrated in color opposite are painted with Italian Comedy scenes by Gillot. Note the great delicacy of the treatment of the paneling above and below the central panels. (Château de Courances.)

DRAWING-ROOMS (GRANDS SALONS)

DURING THE XVIIITH CENTURY the use of mirrors became more and more fashionable as the technique of making large mirrors was gradually mastered. Eventually this decorative system was abused, for it became the fashion to create " mirror rooms, " the walls of which were entirely covered with mirrors. Mirrors were often framed into the paneling of the wall itself either over chimneypieces or as part of the decoration of walls and doors. Their effect was to increase the apparent size of the room. The example illustrated below, in which a large mirror is set into the white and gold paneling of a wall carved with rococo ornament, was actually made at Paris in 1770 for the French Embassy at Vienna. The Régence chest of drawers with gilt bronze sprays which are raised to form the handles, is signed by Cressent.

TOWARDS THE END OF THE REIGN OF LOUIS XV there was a tendency for wall decoration to become rather more severe, thus foreshadowing the new styles which were to triumph in the following period. Although the white and gold paneling illustrated (right) was actually executed during the reign of Louis XV, its simple architectural lines clearly relate it to the Louis XVI style. The paneling forms the background for a set of Louis XV chairs of exceptional quality. The six armchairs with richly carved frames of gilded wood are stamped by Nicolas Heurtaut, and come from a château in Normandy. On the wall hangs a Beauvais tapestry: " A Lesson in Flute-playing. " Gilt bronze plays an important part in the decoration of this room; the wall lights attached to the paneling, the candlesticks and mounted porcelain vases visible in the foreground of the room are all of this material.

(color plate opposite.)

THE TASTE FOR INTIMACY and comfort so characteristic of the Louis XVI period is present in every feature of this room with its combination of wall paneling and elegant textiles. The delicately carved paneling of the walls (the work of the brothers Rousseau) includes an alcove in which there is a bed, spread with silk embroidered with flowers in silver thread. At the back of the alcove hangs a large decorative panel of embroidered silk. The Louis XVI rug is woven in the Salembier style. The two Louis XVI chairs "à la Reine" carry the stamp of the cabinetmaker Demay.

THE WALLS OF THIS OVAL BOUDOIR are covered with Louis XV paneling, painted olive-green, with moldings accented in antique gold. A panel of mirrors, set into a false alcove, increases the apparent size of the room. Small rooms, like this one, were often decorated with mirrors and pictures. The careful balance established here, between the proportions of the room and those of the furniture and bibelots, results in an overall impression of ease and harmony. The style of décor is Louis XV throughout, with the single exception of the small table between the sofas.

LOUIS XV ROOMS are particularly charming because of their low ceilings. Their beautifully carved woodwork makes them look like exquisite jewel-boxes. The picture at left shows a room, reconstructed in Paris, containing the original white and gold paneling from Mme. de Pompadour's boudoir in the Château de Belleville. All of the furniture once belonged to royalty: the guitar was owned by Princess Élisabeth d'Orléans, Duchesse de Lorraine. The little Louis XV vanity is set with plaques of Sèvres porcelain.

THE KNOT, THE GARLAND, the medallion and the beribboned floral bouquet are typical motifs of Louis XVI décor. They give a somewhat more feminine character to interiors than the solemn volutes and scrolls characteristic of the late Louis XV style. A Parisian interior decorator has recreated the atmosphere of a late XVIIIth century drawing-room in a setting of Adam-green Louis XVI wall paneling which provides an admirable background for fine furniture dating from the same period. The chest of drawers, for instance, below the central panel, is by Riesener, one of Queen Marie-Antoinette's favorite cabinetmakers. As was sometimes the practice at the period, the decorator has not hesitated to mix medallion-backed Louis XVI chairs with Louis XV armchairs upholstered with a material which matches the color of the paneling. These pieces are stamped by Nogaret. Even the back of the chair-frames (e.g. the armchair in the foreground at left) is carved with incised decoration, a very rare feature, seldom found except on chairs which were intended for royal palaces or important clients.

NEO-CLASSICAL TASTE tended to give interiors a very architectural character, as can be seen in the Louis XVI room illustrated at the left: motifs such as architectural friezes, balusters, pilasters, columns and capitals are enclosed within a framework of geometric design entirely based on straight lines and right angles. While the paneling of the Louis XV period rises in uninterrupted slender lines from floor to ceiling, that of the Louis XVI period was often cut by horizontals which accentuated its monumental character. Here the over-doors are no longer merely enclosed by a prolongation of the uprights at the sides, but rather they become isolated members, resting on a cornice supported on two console-brackets.

BOUDOIRS

THIS LATE XVIIIth CENTURY BOUDOIR has been preserved absolutely intact ever since it was created. The paneling comes from a splendid old house in the Chaussée d'Antin which was then a very fashionable quarter. The simplicity of its form was inspired by antique art, as can be clearly seen in the slender shape of the columns painted to imitate marble, the cornice carved with ovoli and palmettes, the sky-blue dome of the ceiling and the parquetry of repeated cubes on the floor. The alcove is hung with pink silk and contains a divan upholstered in blue.

SMALL CIRCULAR ROOMS were particularly fashionable in the second half of the XVIIIth century. The paneled entrance hall (opposite) comes from the former Hôtel Ferrari and is an example of the purest type of late Louis XVI decoration, with its denticulated cornice, and its over-door panels carved and painted in the style of Salembier. Two large vases of blue faience mounted with gilt bronze are set into the round niches, and lighting is concealed behind the small sofa with its frame of gilded wood.

THIS IS A GENUINE LOUIS XV DINING-ROOM. The walls are entirely paneled and painted white with the exception of two shallow niches painted a delicate blue, one of which (illustrated above) contains a remarkable water cistern in the form of a classical tank surmounted by a spreading palm-tree. Only the skirting boards were altered during the Empire period. The original black and white marble flag-stones of the floor remain intact. The Louis XV chairs signed by Lelarge are covered with red leather and their frames are painted the same white as the paneling.

DINING-ROOM FURNITURE always requires a really worthy background.
Such a setting has been provided in this Parisian apartment where the architecture of the room has been modified by adding a modillion cornice and a
paneled skirting board. The walls are sheathed in a veined pink marble and
hung with mirrors and painted canvases of a decorative character arranged
alternately and both framed in gilt wood. These relatively simple features
are sufficient to recreate the atmosphere of the period and provide a worthy
setting for the chairs with frames painted gray and upholstered with natural-
colored leather and for the marble-topped side table. The elegant drapery
of the bay-window harmonizes with the rest of the decoration of the room.

1. THE INTERIOR DECORATION of Provençal houses is often of great refinement, but it is seldom totally devoid of a certain rustic quality. In this library no attempt has been made to conceal the supporting beams in the ceiling, and the floor is made of the red tile so typical in the farmhouses of Southern France. Exotic woodwork of ebony and mahogany was highly appreciated in the late XVIIIth century and can be found particularly in the Bordeaux area and in Provence. The arrangement of the paintings on the walls is typical of the way "picture galleries" were hung of this period. (Château de la Verdière, Aix-en-Provence.)

2. IN THE CHATEAUX OF SOUTHERN FRANCE, wood-carved wall-paneling was often replaced by remarkably delicate "gypseries:" carved and molded plaster-work in relief. The plaster-work illustrated here, from the drawing-room of the Château de la Verdière, dates from 1760 and consists of rococo moldings designed to frame the Flemish tapestries. The painted frames of the Louis Quinze and Louis Seize chairs (in the provinces it was quite usual to mix styles in this way) blend with the colors of the plaster-work.

ITALIAN PLASTERERS who were highly skilled craftsmen did a great deal of work in Provence because of the fine quality of the gypsum obtained in the quarries in the neighbourhood of Aix. At La Verdière their technical abilities were allowed free rein, and relief decoration in plaster not only covers the walls but even runs over into the coved cornice of the ceiling. Garlands and scrolls of the greatest delicacy in white on an apricot-colored ground, run all round the hall whose walls are inset with large canvas panels painted to imitate Genoese embossed leather with a white ground.

IN THE XVIIITH CENTURY even simple provincial craftsmen could sometimes achieve striking results as decorators. This huge sideboard at the Château de La Verdière was the work of a mere local carpenter who boldly harmonized the complex forms of the sideboard to blend with the lines of the wall decorations. The paneling of the cupboard doors in the sideboard stand out in white on a background of two tones of gray and exactly reproduces the moldings of the doors. The fleur-de-lys at the top of the piece is the emblem of the counts of Provence.

THIS DRAWING-ROOM paneling is painted in no less than seven different tones of gray (color plate opposite). The long interval which passed before a Paris fashion penetrated into the provinces can be seen in the furniture of this room which is signed by Gourdin Père: it is still in the Louis XV style, although the setting of the room (wall paneling, side tables, chimneypiece, etc.) is in the fully-developed Louis XVI style. (Château de Montgeoffroy.)

IN THE XVIIIth CENTURY architects took care to plan sets of rooms so that the door openings were arranged one behind the other, usually terminating in a door or a French window opening on to the garden so that impressive perspective effects were obtained. The Louis XV furniture, the wall-clock and barometer both framed in gilded wood, the parquet floor "in the Versailles style," are part of the traditional decoration of a French country house.

WHEN BOOKCASES are set into the paneling, the books form a part of the decorative setting. In the room illustrated above the bindings are surrounded by paneling of a Louis XVI character with a cornice of architectural design; a more lively note is struck by the elegant gilt bronze wall lights, mounted on the paneling.

THIS LIBRARY (right) is a modern interpretation of a Louis XV example: the simple light-colored oak paneling follows the arrangement of the walls exactly, and its color is heightened by contrast with the white of the marble chimneypiece and the heavy window-curtains of red velvet. The total effect is one of warmth, combining modern comfort with traditional design. (Château de Vandes.)

EVEN THE MOST CHARACTERLESS type of room can be given style by modifying its interior. The Louis XVI motifs of the white and gold paneling illustrated here (color plate at left) suggest the style of the period rather than copy it exactly. The bright colors of the curtains and the play of the reflections in the mirrors emphasize the sumptuous character of the furnishings: chairs by Séné upholstered with natural-colored leather in the style known as "à la reine;" the Savonnerie carpet woven with the arms of the Abbey of St. Denis; together with original plaster sculptures by Houdon and Chinard.

THE TYPICAL LOUIS XV STUDY is usually walled with paneling of a distinguished character. The one illustrated is in a chateau in Normandy built during the middle of the XVIIIth century by the owner of a foundry (the emblems of Mercury and Minerva carved in the oval medallions of the wall-paneling are a discreet allusion to his profession). The four bookcases built into the walls on each side of the chimneypiece were not an uncommon arrangement at that period. (Château d'Omonville.)

CANOPIED BEDS were in fashion all through the XVIIIth century. They are a reminder of the not-too-distant days when it was customary to receive one's visitors in the bedroom. Canopies can be of varying degrees of elaboration but must always be hung with the same material as used on the bed. The contemporary "toile de Jouy" which is printed with pink designs on a white ground—used in the bedroom illustrated at left—was clearly intended for a country residence. The wall paneling is simply painted a plain white and contrasts strongly with the rich pattern of the elaborate parquetry floor; it also emphasizes the importance of the bed, the principal piece of furniture in the room. (Château d'Omonville.)

BEDS set lengthwise along the wall, somewhat like sofas, were a first step towards a more informal conception of the bedroom. Here the head and foot panels of the bed are linked by a third along the inner side, all three being upholstered with painted material like that used on the draped canopy above. The light design of the canopy is in keeping with the feminine character of this room, with its pink and white paneling. As was often the case in the past, the dressing table consists merely of a simple table of unstained wood hung with a double thickness of some antique material. (Château d'Omonville.)

SOMETIMES A BED placed within an alcove is even then surmounted by a canopy. This is another step in the evolution of the bedroom towards a greater air of elegance. Towards the end of the XVIIIth century, cupboards and small chambers were cut out of the corners and sides of the room to form store rooms, bath rooms, etc., thus reducing the size of the room itself. This room in a Louis XVI château retains all its original character. The bed, with its curious dome-shaped canopy, is hung with the floral cretonne used on the walls of the alcove. This is a typical bedroom of the period as it appears so often in contemporary engravings by Baudoin and others. (Château de Léchères.)

THE INNER WALLS of a traditional Louis XV alcove are generally hung with a flowered material which gives it a warm and comfortable character. The bed is simply placed against the back wall as in the example below. The design of its covering should match that of the background which, in its turn, should contrast with the wall paneling, usually painted a light color. (Château d'Omonville.)

IN THE SMALLER TYPE OF LOUIS XVI BEDROOM, curtains and upholstery are used to create a soft, quiet atmosphere. This four-poster bed is hung with curtains and pelmets of the same material as is used on the walls: its design of roses is enclosed in a trellis-work pattern. The entire furnishings of this chateau were ordered as a single commission by the original owner. Similar pieces of furniture are found in all the rooms. The chest of drawers veneered with tulip-wood and of a provincial neo-classic character was made by Garnier. The bergère arm-chair in the late Louis XV style is stamped by Gourdin. (Château de Montgeoffroy.)

AN INTERIOR SETTING, characteristic of the revolutionary period, has been created in a modern Parisian flat by means of an enormous curtain of satin, striped in gray, green, pink and black. This wall decoration strongly accentuates the style of the furniture which, with its uninterrupted rectilinear outlines, foreshadows the Directoire style. Pictures and books have been deliberately arranged asymmetrically in order to soften the stiffness of the setting.

THE ATMOSPHERE OF THE XVIIIth CENTURY is one that collectors find particularly attractive today. The perfection of forms created throughout the period makes it possible to assemble those of different dates side by side in the same room. In the drawing room illustrated opposite (color plate) there are Louis XVI armchairs flanking a Louis XV table. Bronzes of an earlier date stand on the *Régence* side table in the background.

LIST OF ILLUSTRATIONS

Color plates are indicated by heavy type

225

TAPESTRIES, CARPETS AND TEXTILES

SCULPTURE

INTERIOR DECORATION

GLOSSARY

PAINTING

Chinoiserie: a word used to describe objects or paintings in the Chinese style, but generally of a fantastic character and imitating oriental originals very freely rather than copying them exactly. The word **Turquerie** is similarly used to describe objects or paintings in the Turkish taste.

Fête Galante, a painting of a half real, half fantastic character, its setting being that of carefree rural life, and its costume largely borrowed from the Italian comedy with its Pierrots, Pantaloons, Scaramouches, etc. It descends through Rubens from the classical idylls of sixteenth century Venice but was developed with great lyrical intensity by Watteau with whose name this type of painting is imperishably associated.

Trompe l'Œil, a painting or a piece of marquetry representing everyday objects with such fidelity as to be actually deceptive and producing an effect of startling reality.

FURNITURE

Bergère, a comfortable type of armchair with rounded back, padded arms and upholstered sides. The shape varies considerably and is sometimes supplied with wings also. The type made its appearance in France about 1725 while the same word anglicized as "berger" is occasionally found in English.

Bombé, literally blown-out, and hence used to describe forms which are bulbous on two axes.

Chiffonier, a piece of furniture containing a series of drawers one above the other intended to hold papers, jewels or "chiffons." Smaller and taller than a chest of drawers and more like an unusually narrow English tall-boy.

Ébéniste, literally one who works in ebony, and by extension one who works in veneers. In practice the word corresponds very roughly to the English word "cabinet-maker."

En-cas table, a small occasional table, which could be used for a wide variety of purposes.

Espagnolette or Espagnolette Head, as a decorative motif consists of a female head backed by a large, stiff lace collar of a type favored by Spanish women. A device popularised by Gillot and his pupil, Watteau, in the early decades of the eighteenth century; it was adapted from them by furniture designers and appears particularly on *Régence* writing tables and chests of drawers.

Guéridon or Guéridon table — a small piece of furniture intended to support some form of light such as a candlestick or candelabrum. The early ones often took the form of a carved figure of a negro and the name derives from a celebrated Moorish galley-slave, Guéridon.

Lambrequin, a decorative motif sometimes in the form of a piece of drapery sometimes imitating the designs of wrought iron, or lace; generally with a shaped or scalloped edge often bordered with a fringe. It can be chased, engraved, applied in relief or painted.

Lit à la Polonaise, a type of bed with a domed central canopy supported on a curved iron framework resting on upright posts at each corner of the bed. The supporting framework was concealed with curtains of the same material as the cover of the canopy which was itself usually surmounted with a plume of feathers.

Menuisier, literally, one who works on a small scale (in wood). The word embraced those who made chair-frames, carved side-tables, etc; i.e. woodwork which was not veneered, and it corresponds very roughly with the English word "carpenter." It also included those who prepared paneling and even timbers for the construction of a building.

Quatrefoil, a four-cusped decorative figure formed of four leaves arranged at right angles in relation to a central button or circle. The motif is generally enclosed within a geometrical figure.

Torchère, similar to a guéridon, but taller.

Transitional style, the name given to the style intermediate between the Louis XV and Louis XVI styles. Its forms are generally of a more or less Louis XV character and its decoration neo-classic. It begins to appear about 1755 and its gradual development into the full Louis XVI style is complete by about 1770.

Vernis Martin, a genre name for all varnishes and lacquers applied to interior decoration, carriages, furniture, fans, small boxes etc. It derives its name from the brothers Martin who in 1730 and again in 1740 were granted patents allowing them a monopoly to make lacquer in relief in the style of China and Japan.

CERAMICS

Barbeau: the common country name for the ordinary cornflower, hence, by extension, used to describe the simple pattern of cornflowers so frequently used on porcelain produced at Sèvres and the various Paris porcelain factories. The word Bouquet is similarly used to describe an all-over floral pattern.

Biscuit: a piece of white porcelain as it emerges from the oven before being glazed or colored in any way. It is chiefly used to describe the groups and statuettes which were produced at Sèvres and became very fashionable from the middle of the XVIIIth century onwards, both when produced in soft paste and hard paste porcelain.

Combed Decoration: a motif used especially in the border of plates and dishes in the form of parallel curving lines of color drawn towards the edge as though with a comb. The color is strongest at the edge and gradually fades and blends with the color of the background on the inner part.

Faience with "High Temperature" Colors: the decoration is painted on the glaze and both are fired at the same time and at a high temperature. Only a few of the metallic oxides used as a basis for ceramic colors can stand up to so high a temperature without blackening or changing color, and as a result only a limited range of colors is available, though these are generally bright. No retouching is possible and, as a result, the painting is usually bold and vigorous.

Faience with "Low Temperature" Colors: the decoration is painted on top of the glaze after it has been already fired once. This gives a double advantage; firstly, a much greater precision and delicacy is possible in the painting, and retouching can be easily done; secondly, a vastly greater range of colors is available, since they fuse at a much lower temperature. A wide variety of half-tones, shades, effects and mixtures of colors is thus possible. The "low temperature" process was discovered by Paul Hannong at Strasbourg about 1748 and enjoyed immediate and widespread success.

Kakiemon, the name of a Japanese family of potters loosely associated with a type of white porcelain decorated in bright blues, reds, greens etc. with free fluent designs of flowers, foxes and other animals, "hedges" etc. First imported into Europe by the Dutch in the XVIIth century when it was incorrectly known as "Korean ware" and frequently copied by the first European makers of porcelain.

Kaolin: a clay of a special type essential for the production of hard-paste porcelain. When finely ground and formed into a paste with water, it can be modeled or molded and heated to a high temperature when it fuses and becomes semi-translucent.

Soft Paste Porcelain (pâte tendre), also sometimes known as artificial porcelain because it lacks kaolin **(q. v.),** the essential constituent of true (hard paste) porcelain. The paste was composed of calcareous marl and frit obtained by fusing together a variety of mineral salts; sand, sea-salt, soda, nitre, alum. It was difficult to "throw" or mold, and anything but easy to fire; hence its products were extremely expensive to produce. Soft paste porcelain is of an extremely attractive, creamy character and the colors are slightly melted into the ground which gives an inimitably soft effect without any loss of brilliance. The technique was invented at Rouen about 1673 but was hardly developed at all until it was adopted at the Saint-Cloud factory about 1700.

Terre de Pipe or pipe-clay: a ceramic paste of a hard white character with a very fine grain and easily modelled, being especially suitable for decoration in relief, cast in molds and applied to the surface of a vase, jar, cup etc. The glaze is exceedingly thin and transparent. The development of this technique proved a serious embarrassment to the faience trade. It was extremely inexpensively produced in England where it had been invented. After the treaty of commerce signed between the two countries in 1783, it was imported into France in great quantities and many faience factories were ruined and had to close down. Indeed, the manufacture of French faience has never recovered from the blow it received then.

GOLD AND SILVERWARE

Gadrooning: convex curves in a series forming an ornamental edge, like inverted fluting. Often used on the edge of a plate or the foot of a drinking vessel. It can also be applied vertically or spirally to the body of a piece.

Torus molding: a large convex molding of semi-circular or similar shape used especially at the base of a column; sometimes of a twisted character.

GILT BRONZES

Burnished, polished and made to shine and reflect light. Used especially of metal work on which the gilders produced a high polish by means of a **brunissoir,** a special tool made of steel or agate.

Mat or Matt, with a dull, lusterless finish. Used to describe those parts of a metal object left unpolished.

Or Moulu: finely ground gold used in combination with mercury for gilding metal objects. Hence by extension the gilded metal itself (generally gilt bronze). The word was commonly used in the XVIIIth century but passed into desuetude in the XIXth century. It is now in use as the word "ormolu."

Rocaille, literally small rocks and originally used to describe the rock-work of grottoes etc.; hence a decorative device consisting of rock and shell forms, much used in the earlier phases of the rococo style.

WOOD PANELING

Crossette: a projection in the architecture of casing round a door or in the border of a panel. In paneling it begins almost as a flat ornamental motif gradually gaining in relief and developing into voluted and scrolled shapes.

CARPETS, TAPESTRIES AND TEXTILES

Hungarian embroidery: a type of embroidery of geometrical design in the form of imbricated triangles. Each element of the pattern is in a single color, but shaded.

Mille Fleurs, a type of medieval tapestry in which the ground was sprinkled with floral motifs.

GENERAL

Encyclopédistes, the group, headed by Diderot and d'Alembert, responsible for producing the **Encyclopédie ou Dictionnaire des Sciences et des Métiers,** issued in a large number of volumes between 1751 and 1777. Primarily a technical publication, it was strongly imbued with liberal, rationalistic and anti-religious views and exercised a wide influence on the French Revolution and on the later XVIIIth century in general.

HISTORICAL FRAMEWORK

Louis XIV, 1643-1715.
Regency of the Duke of Orléans, 1715-1723.
Louis XV, 1715-1774.
Louis XVI, 1774-1793.
French Revolution begins 1789.
Directoire, 1795-1799.

It is important to realize that artistic styles do not coincide precisely with historical reigns or political periods. Thus traces of the *Régence* style can be found as early as 1700 and the Louis XVI style was fully developed by 1770, some years before Louis XV's death.

Note. The term *Régence* has been preserved throughout for the style of that name to avoid confusion with the English Regency style of the early XIXth century.

BIBLIOGRAPHY

GENERAL

Nouvelle Encyclopédie illustrée de l'Art français. L'Art au xviiⁱᵉ siècle, publ. Guy Le Prat.
Arts, styles et techniques, Larousse.
    Émile DACIER : Régence Louis XV. 1951.
    Louis REAU : Louis XVI. 1952.
    P. VERLET : Le style Louis XV. 1943.
    E. DACIER : Le style Louis XVI. 1944.
    R. SCHNEIDER : L'Art français au xviiⁱᵉ siècle. 1926. Laurens

DICTIONARIES

    BELLIER de la CHAVIGNERIE et AUVRAY : Dictionnaire général des artistes de l'école française. 1882-1885.
    Ch. DU PELOUX : Répertoire biographique et bibliographique des artistes du xviiⁱᵉ siècle français. 1930-1941.
    HAVARD : Dictionnaire de l'ameublement et de la décoration. 1887-1890.
    D. GUILMARD : Les maîtres ornementiistes. 1881. Plon.
    Louis REAU : Dictionnaire d'art et d'archéologie. Larousse.

PAINTINGS

    L. REAU : Histoire de la peinture française au xviiⁱᵉ siècle. 1926.
    M. FLORISOONE : La peinture française. Le xviiⁱᵉ siècle. 1948.
    L. DIMIER : Les peintres français du xviiⁱᵉ siècle. Histoire des vies et catalogue des œuvres. 1929-1930.
    J. LOCQUIN : La peinture d'histoire en France de 1747 à 1785. 1912.
    L. DUMONT-WILDEN : Le portrait en France au xviiⁱᵉ siècle. 1909.
    E. DACIER et P. RATOUIS de LIMAY : Pastels français des xviiⁱᵉ et xviiⁱᵉ siècles. 1927.
    P. RATOUIS de LIMAY : Le pastel en France au xviiⁱᵉ siècle. 1946.
    Ch. STERLING : La nature morte de l'antiquité à nos jours. 1952.
    Jules et Edmond de GONCOURT : L'Art au xviiⁱᵉ siècle. 2nd. ed. 1873. 3rd. ed. 1880.
    Pierre de NOLHAC : Mme Vigée-Lebrun, peintre de Marie-Antoinette. 1912.
    Florence INGERSOLL SMOUSE : Joseph Vernet. 2 vol. 1926.
    Baron PORTALIS : Honoré Fragonard, sa vie et son œuvre. 1889.
    Lady DILKE : French Painters of the xviiⁱᵗʰ century. 1899.
    J. et E. de GONCOURT : French xviiⁱᵗʰ century Painters, selected and translated by Robin Ironside. 1948.
    F. FOSCA : The xviiⁱᵗʰ century : Watteau to Tiepolo. 1952.

FURNITURE

    H. VIAL, A. MARCEL, A. GIRODIS : Les artistes décorateurs de bois. Répertoire alphabétique des ébénistes, menuisiers, sculpteurs, doreurs, etc., ayant travaillé en France aux xviiᵉ et xviiⁱᵉ siècles. 1912-1921.
    A. THEUNISSEN : Meubles et sièges du xviiⁱᵉ siècle. Menuisiers, ébénistes, marques, plans et ornementation de leurs œuvres. Paris. 1934.
    Comte de SALVERTE : Les ébénistes du xviiⁱᵉ siècle. 4th ed. 1953.
    Comte de SALVERTE : Le meuble français d'après les ornemanistes. 1660-1789. Paris, 1930.
    J. NICOLAY : L'Art et la manière des maîtres ébénistes français au xviiⁱᵉ siècle. 1955.
    H. CLOUZOT : Les meubles du xviiⁱᵉ siècle. Étude technique du meuble, étude graphique des éléments et de l'exécution; répertoire des ébénistes. 1922.
    H. CLOUZOT : L'ameublement français sous Louis XV. Bibliothèque de l'Art décoratif. 1912.
    P. VERLET : Les meubles du xviiⁱᵉ siècle. I. Menuiserie. II. Ébénisterie. 1955.
    P. VERLET : Le mobilier royal français. Meubles de la Couronne conservés en France. 1945-1956.
    P. DEVINOY et Madeleine JARRY : Le siège en France du moyen âge à nos jours. 343 photographies. 1948.
    P. DEVINOY : Le meuble léger en France. 324 photographies. 1952.
    J. MOTTHEAU : Meubles usuels. I. Régence et Louis XV. II. Louis XVI. 1950-1951.
    C. DREYFUS : Musée du Louvre. Le mobilier français. Tome I : Époques Louis XIV et Louis XV. Paris, 1922. Tome I : Époque Louis XVI. Paris, 1922.
    Roger de FELICE : Le meuble français sous Louis XV. 1922. dº Louis XVI. Engl. trans., 1921.
    G. JANNEAU : Les sièges. Vol. I : De l'art antique au style Régence. Vol. II : Du style Louis XV au style Restauration, l'art oriental. Paris, R. Ducher, 1928.
    G. JANNEAU : Les beaux meubles français anciens. I. Les commodes. II. Les petits meubles. III. Les grands meubles. IV. Les lits de repos et lits. V. Les sièges Charles Moreau, 1928-1930.
    G. JANNEAU : Le mobilier français. Presses universitaires, 1941.
    SEYMOUR de RICCI: Les styles Louis XIV et Régence. Décoration et mobilier. 1912. Engl. trans., 1929. dº Louis XV. Engl. trans., 1927.
    SEYMOUR de RICCI : Le style Louis XVI. Mobilier et décoration. 1912. Eng. trans. 1929. dº Louis XV. Eng. trans. 1927.
    Lady DILKE : French furniture and decoration in the xviiⁱᵗʰ century. 1901.
    Charles PACKER : Paris furniture by the Master Ebenistes. 1956.
    F. J. B. WATSON : Wallace Collection Catalogues : Furniture. 1956.

CERAMICS

    Dr. CHOMPRET (sous la direction du) : Répertoire de la faïence française. 1935.
    Comte de CHAVAGNAC et Marquis de GROLLIER : Histoire des manufactures françaises de porcelaine. Paris, Picard et Fils, 1906.
    Paul ALFASSA et Jacques GUERIN : Porcelaine française. Paris, 1930.
    Alexandre BRONGNIART : Traité des arts céramiques. Paris, 1844.
    Albert JACQUEMART : Les merveilles de la céramique. Paris, 1874.
    Édouard GARNIER : Histoire de la céramique. Tours, 1882.
    P. VERLET, GRANDJEAN, Marcelle BRUNET : Sèvres. Le Prat, 1955.
    Arthur LANE : French Faïence. 1948.
    W. B. HONEY : French Porcelain of the xviiⁱᵗʰ century. 1950.
    W. B. HONEY : European Ceramic Art. 1949.

GOLD AND SILVERWARE

    Henri BOUILHET : L'orfèvrerie française au xviiⁱᵉ siècle et au xixᵉ siècle d'après les documents réunis au Musée centennal de 1900. 1908-1912.
    Henri HAVARD : Histoire de l'orfèvrerie française. 1896.
    Henry NOCQ : Le poinçon de Paris. 1926-1931.
    H. NOCQ, P. ALFASSA et L. GUERIN : L'orfèvrerie civile française. 1927.
    E. MAILLARD, N.-G.VEDRES, J. BABELON, G. YVER, S. FOUQUET, G. FOUQUET : L'orfèvrerie et la joaillerie. 1942.
    Henry NOCQ, Carl DREYFUS : Tabatières, boites et étuis; orfèvrerie de Paris xviiⁱᵉ siècle et début du xixᵉ, du Musée du Louvre. 1930.
    Louis CARRÉ : Les poinçons de l'orfèvrerie française. 1928.
    Germain BAPST : Études sur l'orfèvrerie française au xviiⁱᵉ siècle. Les Germains orfèvres-sculpteurs. 1887.
    J. BABELON : L'orfèvrerie française. 1946.
    BEUQUE et FRAPSAUCE : Dictionnaire des poinçons des maitres orfèvres français. 1929.
    Ed. GELIS : L'horlogerie ancienne. Histoire, décor et technique. 1949.
    Louis CARRÉ : A Guide to Old French Plate. 1931.

GILT BRONZE

    METMAN et VAUDOYER : Musée des Arts décoratifs. Le bronze, le cuivre, l'étain. 1909-1910.
    A. de CHAMPEAUX : Dictionnaire des fondeurs, ciseleurs, modeleurs en bronze et doreurs. 1886 (paru lettres A-C, la suite manuscrite à la Bibliothèque du musée des Arts décoratifs).
    J. ROBIQUET : Gouthière, sa vie et son œuvre. 1912.
    Baron DAVILLIERS : Le cabinet du duc d'Aumont et les amateurs de son temps... Accompagné de notes... sur P. Gouthière et les principaux ciseleurs du temps de Louis XVI. 1870.
    Lazare DUVAUX : Livre Journal, 1748-1758, éd. Courajod. 1873.
    Collection Georges HŒNTSCHEL : Vol. IV. 1908.
    G. DUMONTHIER : Les bronzes du Mobilier national. Bronzes d'éclairage et de chauffage. 1909.
    G. DUMONTHIER : Les bronzes du Mobilier national. Pendules et cartels. 1910.
    HENRIOT : L'Encyclopédie du luminaire. 1934.
    TARDY : La pendule française des origines à nos jours. 1950.

WOOD PANELING

    L. METMAN et G. BRIÈRE : Le musée des Arts décoratifs, Le Bois. 1905-1906.
    M.-J. BALLOT : Le décor intérieur au xviiⁱᵉ siècle à Paris et dans l'Ile-de-France. Boiseries sculptées et panneaux peints. 1930.
    Collection G. HŒNTSCHEL : 1908. Vols. II and III.
    S. ROCHE : Cadres français et étrangers du xvᵉ au xviiⁱᵉ siècle.
    Fiske KIMBALL : The Creation of the Rococo. 1943.

TAPESTRY, CARPETS, TEXTILES

    F. SALET : La tapisserie française du moyen âge à nos jours. 1946.
    G. JANNEAU : Évolution de la tapisserie. 1947.
    J.-J. GUIFFREY : Histoire générale de la tapisserie. Tapisseries françaises. 1880.
    H. GOBEL : Wandteppische und ihre Manufakturen, Leipzig. 1923-1924. Vol. II.
    M. FENAILLE : État général des tapisseries des Gobelins. 1903-1923.
    J. BADIN : La manufacture des tapisseries de Beauvais. 1909.
    C. PERATHON : Essai de catalogue descriptif des anciennes tapisseries d'Aubusson et de Felletin. 1894-1902.
    J. BABONNEIX : Le tapis et la tapisserie d'Aubusson. 1935.
    E. DUMONTHIER : Recueil de dessins de tapis et de tapisseries d'ameublement du mobilier de la Couronne. 1911.
    E. DUMONTHIER : Mobilier national. Étoffes et tapisseries d'ameublement aux xviiᵉ et xviiⁱᵉ siècles. 1910.
    R. CHAVANCE : Tissus du xviiⁱᵉ siècle. 1950.

SCULPTURE

    Luc BENOIST : La sculpture française. 1945.
    St. LAMI : Dictionnaire des sculpteurs de l'école française au xviiⁱᵉ siècle. 1910-1911.
    M. FURCY-RAYNAUD : Inventaire des sculptures exécutées au xviiⁱᵉ siècle pour la direction des Bâtiments du Roi. 1925-1926.
    Lady DILKE : French architects and sculptors of the xviiⁱᵗʰ century. 1900.
    Louis REAU : Les Lemoyne. 1927.
    Louis REAU : Étienne-Maurice Falconet, 2 vol. 1922.
    Louis REAU : Jean-Baptiste Pigalle. 1951.
    Louis REAU : Houdon (Les Grands Artistes). 1930.
    Henri STEIN : Augustin Pajou. 1912.
    GIACOMETTI : Houdon, 3 vol. 1918-1919. Illus. ed. 2 vol. 1929.

INTERIOR DECORATION

    L. BERNEVAL : Intérieurs de style. 1953.
    Fr. CONTET, etc. : Les vieux hôtels de Paris. 1911-1932 (22 vol. parus).
    J. VACQUIER et H. SOULANGE-BODIN : Les anciens châteaux de France. 1913-1933 (14 vol. parus).
    H. DESTAILLEUR : Recueil d'estampes relatives à l'ornementation des appartements aux xviᵉ, xviiᵉ et xviiⁱᵉ siècles. 1863.
    Fiske KIMBALL : See above.

CONTENTS

THIS WORK
WAS FIRST PRINTED ON
OCTOBER 15TH 1956
AT THE
CRÉTÉ PRESS AT CORBEIL-ESSONES
AND THE PAUL DUPONT PRESS AT CLICHY.
THE PHOTOGRAVURE
IS BY CLICHÉS UNION, CORNEVIN BRETON,
COURMONT, L'ILLUSTRATION.
THE BOOK-BINDING BY DIGUET-DENY.
THE LAYOUT
BY R. BRIDOUX